THE DISABLED HOMEMAKER

THE DISABLED HOMEMAKER

By

Hoyt Anderson

With a Foreword by

Edward V. Roberts
Director
Department of Rehabilitation
Sacramento, California

Illustrated by

Morris Gee
Office of Architecture and Engineering
University of California
Davis, California

CHARLES C THOMAS • PUBLISHER
Springfield • Illinois • U.S.A.

Published and Distributed Throughout the World by
CHARLES C THOMAS • PUBLISHER
Bannerstone House
301-327 East Lawrence Avenue, Springfield, Illinois, U.S.A.

©*1981*, *by* CHARLES C THOMAS • PUBLISHER
ISBN 0-398-04077-X (Cloth)
0-398-04078-8 (Paper)
Library of Congress Catalog Card Number: 80-11901

Library of Congress Cataloging in Publication Data

Anderson, Hoyt.
    The disabled homemaker.

    Bibliography: p.
    Includes index.
    1. Home economics for the physically handicapped.
2. Physically handicapped—Rehabilitation.
I. Title. [DNLM: 1. Housekeeping. 2. Handicapped.
3. Self-help devices.   4. Rehabilitation.
HD7255 A546d]
TX147.A63   640'.2'408166   80-11901
ISBN0-398-04077-X
ISBN 0-398-04078-8 pbk.

Printed in the United States of America

OK-1

To

Nona Thomas Anderson

A friend who devotes her life to others

FOREWORD

Hoyt Anderson's book provides a comprehensive collection of information, ideas, and shortcuts that will help people with all sorts of disabilities to manage their own lives more effectively. It covers everything from techniques for cooking and cleaning to time management and clothing modifications. But this is more than a specialized collection of household hints. Underlying the book is a real belief in people and what they can accomplish. There is encouragement here, the encouragement that comes from real life examples of disabled people who have successfully put the pieces of the independence puzzle together and are leading active and satisfying lives. Running all through the excellent, practical advice in *The Disabled Homemaker* is the realization that the goal of independence is possible—that others have tried and succeeded and found it to be well worth the effort.

But Anderson doesn't underplay the risks. He makes it clear that moving away from dependence means taking risks and cautions against unrealistic optimism that could lead to discouragement. At the same time, he points out that the chances you take are not too great a price for the ultimate payoff of personal independence.

I am sure that you will find this book stimulating as well as an invaluable resource in your efforts toward leading a more independent life.

Edward V. Roberts

ACKNOWLEDGMENTS

This book could not have been written without the information, assistance, consultation, and moral support from other people. Therefore, I wish to thank and give credit to the following individuals for their contributions:

Carriann Henriques, Independent Living Skills Coordinator for Resources for Independent Living, who inspired me to write this book through her teaching of a class on the subject at California State University, Sacramento, in 1974.

Joel Bryant and Nancy Seyden, Counselors, at the Center for Services to Handicapped Students at the University of California, Davis, for insightful interviews.

Barbara Charlton, Stan Frost, Elgie Fuson, and Barbara Rugeley, librarians at California State University, Sacramento, who spent hours of their time assisting in the research for this publication.

Georgella Gladden, R.N., nurse at the California State University, Sacramento Health Center, for her medical advice and her review of portions of this manuscript.

Donna Selnick, Home Economics Instructor, California State University, Sacramento, for consultations.

Pat Sonntag, Director of Disabled Student Services at California State University, Sacramento, who granted me interviews and who diligently works to provide ever expanding opportunities and services for handicapped students on campus.

Sterling Ebel, a friend and counselor, who gave support to me in my professional writing efforts.

Kay Galloway and Henrietta Baron, Special Education Instructors at Rio Americano High School in Sacramento, California, both of whom helped to broaden my insight and understanding of the physically handicapped.

Ralph V. Chmelka, principal of Starr King Exceptional School, who assisted in arranging interviews to aid in my research.

Judy Richardson, Instructor of orthopedically handicapped students, and Linda Erickson, senior occupational therapist, in the San Juan Unified School District, Sacramento, who granted me interviews prior to the writing of this manuscript.

Morris Gee, a friend with architectural, drafting, and photographic expertise, who graciously assumed the responsibility for illustrating this book.

Jean Stephens, advisor to the Sacramento City College newspaper, who permitted me to use the photography equipment to prepare the photographs for this book.

H.A.

CONTENTS

Page

Foreword vii

Chapter

1 ANYONE CAN LIVE INDEPENDENTLY............... 3

2 PHYSICAL DISABILITIES AND INDEPENDENT
LIVING 16

3 TAKE CARE OF YOUR BODY 32

4 DOING THINGS THE SIMPLE WAY 89

5 PLANNING YOUR KITCHEN 97

6 COOKING MADE EASY 114

7 KEEPING YOUR HOME NEAT AND SPOTLESS 167

8 DOING YOUR LAUNDRY 180

9 STORAGE ORGANIZATION THAT WORKS
FOR YOU 208

10 STRUCTURAL MODIFICATIONS AND HOME
ADAPTIONS 230

11 COMFORTABLE CLOTHING 265

12 CARING FOR YOUR CHILD 279

Appendices 313

Suggested Readings 321

Index 327

THE DISABLED HOMEMAKER

---- *Chapter 1* ----

ANYONE CAN LIVE INDEPENDENTLY

If you were born with a disability or acquired one later in life, you can achieve some degree of independence with determination and willpower, no matter what the extent of your limitations. Today, tremendous strides are being made in helping those with physical disabilities to become self-reliant. However, this has not always been the case. Traditionally, handicapped people who could no longer live with their families had few alternatives other than to stay in state hospitals, boarding and nursing homes, or convalescent facilities. For instance, Diane, who was confined to a wheelchair, yearned to leave home, find a job, and live in an apartment. Unfortunately, this wish never came true. One night while her parents drove home from a party, an oncoming vehicle crashed into their car and killed them instantly. Since Diane had no relatives, a social worker placed her in a convalescent hospital. Now, every morning nurses dress, groom, and feed her. After breakfast she sits watching T.V., trying to forget her ever present feelings of confinement, boredom, and despair.

However, times are changing. Slowly a new awareness is taking place. More handicapped people have the opportunity to live away from sheltered environments and to assume greater responsibilities.

HAPPINESS AND FREEDOM COME WITH BEING SELF-RELIANT

When many disabled people reach their late teens or early twenties, they have a strong desire to live independently. For many this is possible.

Cindy, a twenty-six-year-old cerebral palsied college student, obtained a B.A. degree and applied for admission to a graduate program at a university 500 miles from her home. When she went for an interview, some of the instructors wondered if Cindy could live alone and still maintain satisfactory grades. Finally, the faculty rejected her application but suggested she enroll in summer classes so that they could evaluate her performance.

For the next two months Cindy made plans, and on the day before school began, a friend drove her to campus. During the first week of school she felt homesick, but as Cindy made friends and became involved in her classes, the feeling of loneliness disappeared. Soon, despite the exhausting schedule, which usually began at five o'clock in the morning with a hot shower and ended about 11 PM after she completed her homework, Cindy enjoyed her new experience. As summer school drew to a close, she felt proud of her accomplishments, especially her B average. That fall when she reapplied for admission to the program, the faculty accepted her, no longer doubting her abilities.

While many disabled people like to live alone, others want to share their lives with someone else. A good example was Marlene, who had a desire to leave her boarding home and marry. One weekend while attending a convention, she met Paul, and they spent much time together. During the next eight months, he dated her often and finally proposed. Marlene then discussed her plans with a social worker who suggested she enroll in an independent living program to learn cooking, cleaning, and housekeeping skills. Six months later Marlene and Paul married. Today, after almost four years, they are still living together, caring, helping, and loving each other.

While many handicapped people have a choice of life-styles, some must either become self-reliant or face the prospect of living in an institution. John, a quadriplegic, had to make this choice during his senior year of high school. One afternoon he received a message to contact Mrs. Blake, his guardian, immediately. When John did, she told him that his mother had suffered a heart attack and was lying in critical condition at a nearby hospital.

That evening he stayed with his aunt. While they were eating dinner, the phone rang, and she picked up the receiver but only talked briefly. Then, with tears in her eyes, she turned to him and said, "John, your mother is dead."

Shocked, not wanting to accept this news, he grieved for almost a month before resuming classes, still worried about who would help him in caring for his personal needs.

Six weeks later, during a visit with Mrs. Blake, she told John his aunt could no longer care for him. Therefore, he had to make a decision either to move into a convalescent hospital or to try living in an apartment with an attendant assisting him. Determined never to live in a nursing facility but still somewhat apprehensive about managing his own home, he finally decided to try living independently. Mrs. Blake helped him hire an attendant and find an apartment. For the first few months, adjusting to his new surroundings was difficult. However, as time passed he soon learned to cope with and even to enjoy this life-style.

As these young people did, you too can experience the feeling of personal freedom as you become more self-reliant.

DEFINING INDEPENDENT LIVING

Just what is independent living? It can have different meanings, depending on your point of view. As with all Americans, however, handicapped people want to control their own affairs. Joel Bryant, director of the Disabled Student's Program at the University of California in Davis, California, who is also confined to a wheelchair, explains the concept this way.

"For me it really means autonomous living; someone having the ability to direct his own life even though he cannot perform all of the tasks himself. This involves taking responsibility and being able to plan your own life without supervision." Even someone needing much physical care can often live in his own home if he is able to arrange for others to assist him (*see* the section on attendant care in Chapter 3).

MAYBE YOU SHOULD THINK ABOUT LIVING INDEPENDENTLY

Although some handicapped people find it difficult to leave home, often those who work with the disabled urge them to move into a more independent living situation.

INDEPENDENCE DEVELOPS BETTER INTERPERSONAL RELATION-SHIPS. All children as they mature depend on their parents;

however, this is sometimes more true of the handicapped. It is often less difficult for them to ask another member of the family to do something than to struggle with it themselves. For example, Peter, a teenager with poor finger dexterity, had trouble lacing and tying his shoes and often became frustrated, spending fifteen or twenty minutes at the task. It was much easier to ask someone else for help. However, doing this did not help him improve so that he could do it faster in the future. When Peter's parents saw him struggling, they immediately came to his aid instead of allowing him to become more self-reliant.

Some disabled people, on the other hand, may not feel comfortable relying on others. For instance, even though Bill wanted to take girls out on dates, he felt awkward about asking any girl because he would need to depend on her for transportation. Since Bill did not drive, he felt this was imposing on her, which might cause a strained relationship—especially if he took the same girl out several times.

You can see how too much dependence on others can interfere with interpersonal relations.

SELF-RELIANCE BUILDS CONFIDENCE AND INITIATIVE.   A handicapped person may be reluctant to try something new because he thinks it might be impossible. There are many reasons why disabled people might feel this way. But, do not think pessimistically. Often you can accomplish more than you realize. Jerry, a paraplegic, had such an experience.

One summer following his graduation from college, a vocational counselor located him a job in a city 10 miles away. Since Jerry was injured five years previously, he had lived with his parents but now had to leave home and live in an apartment. Even though he was happy about this employment opportunity, Jerry felt uncomfortable about his new living situation. At one point he was on the verge of rejecting the position, but when his vocational counselor threatened to close his case, Jerry decided to accept.

Two weeks later, still having mixed feelings and reservations, Jerry made the move. At first he sometimes lay awake at night, wondering if he could cope. However, like many disabled individuals after a short while, Jerry became confident and tackled things he had never done before. This is just one more example of how another disabled person became independent.

Are you still living at home but want to become self-reliant? It may be possible. Begin by developing confidence in your abilities. Remember, once you accomplish something and learn to do more and more things, you gain courage. Think positively and always be willing to try.

CHOOSING TO LIVE INDEPENDENTLY PREPARES FOR THE DEATH OF PARENTS. There is an old saying, "Everybody must go sometime." However, for a physically handicapped person, the death of his parents could mean a life of dependency on others in an institutionalized setting. In some cases although disabled people might want to be independent, they simply may not have the skills necessary. The two cases of Diane and John described earlier in this chapter demonstrate what a profound impact the death of parents can have on some handicapped young people.

So that you will not face a similar situation, perhaps you should begin thinking about your own housing while your mother and father are still alive. Here are three good reasons for making this decision.

First, as your parents grow older, they may become less able to care for you. This could be a more critical circumstance when one parent has died, since your only option may be to reside in a convalescent hospital, nursing home, or board-and-care facility in the event of the other parent's death. To avoid this happening, why not begin some preparation for becoming self-reliant now?

Another good reason for moving away from your parent's home while your mother and father are still living is that they may be able to help you make the transition. Most parents want their son or daughter to succeed and sometimes can offer assistance, so enlist their support and listen to any advice they may offer.

Finally, leaving your parents' home while they are still living insures that you will have a place to return to if you so desire. Always remember if you should make that decision, do not feel discouraged, because often young, able-bodied people return home several times before moving out permanently.

BE READY

Before trying to live independently, ask yourself one important question: Are you ready? This may sound obvious, but some disabled people who have this desire may not be prepared. For instance, Kate, a nineteen-year-old college freshman who was confined to a wheelchair, moved into an apartment shortly before enrolling in school for the first time. Since Kate had always lived at home and relied on her mother to cook, clean, and do the laundry, she was unaware of how long each daily living task would take. However, when her college classes began and the instructors started assigning homework, Kate soon discovered it was quite a struggle to do the numerous household chores and still find time to study. In fact, because of her heavy schedule, she often fell asleep during classes. Consequently, since her parents lived nearby, Kate returned home and was then able to cope with college life better.

FINANCIAL RESOURCES. One of the first things to think about is how to finance your plans. This means determining the cost of housing and other living expenses. One prime source of income for some disabled Americans is the Federal Supplemental Security Income program, more commonly known as SSI. This program, administered through the Social Security Administration, helps meet the financial needs of the handicapped and elderly people whose monthly income is below a fixed level. Although a person is allowed a certain amount of money or valuables such as jewelry, stocks, and bonds, he is still entitled to receive some types of limited resources. Other kinds of income, such as social security, veteran's benefits, and annuities, generally lower your SSI grant. Furthermore, the amount of your check may also depend on your living arrangements. If you cannot afford to live independently any other way, why not consider this program as one possible solution?

When it comes to housing, since most handicapped people rent, probably one of the best ways to calculate what you must spend is to look in the classified section of your daily newspaper and check the prices; then you might also want to make some phone calls. Be sure to inquire whether utilities are included in the rent. If not, this will be an added expense.

In your search for the least expensive place to live, do not forget that in 1974 the United States Congress established the Section Eight Housing Program, which provides assistance for lower income, disabled, and elderly citizens to secure adequate housing.

Under this program, public housing authorities in the community where handicapped individuals live will help them apply for subsidized housing. In such cases, a person whose yearly income falls below a certain amount is expected to pay no less than 15 percent or no more than 25 percent of their rent, while the Housing Authority pays the rest.

Aside from housing, there are other expenses to take into account, including food, clothing, and transportation, to mention a few. Be sure to consider each item carefully in estimating your necessary income to live independently.

ANALYZE YOUR ABILITIES.   Living in your own home means being as self-reliant as possible. But have you ever sat down and thought about all the daily living activities associated with independent living? How many can you do for yourself? With how many would you need help?

Making an assessment is easy; just use the chart in Table 1-I. For every item that applies to you, decide whether you can do it yourself or whether you will need help. Then check the appropriate column.

Table 1-I
LIVING SKILLS PROFILE

	I CAN	I NEED HELP
EATING		
1. Finger feed	_____	_____
2. Use fork for solid foods....................	_____	_____
3. Use spoon................................	_____	_____
4. Drink with cup or glass	_____	_____
5. Cut with knife...........................	_____	_____
6. Butter bread	_____	_____
7. Eat entire meal unassisted	_____	_____
8. Clean up table...........................	_____	_____
PERSONAL GROOMING		
1. Brush teeth or dentures	_____	_____
2. Reach and turn faucets on and off	_____	_____
3. Wash face	_____	_____
4. Wash hands	_____	_____
5. Wash entire body	_____	_____
6. Dry entire body	_____	_____
7. Use tub or shower	_____	_____
8. Use deodorant	_____	_____

	I CAN	I NEED HELP
9. Open and use jars or tubes		
10. Shave		
11. Put on makeup		
12. Comb hair		
13. Shampoo hair		
14. Set hair		
15. Groom nails		
16. Use facial tissue		
17. Take care of female hygiene		

TOILETING

	I CAN	I NEED HELP
1. Drain urinal		
2. Manage daily catheter care		
3. Change catheter		
4. Manage bowel care		
5. Take clothing on and off		
6. Transfer to toilet or commode		
7. Cleanse self after toileting		
8. Flush toilet		

DRESSING

	I CAN	I NEED HELP
1. Button and unbutton clothing		
2. Use zippers		
3. Take on and off		
a. slacks		
b. undergarments		
c. bra		
d. stockings		
e. support hose		
f. socks		
g. shirt		
h. corset		
i. coat		
j. braces		
k. splint		
l. artificial limbs		
4. Get clothes from closet and drawers		

CLEANING TASKS

	I CAN	I NEED HELP
1. Pick up objects from floor		
2. Wipe up spills		
3. Make bed (daily)		
4. Change sheets on bed		
5. Use dust mop		
6. Shake dust mop		
7. Dust high surfaces		
8. Dust low surfaces		
9. Wash kitchen floor		

	I CAN	I NEED HELP
10. Sweep with broom	———	———
11. Use dust pan	———	———
12. Use vacuum cleaner	———	———
13. Use vacuum cleaner attachments	———	———
14. Carry light cleaning tools.................	———	———
15. Use carpet sweeper	———	———
16. Clean bathtub	———	———
17. Carry pail of water.......................	———	———

COOKING

	I CAN	I NEED HELP
1. Turn on water...........................	———	———
2. Turn on gas or electric stove	———	———
3. Light gas with match	———	———
4. Pour hot water from pan to cup	———	———
5. Open packaged goods	———	———
6. Carry pan from sink to stove	———	———
7. Open screw top jars	———	———
8. Use can opener	———	———
9. Use can punch	———	———
10. Use bottle opener	———	———
11. Handle milk bottle.......................	———	———
12. Dispose of garbage	———	———
13. Remove things from refrigerator...........	———	———
14. Bend to low cupboards	———	———
15. Reach to high cupboards	———	———
16. Peel vegetables..........................	———	———
17. Cut up vegetables	———	———
18. Handle sharp tools safely	———	———
19. Break an egg	———	———
20. Stir against resistance	———	———
21. Use measuring cups and spoons	———	———
22. Use flour sifter	———	———
23. Use an egg beater	———	———
24. Remove batter to pan	———	———
25. Open oven door	———	———
26. Carry pan to oven and put it in	———	———
27. Stir mixture in pan on stove	———	———
28. Fry item on stove	———	———
29. Cut meat...............................	———	———
30. Use electric frying pan	———	———
31. Roll cookie dough or pie crust	———	———
32. Use electric mixer.......................	———	———
33. Use electric hand mixer..................	———	———
34. Cut with shears.........................	———	———
35. Make a sandwich	———	———
36. Crack a soft boiled egg	———	———
37. Squeeze citrus fruit......................	———	———

	I CAN	I NEED HELP
38. Put on an apron	———	———

SERVING MEALS

1. Set table	———	———
2. Carry hot casserole to table	———	———
3. Clear table	———	———
4. Scrape and stack dishes	———	———
5. Wash dishes	———	———
6. Wipe silver	———	———
7. Wash pots and pans........................	———	———
8. Wipe up stove and work areas..............	———	———
9. Wring out dish cloth	———	———
10. Put dishes away	———	———

LAUNDRY

1. Sort clothes	———	———
2. Wash lingerie	———	———
3. Wring out, squeeze dry	———	———
4. Hang on rack to dry	———	———
5. Hang on line to dry	———	———
6. Sprinkle clothes	———	———
7. Iron shirt or dress..........................	———	———
8. Fold shirt or dress..........................	———	———
9. Iron flat pieces	———	———
10. Set up and take down ironing board	———	———
11. Use ironer (hand controls)	———	———
12. Use washing machine	———	———
13. Use dryer	———	———

SEWING

1. Thread needle and make knot	———	———
2. Sew on buttons	———	———
3. Mend rips.................................	———	———
4. Darn socks	———	———
5. Use sewing machine	———	———
6. Knit	———	———
7. Crochet	———	———
8. Embroider	———	———

HEAVY HOUSEHOLD TASKS

1. Household laundry—washing	———	———
2. Hanging clothes	———	———
3. Clean range	———	———
4. Clean refrigerator	———	———
5. Wax floors	———	———
6. Turn mattresses...........................	———	———
7. Wash windows	———	———
8. Put up curtains...........................	———	———

	I CAN	I NEED HELP
MARKETING		
1. Make out shopping list	——	——
2. Order over the telephone	——	——
3. Put groceries away	——	——
FINANCIAL MANAGEMENT		
Basic figuring		
1. Calculate basic math concepts	——	——
2. Know value of money	——	——
3. Make change	——	——
4. Use coin-operated machines	——	——
5. Use pay phones	——	——
Banking and checking account procedures		
1. Open a checking and savings account	——	——
2. Keep financial record of checking account	——	——
3. Balance bank statement	——	——
4. Write checks	——	——
5. Cash checks	——	——
6. Understand overdrawn term	——	——
7. Stop payment on check	——	——
8. Withdraw money from bank	——	——
9. Understand service charges	——	——
10. Figure interest	——	——
Personal finances		
1. Understand and pay bills	——	——
2. Budget monthly income	——	——
3. Make purchases in stores (food, etc.)	——	——
4. Use credit wisely	——	——
5. Pay taxes	——	——
6. Purchase insurance needed	——	——
CHILD CARE		
1. Bathe baby or child	——	——
2. Diaper baby	——	——
3. Dress child	——	——
4. Comb hair	——	——
5. Feed child	——	——
6. Lift child to chair or bed	——	——
7. Put child on floor	——	——
8. Put child in bed or crib	——	——
9. Put child in play pen	——	——
10. Supervise outdoor play	——	——

If you feel after making a personal evaluation that you will need much assistance, do not think living in your own home is impossible.

As was stated earlier, some people with severe disabilities hire attendants to help them with daily living activities they cannot perform. Nevertheless, before considering becoming more self-reliant, have a clear idea about the various types of help you will need.

CONSIDER THE TIME FACTOR. Disabled people should always think about how much time is needed for each daily living task they must perform. Often, the simplest things take longer to accomplish. For instance, Larry, who is confined to a wheelchair, has a job with the California State Department of Health. However, in order for him to arrive at work by 8:00 AM, he must be awake at 5:00. It takes him this length of time to get out of bed, shower, shave, and eat breakfast. Then Larry must wait forty-five minutes for a specially equipped wheelchair bus to come and drive him to work. Despite this careful planning, he is sometimes late.

Larry's situation is typical of the difficulties many handicapped people face. Therefore, before moving into an independent living situation, think about the time you will spend performing your daily living activities and be prepared to adjust your life-style accordingly.

YOUR LIVING ARRANGEMENTS. Do you want to live alone or with another person? This is an important question in making your plans. Some people enjoy the peace and solitude of life alone, while others may find it dull, boring, and even depressing. If you feel you might be lonesome by yourself, consider finding a roommate. You can then leave your sheltered environment, have someone with whom to share many of your experiences and still become more self-reliant.

This chapter discussed some of the reasons for becoming independent and prime considerations to keep in mind when you are thinking about living in a home of your own. Remember that even though you have severe physical limitations you can develop a greater degree of independence. However, to succeed, you must have a strong desire and a firm personal commitment to keep working toward your goal of becoming self-reliant.

POINTS TO REMEMBER

1. *Anyone can live independently*. Many severely handicapped

people, regardless of physical limitations, can live in a home of their own and become more self-reliant.

2. *One definition of independent living.* The ability to direct your life, even though you cannot perform all the daily living tasks yourself.

3. *Some reasons for becoming self-reliant.* Independence develops better inter-personal relationships, builds self-confidence and initiative, and prepares for the death of parents.

4. *Be ready.* Consider financial resources, physical abilities, the time factor, and your living arrangements.

Chapter 2

PHYSICAL DISABILITIES
AND INDEPENDENT LIVING

W hat are some of the problems a physically handicapped person might encounter when he begins trying to live independently? This all depends on the extent of his impairments. Some individuals have visible injuries such as an awkward gait, while others have invisible disabilities that nevertheless interfere with or restrict the homemaker's activities, for example, cardiac problems.

People's impairments can also be divided into two groups—ambulatory or nonambulatory. An ambulatory person may walk with some difficulty, may use crutches, cane, or walker, or may wear leg braces. Someone nonambulatory is confined to a wheelchair.

Within these two general classifications there are countless specific disabilities. The next section will examine some of them and discuss how they can apply to homemaking.

HEMIPLEGIA AFFECTS RIGHT OR LEFT LIMBS

Hemiplegia paralyzes either the right or left side of the body and results from damage to part of the brain on the opposite side. In other words, a lesion in a person's left brain hemisphere will impair the right limbs or vice versa. The regions of the brain most affected are the cerebral cortex, the brain stem, and the pyramidal tracts.

The hemiplegic individual often moves his limbs involuntarily and could have muscle contractures; flexed elbows, wrists, and fingers; shoulders that rotate toward the middle of the body; legs and hips that also rotate inwardly; and bent knees and ankles. In

16

addition, the person often swings his disabled leg outward in a semicircle as he walks.

Besides paralysis' affecting one side of the body, people might have other impairments as well. Some of these could include weakness to the lower two-thirds of the face; an altered response to sensations of touch, temperature, and pain; impairments to vision and hearing; personality changes consisting of irritability, lapse of memory, and poor judgment; aphasia; and loss of language. An individual with a communication handicap may be unable to speak, write, tell time, read, do arithmetic, spell, type, count, recognize objects, or understand what others are saying.

People of all ages are disabled with hemiplegia, but most often they are over fifty. This handicap in younger children is usually classified as one type of cerebral palsy, which will be discussed later. While a tumor or cerebral anoxia may cause this impairment, cerebrovascular accidents or strokes that cut off the blood supply to the brain are usually the principle reasons. A stroke is a result of either *atherosclerosis*, fatty or other substances collecting in the inner lining of the arteries and blocking the passage of blood; *cerebral thrombosis*, where a clot forms in an artery and completely shuts off the blood flow; *embolus*, a traveling blood clot that may lodge in a small artery in the brain or neck; a *cerebral hemorrhage* or a weak spot in a broken blood vessel; or in rare cases, a *tumor* that presses against a blood vessel and shuts off the blood supply.

A homemaker with any of these afflictions could be affected in several different ways. First of all, an individual could be limited to working with one hand; however, in some cases the person might use the other hand as a functional helper to assist in performing such tasks as holding things down. As stated earlier, hemiplegics usually have some loss of sensation and may not be able to feel whether things are hot or cold. Therefore, any household task exposing the homemaker to heat could be potentially dangerous. One way of solving this problem is for the person to wear thickly padded, heat resistant asbestos mitts (*see* the section on ranges and ovens in Chapter 6). Some homemakers with hemiplegia are also aphasic—they would be unable to read or understand a cookbook. Of course, mobility is often a problem, and the person might find climbing stairs or entering a house with front steps difficult.

SPINAL CORD INJURY AND PARAPLEGIA OR QUADRIPLEGIA

Paraplegia and quadriplegia are functional descriptions of physical conditions resulting from many causes, including congenital abnormalities, infections, tumors, spinal abscesses, and traumatic injuries. Thousands are disabled yearly in automobile, swimming, diving, football, skiing, motorcycle and gunshot accidents.

Dorland's Illustrated Medical Dictionary defines paraplegia as "paralysis of the legs and lower part of the body, both motion and sensation being affected."* Quadriplegia is some involvement of or total paralysis in both legs and arms.

Especially in cases of severe injury, spinal cord damage may result. But before discussing this disabling impairment you should understand a little about human anatomy. The spinal cord is a bundle of nerves approximately 17 inches long, depending on your height, and is an extension of the brain that stimulates the muscles, skin, and internal organs. Thus, any injury to the spinal cord, such as concussions, compressions, contusions, punctures, lacerations, and transections could cause an interruption in the nerve impulses and bring about paralysis. Dislocations and fractures are two of the most common reasons for spinal injury. A dislocation is any bone out of anatomical position that may cause pressure on nerves, while a fracture is a break that injures the spine. Due to the amount of damage, a person may lose either partial or total use of his limbs along with loss of sensation below the level of the injury or the lesion to the spinal cord.

So that people in the medical profession can describe a person's physical condition in a simple manner, they use a shorthand method to explain it. For example, a typical neck lesion that might result from a diving accident would be C5; C stands for the cervical region of the spinal cord, a 5 means the fifth vertebra (see

----

Dorland's Illustrated Medical Dictionary, ed. Philadelphia, Saunders, 1974, 25th ed.

Fig. 2-1). Likewise, *T8* and *D8* are the eighth thoracic and dorsal chest vertebrae, while *L* stands for the lower back, or lumbar, vertebrae. The spinal cord ends between *L1* and *L2*. Bear in mind also that no two people with the same type of lesion at a certain level necessarily have identical disabilities; this all depends on the severity of the damage.

What are some of the problems a person with paraplegia or quadriplegia should consider before attempting to become self-reliant? Table 2-I lists some of the daily living tasks and the level of injury at which people can still accomplish them. Note also that many people with paraplegia or quadriplegia can use adaptive devices to become more independent.

One of the most important things for spinal injured individuals with no sensation in their buttocks is to avoid developing decubiti, or pressure sores, which can occur as a result of prolonged sitting or lying in the same position. Since many paraplegics and quadriplegics have little or no feeling below the waistline, they must consciously remember to move periodically while sitting. If the person does not take this precaution, he might need surgery to graft new skin over the exposed sore.

Many people with spinal cord injury also have poor bladder and bowel control because the pathways that carry messages to the brain have been damaged. Therefore, the person may not know when to void and be unable to restrain his urine, making catheterization necessary. Moreover, if the individual has no sensation or muscle control, he does not have enough strength to move his bowels. In these cases sometimes another person must physically remove the feces from the rectum.

To help with bowel and bladder problems as well as give assistance with other aspects of daily living, quadriplegics always need some attendant care. However, someone with paraplegia may or may not need help, depending on the level of their lesion. For instance, a person with damage to the cervical region might be unable to walk but have no loss of sensation. Someone having a high thoracic lesion could be able to use his arms.

UPPER EXTREMITY WEAKNESS

Various disabilities cause upper extremity weakness, including

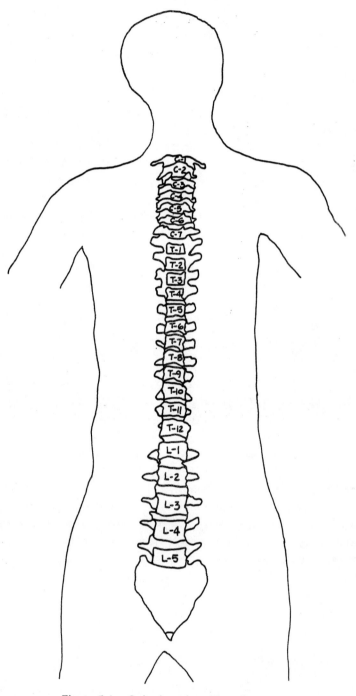

Figure 2-1. Spinal cord and vertebrae.

Table 2-I
LIMITATIONS OF THE SPINAL CORD INJURED

Daily Living Tasks	Level of Spinal Cord Lesion						
	C4	C5	C5-C6	C6	C7	C6-T4	T4 or Lower
Eating	NSR[a]	SRA[b]	SRA	SR[c]	SR	SR	SR
Hygiene							
Teeth	NSR	SRA	SRA	SR	SR	SR	SR
Hair	NSR	SRA	SRA	SR	SR	SR	SR
Shave (Men)	NSR	SRA	SRA	SR	SR	SR	SR
Makeup (Women)	NSR	SRA	SRA	SR	SR	SR	SR
Wash	NSR	SRA	SRA	SR	SR	SR	SR
Bathing	NSR	NSR	SRA	SR	SR	SR	SR
Dressing							
Upper Extremity	NSR	NSR	SRA	SR	SR	SR	SR
Lower Extremity	NSR	NSR	NSR	SRA	SR	SR	SR
Fastenings	NSR	NSR	SRA	SRA	SR	SR	SR
Toileting							
Bowel Care	NSR	NSR	NSR	SRA	SRA	SR	SR
Bladder Care	NSR	NSR	NSR	SRA	SRA	SR	SR
Bed mobility							
Sitting	NSR	NSR	NSR	SR	SR	SR	SR
Positioning	NSR	NSR	SRA	SR	SR	SR	SR
Transfers							
To Bed	NSR	NSR	NSR	SRA	SRA	SR	SR
To Toilet	NSR	NSR	NSR	SRA	SRA	SR	SR
To Car	NSR	NSR	NSR	SRA	SRA	SR	SR
Ability to Push Wheelchair							
Indoor	NSR	SRA	SRA	SR	SR	SR	Ambulatory
Outdoor	NSR	NSR	SRA	SRA	SRA	SR	Ambulatory
		(—with electric model—)					

[a] NSR—not self-reliant

[b] SRA—self-reliant with adaptive devices

[c] SR—completely self-reliant

hemiplegia, spinal injury, multiple sclerosis, polio, muscular dystrophy, and Parkinson's disease. Lack of strength in the arms can interfere with independent living in many ways. An individual with this type of impairment may have difficulty lifting, reaching, and carrying. One way to move objects without picking them up is to slide the items rather than carry them. Also, remember that a pot with a little water is easier to handle; there is no need to fill it up completely. A table on wheels or metal serving cart is also useful for someone with this disability (*see* "Basic Cooking Activities" in Chapter 6).

For a person with reduced strength in the limbs, be sure to plan all storage and work areas carefully to avoid needless reaching. People with limited upper extremity strength might also be unable to grasp and control finger movements. This could affect the homemaker's ability to dress, to groom, and to prepare meals. For instance, when cooking, the individual may find it difficult to place a knife in a knife rack but could put it on a magnetic holder easier.

ARTHRITIS AFFECTS JOINTS

Today in the United States 2 million people suffer from arthritis with an additional 600,000 new cases reported each year. One in ten people will have this disease during their lives, and it affects somebody in one of four families.

Literally, the word arthritis means *inflamation of a joint*. Although there are many different types causing aches and pains in joints and connective tissues throughout the body, two of the most common forms include rheumatoid arthritis and osteoarthritis.

Rheumatoid arthritis usually attacks the joints but can also lead to diseases of the lungs, skin, blood vessels, muscles, and heart. The symptoms are never quite the same in any two cases and may stay for a few days, disappear, and then come back again, only to return in a more severe form. When a person has an attack, he might describe his discomfort as feeling sick all over, having a fever and anemia, tiring easily, not having an appetite, or losing weight. The individual's glands and spleen might also swell. Joints in a person's hands, arms, legs, and feet can stiffen, making a complete range of motion difficult. Weeks or months may pass between arthritic attacks in the initial stages; however, in many cases gradually the condition begins to appear more often until some people cannot ignore the almost constant pain.

Osteoarthritis is also a disease of the joints, involving a

breakage of the cartilage and other tissues. Unlike rheumatoid arthritis, it causes little or no inflamation, although pain and limitation of motion sometimes occurs. With osteoarthritis there is a softening, pitting, and fraying of the smooth cartilage; the surface then loses its elasticity, making damage more likely. The cartilage often continues to wear away, exposing the smooth bone, which will rub against another one and cause pain. With these gliding surfaces gone, it becomes more painful to move the joints that have lost shape. The underlying bone ends grow thicker, and bony spurs develop where ligaments are attached. Cysts sometimes form in the bone near the joints as fragments of bone or cartilage become loose. In severe cases, osteoarthritis destroys the entire joint structure. One sign of this affliction is Heberden's nodes which appear most often on the hands of women over forty. These start on one finger, then spread to the others. Even though they may be painless, sometimes redness, swelling, and aching suddenly develop. Those with Heberden's nodes might experience numbness, tingling of the fingertips, and clumsiness of the hands. A second indication of this disability is a deformity of the finger's middle joint known as "boutonniere." Sometimes the first joint is also affected and the finger takes the form of a "swan's neck" due to the contraction caused by the impairment and pulling of the tendons.

As a result of these problems, homemakers with arthritis cannot perform certain household tasks. Often the person has severe hand involvement with limited motion in the fingers and wrist; therefore, the individual must protect his hands as much as possible by avoiding tasks that require too much strength. Such activities might include prying open screw-top jars, opening cans with a small can opener, or stirring heavy batters. You can modify these jobs using a jar opener, an electric or wall can opener, and a lightweight or portable mixer.

People with arthritis also have a reduction of manual strength; this is especially true when joints are inflamed. Since inflamation can aggravate the condition, a person should try to refrain from doing heavy manual activities such as lifting or carrying.

Because these homemakers should keep their joints mobile, they ought to avoid prolonged standing or holding. For this reason it is unwise for them to start a task unless they can stop or take a break to reduce pressure on their hands and other parts of the body. For example, a person should rest periodically while peeling or handling vegetables.

The arthritic must always watch to prevent ulnar deviation, a pressure that pushes the fingers towards the little finger. The fingers of someone with arthritis often tend to bend to one side. Obviously, if the condition becomes severe, it can greatly reduce the homemaker's ability to use one or both hands.

PROBLEMS OF INCOORDINATION
AND INDEPENDENT LIVING

Many handicaps and illnesses cause incoordination. Probably one of the best known of these is cerebral palsy, which affects about 750,000 children and adults in the United States. Every year 1 infant in 200 is born with this disability; at the present birth rate, approximately 15,000 babies are born annually with this disability. A literal definition of the word cerebral palsy is brain paralysis (*cerebral* referring to the brain and *palsy* meaning paralysis). One could define this condition as a nonprogressive disorder of movement or posture beginning in childhood because of a malfunction or damage to the brain. According to some estimates, in 86 percent of the cases a child was injured at birth, while the other 14 percent are due to skull fractures, brain hemorrhages, clots, and tumors occurring later in life. Depending on the nature of a person's injury, he could have either one of the following five types of cerebral palsy:

1. Spasticity. The person has tight limbs and difficulty using them.
2. Athetosis. Limbs often move involuntarily. An individual's purposeful movements may be contorted.
3. Rigidity. A severe form of spasticity. Most people having this form of cerebral palsy are confined to wheelchairs.
4. Ataxia. The person has an impaired sense of balance, positioning in space, and incoordinated movements.
5. Tremor. People's limbs begin to shake, especially when they attempt to use them.

Spasticity, athetosis, and ataxia are the three most common

forms of cerebral palsy; however, someone might show signs of more than one type. For example, people who are quadriplegics as a result of this impairment usually have a combination of spasticity and athetosis.

Other physical handicaps may also cause incoordination; some of these include multiple sclerosis, Parkinson's disease, and Friedreich's ataxia.

An individual with a disability involving incoordination could have numerous difficulties when attempting to live independently. These can range from gross motor skill deficiencies, such as walking, standing, and maintaining balance, to fine motor skill problems, such as threading a needle, buttoning clothing, or feeding oneself. For instance, when the person is eating, he might spill his glass of milk while trying to drink it, or throw food on the floor while attempting to put it in his mouth.

THE WHEELCHAIR HOMEMAKER

People use wheelchairs for many different reasons. Individuals with a number of disabilities, including those already mentioned in this chapter, may be unable to use the lower extremities. Others, such as those with arthritis, may be confined to a wheelchair when their condition reaches an acute or severe stage and can walk independently or with the aid of a cane or crutches when the arthritic attack subsides. In different cases a person might be paralyzed or have poor muscular control of his legs and be chairbound permanently. Throughout this book various ways of making life easier for those in wheelchairs will be presented as well as structural modifications to provide greater accessibility and convenience in the home; however, here is a brief description of some of the problem areas:

HEIGHT CONSIDERATIONS.   All work surfaces must be lower, so that the person can reach them comfortably.

EXTENDED FOOTRESTS.   Without some modification, extended footrests make it impossible for a person to move close to such places as bathroom vanities or kitchen sinks.

SPACE LIMITATIONS.   Often wheelchairs are much wider than doorways. This is especially true in public restrooms or bathrooms in commercially built tract homes.

REDUCED LEVERAGE FOR OPENING DOORS.   Often a chairbound

person is unable to open a double door, since frequently when pushing one side with his right hand and pulling the other door with his left, the chair may turn; so after opening it he cannot push his chair inside.

ENTRANCES MUST HAVE RAMPS. To make homes and public places accessible to people in wheelchairs, all buildings must have ramps. Chapter 10 discusses how to construct them so they will be safe and easier for a disabled person to use.

Some people in wheelchairs have poor trunk balance. In these cases the person might find it difficult to remain sitting in an upright position. Consequently, activities such as handling cooking utensils from the standard height counter or range may be strenuous or impossible.

LOWER ENERGY LEVEL. Disabled people must expend more energy in doing daily living tasks, since pushing themselves in a wheelchair 100 yards is equal to an able-bodied person walking a mile.

DAILY TASKS WITH CRUTCHES

People with various disabilities use crutches; however, frequently they have balance problems. This can complicate various household tasks. Take, for instance, cleaning a living room rug. Micky has difficulty managing a tank type of vacuum since she must hold the hose with one hand while balancing herself with a crutch. Often Micky has the sensation of falling; in fact, she has tripped and fallen many times. Although she could vacuum from a wheelchair, she can do it faster from a standing position.

If you walk with crutches, there is a way of maintaining your balance while grocery shopping. Always use a basket so that you can put your crutches inside. Then grab the handle tightly to help stabilize yourself. This way you can remove items from the shelf with one hand, while holding on firmly to the grocery cart with the other, securing yourself so you will not fall when taking things off the shelf.

People using crutches also find it impossible to carry items as they walk. However, with a little ingenuity you can solve this problem. Marlene, an amputee, found a way to take her clothes outside and put them on the line to dry. In order to do this easily without asking for help, Marlene sewed a strip of heavy wide hem tape to a cloth bag. Then on laundry days she filled the bag with clothes and put the strap over her shoulder to pull the bag of clothes behind her as she walks.

A person walking with crutches may also become tired from prolonged walking or standing. Because of this, an individual may need to use a wheelchair for some daily activities. For instance, Francis, a college freshman, is ambulatory with crutches around the house but uses a motorized wheelchair to save time and energy traveling long distances at school between classes.

UPPER EXTREMITY AMPUTEES

An amputee may work with only one hand, while some use the remaining part of their amputated limb as a functional helper in daily activities; still others learn to function with a prosthesis. This depends partly on the level of amputation. Generally, a person is more capable with an arm removed below the elbow and can manage better with an artificial limb than someone whose amputation was at a higher point. Therefore, the level partly determines whether or not an individual has a prosthesis.

There are different types of artifical limbs. Some have hooks for grasping objects, but others are more for cosmetic purposes and are less functional. To illustrate this point, Penny, a high school student, wears a prosthesis resembling a regular arm and hand with fingers; however, she is unable to hold anything. Therefore, she can only use it for activities such as steadying a piece of paper.

Other people cannot use or do not feel comfortable wearing a prosthesis; consequently, they function one handed, although as stated earlier, depending where the limb was amputated, they can use it as a functional helper. For example, Doris, with her left hand removed at the wrist, uses her arm to hold a mixing bowl next to her chest as she stirs cake batter.

Finally, some therapists believe that amputees born with congenital defects learn many of the daily living skills much easier than those who lose limbs later in life.

As stated previously, amputees must learn to perform daily living tasks either with or without a prosthesis. Those with an artificial limb can be taught ways of positioning kitchen utensils and other items correctly for basic activities such as cutting, holding large objects, carrying pans, and washing dishes.

CUTTING.   Always hold the knife with your functional hand. If you use two prostheses, put the knife in the one you use the best. Be sure to steady the fork so it rests on the outside surface of the prosthesis' thumb. When handling a fork, move the wrist unit and rotate it so that the tines touch the plate surface evenly.

If you are concerned about your kitchen utensils slipping, you can put a strip of electric tape around the handle of the ones you are using.

HOLDING OBJECTS.   Point the hooks of your prosthesis upward or downward, and use the rounded part of the hooks to hold the object.

CARRYING PANS.   Place the hook finger of your prothesis parallel with the pan at the same height as your waist. Hold it with your functional hand and push the edge into the opening of your artifical limb. If your amputation is above the elbow, always check to see that the elbow joint is locked.

WASHING DISHES.   To make this task easy, hold the dish in your hand and the cloth or sponge with your prosthesis. Do not use detergents, since they often dissolve the lubricating oil in the hook and wrist of your artificial limb. Keep the threads and bearings clean and well oiled so that frequent use of water will not harm them.

For those who work with one hand, there are other techniques. However, since these also have applications for other disability groups, including those with incoordination, upper extremity weakness, and hemiplegia, they are discussed further in Chapter 6.

DAILY LIVING WITH CARDIAC DISABILITIES

As was discussed at the beginning of this chapter, some physical impairments can be seen, while others cannot. However, in the latter cases they still hinder the homemaker in performing certain daily living tasks. Previously it was mentioned that cardiac disabilities, which according to the American Heart Association affects about 30 million people in the United States, is one group of invisible limitations. Although there are many types, the most common forms are atherosclerosis and hypertension.

Atherosclerosis is the major cause of heart attacks. As stated before, fatty deposits, composed mainly of cholesterol, can accumulate in the arteries. If this continues over a long period of time, the deposits line the artery walls, restricting or completely shutting off the blood flow. Under these conditions, the person can suffer a heart attack if it involves the coronary arteries.

On the other hand, hypertension, commonly known as high blood pressure, results from blood flowing through the arteries at a faster than normal rate, creating a pressure on the walls of the arteries. Consequently, when the rate is higher over a long period of time, the artery walls thicken and lose their elasticity. This increased speed places a strain on the heart, making it more likely the person will suffer a stroke.

It is obvious that the homemaker with heart disease should avoid tension, worry, and anxiety-provoking situations that tend to increase the individual's blood pressure. Furthermore, when the small arteries contract, sometimes the person's cholesterol level temporarily rises.

Someone having a cardiac disability may also become overly tired easily. To prevent this, the person might want to refrain from climbing steps, lifting and pushing, or carrying heavy objects. In addition, people with heart problems may have a lower energy level; they should plan only as much work as they can accomplish comfortably in a day and not exert themselves beyond their endurance.

This chapter has covered several of the disabilities and some of the special problems handicapped people with certain physical limitations may face when living independently. To assist them in reaching that goal, the remainder of this book is devoted to ways of making their lives easier.

POINTS TO REMEMBER

1. *Hemiplegia paralyzes one side of the body.* This condition might also cause weakness in the lower two-thirds of the face, loss of sensation, vision and hearing impairments, personality changes, and aphasia. These homemakers are frequently limited to the use of one hand and may find reading

difficult. They could also have mobility problems.

2. *Paraplegia affects the lower extremities, while quadriplegia involves four limbs.* Spinal cord injury can cause both of these impairments. Paraplegics and quadriplegics must learn to prevent pressure sores, might require catheterizing, and may need help to eliminate fecal matter. Consequently, in some cases these individuals may need attendant care.

3. *Several handicapping conditions often cause upper extremity weakness.* For people with this type of impairment, lifting, reaching, carrying, and grasping is often strenuous or impossible. Furthermore, the person might be unable to control his fingers well enough to accomplish fine movements required for such tasks as fastening buttons.

4. *Arthritis inflames joints.* Two prevalent forms of arthritis are rheumatoid arthritis and osteoarthritis. Frequently, the homemaker has a limited range of motion in the fingers, hands, and wrist. Inflamed joints sometimes accompany this weakness. Arthritics should avoid prolonged standing and holding things; they ought to try to prevent ulnar deviation.

5. *Incoordination may result from various disabilities.* Incoordination could interfere with fine or gross motor skills. In some cases, both are affected.

6. *Wheelchair homemakers have special needs.* Wheelchair homemakers should do their work on lower surfaces with accommodations for footrests. In the community, chairbound individuals often find heavy doors difficult to open, because of the leverage created from a seated position. All buildings must have ramps for them to enter because they must expend a greater amount of energy to push themselves in their chairs than a person who walks. Some chairbound individuals also have poor trunk balance.

7. *People using crutches have a restricted ability to carry items, and they have a tendency to tire easily.*

8. *Amputee homemakers may function one handed or use prosthetic devices.* Some use the remaining part of their amputated limb to assist them in certain tasks.

9. *Atherosclerosis and hypertension are two major forms of*

heart disease. Restriction for these homemakers could include the following: refraining from climbing steps, lifting, pushing, and carrying heavy objects. Often people with cardiac disabilities also have a lower energy level.

Chapter 3

TAKE CARE OF YOUR BODY

From early childhood all of us begin developing habits of personal hygiene and self-care. Staying clean and neat is important for everyone, but this is especially true for someone with a physical disability, since they should always accentuate the positive aspects of their personality to minimize or detract from any impairments.

YOU AND YOUR BED

Feeling good to make a favorable impression on others starts with having a restful night's sleep. To do this, a disabled person must be able to move freely in his bed. Therefore, if you are unable to position your body normally as you lie in bed, you should develop some basic skills to assist you in rolling over, sitting up, and moving forwards and backwards on your mattress.

Rolling Over

Learning to roll over allows you to change how you are lying, reach objects on your nightstand, manage blankets and sheets, and perform dressing tasks easier. However, depending on what your disability is, you might need to learn to accomplish this differently. Following are four ways, with a step-by-step method for each one.

WITH THE ASSISTANCE OF PILLOWS. Persons having a spinal cord injury at the C6 level will need an attendant to lift them, since their legs are paralyzed. If you are disabled this way, always remember to assist the individual helping you by trying to use your arms.

Step No. 1:	Have your attendant lay you on your back near the far side of the bed. Then tell him to place three pillows next to you on the other half of the bed.
Step No. 2:	Instruct the person helping you to cross your left leg over your right one.
Step No. 3:	Place your left arm over your chest, reaching over the pillows, and grab the edge of the mattress with your left hand. Ask your attendant to put his left hand on your left shoulder and his right hand in back of your right knee.
Step No. 4:	Tell him to turn you on your stomach while you try to help by bending your right elbow.
Step No. 5:	Your attendant should then adjust the pillows beneath you if necessary. So this is easier for him, press down with closed fists on the mattress, relieving the pressure as he tries to make you comfortable. (*Note:* To roll back to your original position, reverse the process.)

ROLLING OVER USING YOUR WHEELCHAIR. Someone who cannot grasp may be able to link his wrists under his wheelchair's armrest to help him roll over.

Step No. 1:	Lie near the left side of your bed, being careful not to fall off the edge. Have your wheelchair positioned at the right side of the bed, brakes locked, and facing the foot.
Step No. 2:	Roll to the right and put your left arm across your chest as you reach for the wheelchair.
Step No. 3:	Link your left wrist *over* the armrest, and your right wrist *underneath*.
Step No. 4:	Bend both elbows with force and brace them on the armrest, then slowly pull yourself over towards the chair. With this process, you should also be able to cross and uncross your legs while turning. (*Note:* To reverse the process, use the same procedure except

push rather than *pull* with your wrists.)

USING A ROPE SOMETIMES HELPS. Some people with no voluntary control of the legs may want to use this method if their bed has a headboard with rungs and a side railing. Attach a heavy rope to the bedspring then to the top of the side railing; be sure to leave a portion of it hanging over the railing. Knot the rope in several places to make it easier for you to grasp and to move your fingers along as you turn your body.

Step No. 1:   Take hold of the headboard with your left hand and the rope with your right.

Step No. 2:   Feel the knots along the rope helping you to grasp. Pull on the rope as you start to turn onto your left side.

Step No. 3:   Grab the upper bar of the railing and with your elbow bent; pull yourself over completely.

TURNING WHILE HOLDING THE HEADBOARD AND MATTRESS. If you do not have normal grasping strength but can grab the headboard and mattress of your bed, you might try this method.

Step No. 1:   Lie on your back not too near the edge of your bed and take hold of the rungs on your headboard with your left hand.

Step No. 2:   Reach out and clutch the edge of the mattress with your right hand.

Step No. 3:   Flip yourself over. (*Note:* To roll in the opposite direction, push against the headboard with the heels of your hands until you return to your original position.)

Sitting Up

Mastering techniques of sitting up will enable you to move from a sitting to a lying posture and prepare you for managing tasks that require the use of your hands. Three ways severely handicapped people might be able to accomplish this task are presented here.

WITH AN ATTENDANT'S AID. As indicated before, quadriplegics with a spinal cord lesion at either the C5 or C6 level require assistance to move. In these cases, someone must raise the person's head and shoulders off the mattress to help him. Then the individual can lock his arms and push himself into an upright position in bed. If you want to use this method, follow this procedure:

Step No. 1:   Have your attendant raise your head and right shoulder while you keep leaning on your left shoulder.

Step No. 2:   Tell him to continue supporting your back. He should then bring your head and shoulder up until you are able to lean on both forearms.

Step No. 3:   Shift more weight on your right forearm. Push on the left fist, locking your left elbow first, then your right. Tell the attendant to remove his hand, since you can now balance yourself and sit independently.

USE A ROPE AND YOUR WHEELCHAIR'S ARMREST. Some disabled people can tie a rope and hold on to the armrest of their chair to assist them. To use this procedure, attach a rope to the railing or to the mattress on one side of the bed. Position your wheelchair with its brakes locked on the opposite side.

Step No. 1:   Grab the rope with your right hand and the wheelchair's armrest with your left.

Step No. 2:   Pull yourself into a sitting position.

Step No. 3:   Push with your left hand and extend your left elbow while pulling on the rope with your right hand until you achieve balance.

PUSHING WITH YOUR FOREARMS IN A HOSPITAL BED. For some disabled people it might be easier to sit up in a hospital bed rather than a regular one.

Step No. 1:   Have your attendant crank it up to a 90° angle and lean against the raised portion.

Step No. 2:   Bend your elbows, placing them behind you, and push strongly against the bed portion.

Step No. 3:   Maneuver your head and trunk forward. This bends your hips and will bring you into a sitting position.

Moving Forward and Backward

Another skill some handicapped people must learn is how to slide back and forth on their mattresses. Since many do not have use of the lower extremities, they must devise special ways.

USE A BOARD AND ROPE. A person may want to scoot from side to side, bend forward, and move toward the foot of the bed. Lie on one side and have someone place a board underneath you. It should be smooth and long enough to provide a firm surface for support. Next, your attendant should tie a heavy rope to the right side of the foot of your bed.

Step No. 1: While sitting on the board, hold the rope with your right hand to maintain balance. Grab the board with your left hand as near to your left ankle as possible. Pull on the rope, then shift your weight forward to the left.

Step No. 2: Pull on the rope with your right hand and move forward at the same time. Repeat this process until you are at the end of the board.

USING THE MATTRESS TO SHIFT YOUR WEIGHT. Some disabled people pull themselves along on the mattress while creating momentum.

Step No. 1: Sit up and extend your legs as much as possible.

Step No. 2: Put both fists near your hips on the mattress.

Step No. 3: Bend and thrust your head and trunk forward. Shift your weight to your hands and slide your body ahead. Repeat the process until you move into the desired position.

MAKING WHEELCHAIR TRANSFERS EASIER

People who use wheelchairs and are physically able should learn transfer techniques that enable them to move from the chair to another place. There are many types of transfers, but three of the most common include going from your wheelchair to a bed, toilet, or tub.

Transferring In and Out of Bed

USING ROPES AND A BOARD. To move from your wheelchair into a bed, attach one rope to the head and another to the foot of the bed. Sit on your chair with the brakes locked, facing the bed, and ask your attendant to lift both of your legs onto the bed surface. Then, have your attendant place one end of the board under you and the other end on the bed. Take hold of both armrests, moving yourself forward until you can grasp the two ropes.

Step No. 1: Push your body forward and pull on the left rope, then lean to the side. Your right leg will advance.

Step No. 2: Tug on the right rope and lean that way. Now your left leg will slide ahead.

Step No. 3: Repeat steps one and two until you are on the bed and can roll to the right. Then pull on the rope tied to the head of the bed with both hands; this helps take the pressure off the board so your attendant can remove it and assist you in lying down.

To slide back into your chair follow steps four through six.

Step No. 4: Grab both ropes with your right and left hands. Put most of your weight on the right side so that your left leg will move backwards.

Step No. 5: Shift your weight to the left, enabling your right leg to move backwards.

Step No. 6: Repeat steps four and five until you are far enough backwards so that you can grasp the armrests of your wheelchair. This will give you support until you have slid completely in your seat.

TRANSFER INTO A WHEELCHAIR SIDEWAYS USING A BOARD. Some wheelchairs have removable armrests so you can enter them from the side. To do this, place your wheelchair near the bed, take off the left armrest, and make certain the brakes are locked. Sit on the right edge of your bed, facing the footboard.

Step No. 1. Slide towards the right. Grab the mattress with your left hand to steady yourself. Move your right leg towards the edge of the bed. If needed, use your right hand to assist you in doing this. Move your left leg over in the same way. Repeat the process until both legs are over the edge of the bed.

Step No. 2:   Place your right hand on the back of your
                     wheelchair and the left one on the mattress to
                     balance yourself. Lean to the left so your
                     attendant can put one end of the board
                     under you.

Step No. 3:   Grasp the right armrest with your left hand.
                     Have your attendant push you sideways so
                     you can slide over the board and into your
                     wheelchair.

Step No. 4:   Have your attendant remove the board and
                     help position you in your chair.

Remember, you also must learn to transfer from your wheelchair to the bed. When doing that procedure, just reverse the
order of the steps.

SHIFTING SIDEWARDS WITHOUT A BOARD. Some people who have
greater use of their legs can make a transfer without a board.
Such a person may be able to accomplish this by shifting the
weight from one side to the other on their buttocks until they
can slide into the chair from the side where their armrest has
been removed. Therefore, take off the right armrest, making
certain also that the footrests are in an upright position before
you start the transfer.

Step No. 1:   Steady yourself by placing your right hand
                     on the mattress and your left hand on your
                     wheelchair's seat.

Step No. 2:   Shift your weight from side to side and
                     wiggle to the edge of the bed. When you can
                     place your left hand on the left armrest, you
                     are ready to transfer your body into the chair.

Getting On and Off Your Toilet

There are many ways people confined to wheelchairs transfer
to a toilet. Of course, which one you use may depend partly
on your disability. Here are some of the methods.

RAISED TOILET SEATS. Equipment manufacturers make raised
toilet seats that fit over a regular one, making it the same level
as a wheelchair so that a disabled person does not need to lift
himself up and down. You can use this if you are able to
slide, wiggle, or otherwise move yourself sideways. However,

Figure 3-1.   Raised toilet seat. Illustration furnished by Everest and Jennings.

there must be space alongside your toilet to accomplish the transfer.

Step No. 1:   Remove the right armrest from your wheelchair, and position it near the left side of the toilet.

Step No. 2:   Put your right hand on the toilet seat and your left hand on the left armrest of your wheelchair.

Step No. 3:   While supporting yourself with both hands, slide sidewards onto the toilet seat. Keep sliding until you can grasp the grab bars fastened near the toilet.

TRANSFER TO A TOILET WITHOUT A RAISED SEAT. If a person can lift himself, he may be able to use the same procedure outlined previously without a raised toilet seat.

USE A STRAIGHT CHAIR AS A BRIDGE. If your bathroom door is not wide enough for a wheelchair to pass through, place a small wooden chair between it and the toilet. Perhaps you need more than one chair to bridge the distance between your wheelchair and the toilet seat.

Step No. 1:   Place a wooden chair sideways between your wheelchair and the toilet.

Step No. 2:   Move your wheelchair as close to the doorway of the bathroom as possible.

Step No. 3:   Put your left hand on the seat of your
                   wheelchair, and your right hand on the seat
                   of the wooden chair. Then make your transfer
                   by wiggling from the wheelchair to the
                   wooden chair.

Step No. 4:   Place your right hand on the toilet seat
                   and the left one on the straight chair's seat.
                   Now, move yourself to the toilet.

COMMODE CHAIRS ELIMINATE TRANSFERS. Often when a bathroom door is too narrow for a wheelchair, the disabled person
may use a commode chair. Those chairs are 17¼ inches wide and
have a cutout seat for attending to toilet need. They are also high
enough so someone can wheel them over a toilet seat, and no
transfer is necessary.

Armrests placed along the side of a toilet and free-standing
grab bars are useful for some people, but since installing these
requires some structural modification in the bathroom, they will
be discussed in Chapter 10.

Transferring to the Tub

A major obstacle some individuals in wheelchairs encounter is
the 20 inch high walls of some bathtubs. Disabled people who
have no control of their legs must lower themselves into the tub
using only both hands to support their body. Therefore, such a
transfer can be strenuous. The bottom of the tub, which is
frequently slippery, is also another potential hazard.

However, transferring to a tub may be possible for some people
with no use of their lower extremities but who have the ability to
place their arms on the wheelchair's armrest and grasp a grab bar
installed on the wall above the rim of the tub. The person will
then be able to lower and raise himself into and out of the tub.

To begin the process, wheel your chair a few inches from the
edge of the tub and lock the brakes so you will be able to put one
leg over the side of the tub and then the other leg. Now swing your
footrests aside, unlock the brakes, and pull your wheelchair as
close to the tub as possible.

Step No. 1:   Put one hand on each armrest to steady
                   yourself. Then push on both hands, which

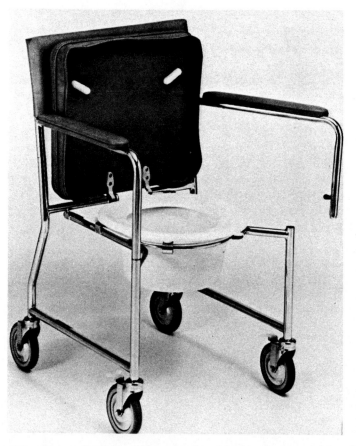

Figure 3-2.   Commode chair. Illustration furnished by Everest and Jennings.

will help slide you forward until you sit on the edge of the tub.

Step No. 2:   Place your right hand on the rim of the tub, and when you are steady move it to the bar. Turn your body slowly, facing the narrow end of the tub.

Step No. 3:   Now, with your left hand hold onto the edge of the tub. Push strongly with both hands as you bend your elbows and slide off the side into the tub. (*Note:* For climbing out of the tub, reverse the process).

Of course, it is impossible to cover all the bed-positioning skills and wheelchair transfer techniques, so you are encouraged to refer to *Activities of Daily Living for Physical Rehabilitation* for further reference (*see* bibliography).

URINARY MANAGEMENT

As stated earlier, people with spinal injury almost always wear an indwelling catheter. Likewise, other disabled individuals such as those with multiple sclerosis and hemiplegia may also use one, since they could be unable to void properly. In other words, when the bladder has filled with urine, catheterization allows it to drain voluntarily without the person having to control this function. Of course, one should always seek medical advice in caring for bladder problems, but here is some information everyone using a catheter should know.

CATHETERIZATION AND URINARY PHYSIOLOGY. Refer to Figure 3-3 to help you understand the following discussion of the urinary structure and catheterization. In males, the catheter is inserted through the penis up the urethra into the bladder. Females have it inserted directly into the urethra, located in front of the vaginal opening.

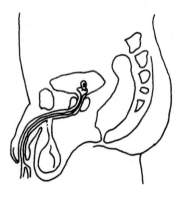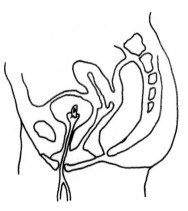

MALE   FEMALE

Figure 3-3.   Catheters in urinary tracts.

USING A CATHETER. Depending on someone's physical condition, he may need the catheter changed at different time intervals. For example, some people may need to have this done once a week, while others use one for a month; there is no specific time, since it is a personal matter. For people using catheters over a long duration, an *indwelling* or *retention* type is prescribed—most often a *Foley catheter*. In some communities the local health agency provides nurses who will visit a person's home and do the procedure for him. Whenever possible, for the sake of cleanliness, one should have medically trained personnel change the catheter. However, a man if he desires could learn to do this himself, while females always need assistance. Therefore, here is a list of the necessary equipment and a description of the procedure for catheterizing males.

Figure 3-4. Foley catheter.

Figure 3-5. Catheter kit. Illustration furnished by Davol Inc.

Equipment:
    1. Catheterization Tray containing
       a. One sterile emesis basin
       b. Three sterile 4 × 4 cotton pads
       c. One paper drape with hole in center or three towels
       d. One 5 or 10 cc syringe (used to fill Foley catheter)
       e. Two 100 cc plastic cups
    2. Sterile gloves
    3. Water soluble lubricant (sometimes known as K-Y® jelly)
    4. Water
    5. Foley catheter
    6. Asepto® syringe (for b.i.d. irrigation)
    7. Drainage bag for collecting urine

Procedure:

Step No. 1:	Lay all the equipment on a clean sterile table.
Step No. 2:	Put on the gloves.
Step No. 3:	Lie down or sit in a comfortable position. If sitting, put the drape over your lap with your penis extending through the hole (see Fig. 3-6), or use three towels.
Step No. 4:	Clean your penis. Put soap and water or a benzalkonium chloride cleaning solution in one cup on the catheterization tray and water for rinsing in the other one. Wash the head of your penis well. If you have not been circumcized, pull back the foreskin and cleanse thoroughly. This is important, since much bacteria gathers there. Now rinse with water.
Step No. 5:	Take the syringe, and fill it with 5 cc of water. Then inject the liquid into the catheter at one end to blow up the Foley bag at the other end to make certain it does not have a hole.
Step No. 6:	Put the water-soluble lubricant on the end of the catheter that you will insert into your penis.
Step No. 7:	Gently push the catheter into your urethra all the way up to the bladder. If this is done correctly, urine will flow out.

Figure 3-6.

Step No. 8:   Put enough water into the syringe to fill
                 the Foley bag, and insert it into the catheter.
                 (Remember, there are two openings at one
                 end of the Foley catheter, one leading to the
                 urine and the other leading to the inflatable
                 balloon. Be sure to inject the water into the
                 balloon end. A sure way of telling is to check
                 which end the urine flows from. Then place
                 the syringe into the other tip.)

Step No. 9:   When the balloon has filled with water,
                 some catheters automatically clamp off. If
                 yours does not, you will have to do it
                 manually so the water cannot drain back out.

Step No. 10:   Strap the urine bag to one leg underneath
                 your clothing.

DOING YOUR B.I.D. IRRIGATION.* Regardless of how often
you have your catheter changed, you should perform an irrigation of the indwelling type two times each day to prevent

_____

*B.I.D. means twice daily. (*Bi* means twice. *D* stands for daily).

infections. This is done to cleanse your bladder so that bacteria will not develop. When irrigating your bladder, use a 50 cc syringe and inject a urological solution that has the same chemical composition as your urine. Be sure to insert the syringe into the urine end of your catheter and not the one that attaches to the leg bag. Let the solution flow up the drainage tube through the urethra into your bladder; then allow it to drain out.

GENITOURINARY COMPLICATIONS. If a person wearing a catheter does not have good personal hygiene habits, some of the following complications might result:

1. Infections. Infections, which may occur from improper cleansing of the bladder, are potentially fatal for those requiring catheterization. Among the symptoms that often appear are nausea, chills, and fever. Usually the condition is treated with antibiotics and the use of ice packs. Furthermore, an individual who develops infections is generally instructed to remain in bed with the scrotum elevated.

2. Stones. Different types of stones can sometimes form and lodge in the urinary tract. Some are soft and easily crushed, while others are hard. Frequently, stones cause infections and might be found in the kidneys or bladder. When they are in the kidneys, the individual often needs to undergo surgery. On the other hand, doctors can either use a special solution to dissolve bladder stones, the procedure of litholapaxy to crush them, or perform an operation to remove oversized ones.

3. Fistulas. Penal or penoscrotal fistulas result from the improper positioning of a catheter. This causes rubbing and pressure on the penis, which over a long period of time could produce sores. To prevent this from happening, make sure your penis can move freely without any restrictions once you are catheterized.

4. Urethral stricture. A urethral stricture is an obstruction of the urethra that blocks the urine flow from the bladder through the penis.

BOWEL CARE

Disabled people with no sensation in their rectum do not have the muscle strength for bowel movements and often need some help. Therefore, to avoid other health problems, the person must put himself on a schedule. For example, Jerry, a quadriplegic, sits on the toilet every morning after breakfast. A handicapped individual like Jerry can use one of three procedures to assist in dislodging his stools. These include digital stimulation, chemicals or agents, and enemas.

DIGITAL STIMULATION. A paraplegic may be able to use this method independently, while a quadriplegic always needs assistance. The purpose of digital stimulation is to stimulate a reflex to enable the person to eliminate his stool. You will need the following equipment. Then be sure to pay close attention to the steps outlined.

Equipment:
1. Disposable unsterile gloves
2. Lubricating jelly (Vaseline®)
3. Toilet tissue

Procedure:

Step No. 1: Put on your gloves and lubricate your index finger.

Step No. 2: Insert your finger through the anal opening, and move it in a circular motion outward toward your spine. (*Caution:* Do not point your finger inward, since you might injure your bladder.) Remove any fecal matter present in the opening of the rectum.

Step No. 3: When the rectum is clear of feces, massage the inner sphincter muscle. Make a circular motion with your finger to open it. Place the finger as far up as it will go in your anus so you can reach that muscle.

Step No. 4: Use toilet tissue to clean your buttocks, and cleanse it with soap and water. Then be sure to wash your hands.

CHEMICALS AND AGENTS. If digital stimulation proves unsuccessful, you might try using chemicals and agents. There are basically three types: glycerine or Dulcolax® suppositories, stool softeners for constipation (which shorten the time of defecation), and laxatives. Senekot® and Colace® are two types of stool softeners, while milk of magnesia is often prescribed as a laxative. However, remember that prolonged use of laxatives can lead to dependency.

ENEMAS. Your last alternative is an enema. Resort to them only when absolutely necessary, since they may also become habit forming. One type is the Fleet® ready-to-use mineral oil enema sold in many drugstores.

CARE OF THE SKIN

Anatomy and Functions

ANATOMY. You have two layers of skin tissues: an *epidermis*, the top portion, and the *dermis*, a lower one. The epidermis is made up of an outer horny thickness of dead cells, which act as a buffer between the outside environment and an inner level of living cells that regenerate new ones to replace those that are sloughed off periodically.

The dermis, containing hair follicles, sweat glands, blood vessels, and nerve endings, is a thick underlying portion with fibrous connective tissues that make the skin strong yet pliable.

FUNCTIONS. The skin shields the body from chemicals and physical agents, microorganisms, and the sun's ultraviolet rays. Your palms and feet also have thicker and tougher layers for added protection.

Your skin has other functions. Nerves in certain areas of the skin, such as the palms, soles of your feet, and eyelids, are sensitive to touch and heat. In addition, the skin regulates fluids and temperature in your body. Water and salts are continually excreted through your sweat glands, even though you are not perspiring. Evaporation assists in regulating body temperature.

General Considerations for Cleanliness

Whether you are bathing or washing your face, you should remember a few basic points.

BE GENTLE TO YOUR SKIN. Avoid harsh rubbing with rough cloths, since you might harm the tissues, particularly if you have poor circulation or a skin irritation.

SELECT THE RIGHT SOAP. Check with your doctor about the

soap you use. He might advise you to purchase a special brand. Some physicians recommend a superfatted soap for people with sensitive skin. People having a more oily type should bathe with a soap that helps in drying and closing the pores.

Individuals with skin problems, such as acne, may want to use an antibacterial detergent. This preparation dries the surface, but it can be washed off easier than soap. However, always remember to rinse your body thoroughly before using a towel.

LOTIONS AND CREAMS GIVE PROTECTION. Lotions and creams can either protect or soften your skin, and some have both qualities. Also, do not forget that some creams soften more, while others protect the skin better.

DEODORANTS AND ANTIPERSPIRANTS REDUCE BODY ODORS. Both men and women should use deodorants and antiperspirants. If your skin is sensitive to one brand, try another one. Did you also know that cornstarch can be applied to reduce moisture under a woman's breast or between the toes?

Bathing Hints

Frequent bathing is extremely important for disabled people, especially if they have difficulty feeding themselves, drool, or have bowel and bladder problems. You should bathe at least twice a week, still better once a day. However, if your skin is dry, perhaps a dermatologist may recommend that you take a bath less often. Sometimes emollient creams or lotions with lanolin help to reduce scaling and drying. When washing, be sure to cleanse your face, underarms, and genital area thoroughly. Since females using a catheter have it exposed to menstrual flow, they should always cleanse themselves well during menses and each time they remove the sanitary pads.

BATHING AIDS. Here are some aids that disabled people find helpful when bathing.

1. Bathtub safety rail. You can grasp the bathtub safety rail when you enter or leave the tub. It is styled so a disabled person is able to grip it firmly with either one or two hands. This safety rail is adjustable to fit 4-, 5-, or 6-inch tub walls. The durable nylon coated steel tubing rail will fit both straight and tapered sidewalls of a tub (See Fig. 3-7).

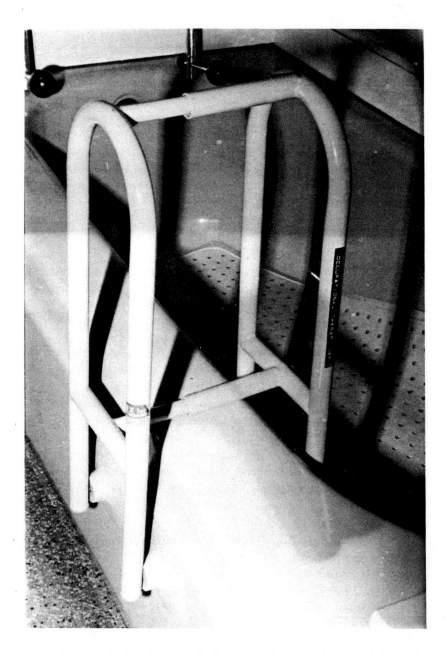

Figure 3-7.   Bathtub and safety rail. Illustration furnished by Cleo Living Aids.

2. Patient lift. The patient lift enables another person to lift someone from a wheelchair into a bathtub easily. Simply help the handicapped individual to transfer into the portable sling, which can be attached with chains to the patient lift. Then turn the crank to activate the hydraulic cylinder, which lifts the person upward. To lower him into the tub, turn it the other way.

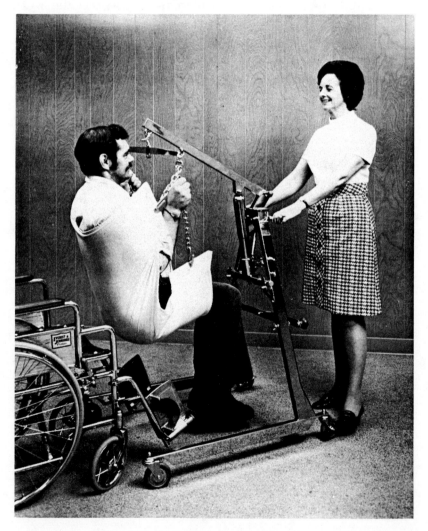

Figure 3-8.   Patient lift. Illustration furnished by Everest and Jennings.

3. The Trevo Lifter®. The Trevo Lifter, which has been tested in more than 10,000 up-and-down cycles with 185 pounds of weight, is a chair that can be put inside the bathtub and that can be raised and lowered. To install this device, remove the aerator from the faucet and install the proper adapter in its place. Mount the Trevo Lift's control on the wall with the lever in an *up* position. Connect the hose to the faucet. In doing this, make certain to pull down on the white plastic ring that you also fasten on the adapter; then release it to lock the hose in place. Open the cold water tap all the way. If the lever is in the *up* position, the chair will rise to the rim of the tub. When the chair has risen to the

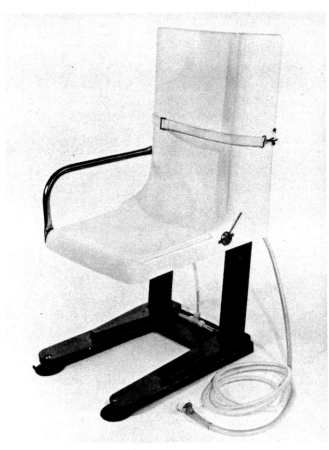

Figure 3-9.   The Trevo Lifter. Illustration furnished by Geddis, Inc.

proper level, move the control lever to the *intermediate* position while you slide onto the chair. Then push it into the *down* position to lower the chair to 1½ inches from the bottom of the tub. When you have finished bathing, lift the lever to the *up* position again, and the chair will slowly rise to the rim of the tub and stop.

4. Soap ball. Some people who lack proper coordination or have limited use of their arms and hands might have difficulty grabbing the soap because the bar floats in the tub. If you have this problem, one solution could be to purchase a soap ball that fastens around your neck with a rope. It is easier for some disabled people to reach and it also prevents the soap from slipping back into the water where one might have a difficult time grasping it again.

5. Back brush. A long-handled brush makes washing your back easier, especially for those with limited reaching ability.

6. Flexible shower hose. A flexible shower hose brings the spray nearer to the handicapped person and can be used as a fixed or a hand-held shower. Often these are easier for someone with a disability to manage, since the individual can direct the water where desired.

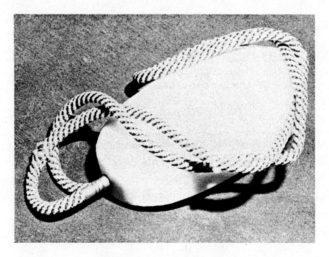

Figure 3-10.   Soap ball.

Figure 3-11.   Back brush. Illustration furnished by Empire Brush Company.

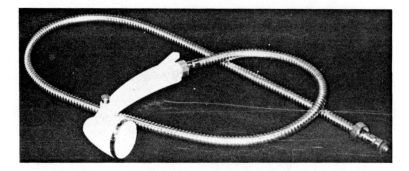

Figure 3-12.   Flexible shower hose. Illustration furnished by Cleo Living Aids.

Drying Yourself

After you have bathed, always remember to dry your body well. For some disabled people with limited arm extension, this can be a difficult task. One way to solve the problem is to sit in a chair or wheelchair with a large cloth over the back to absorb the moisture as you rub against it.

Another helpful aid for drying is a towel that you can double and cut to a desired length, having a loop fastened to each end. In using this, a handicapped individual needs only a limited

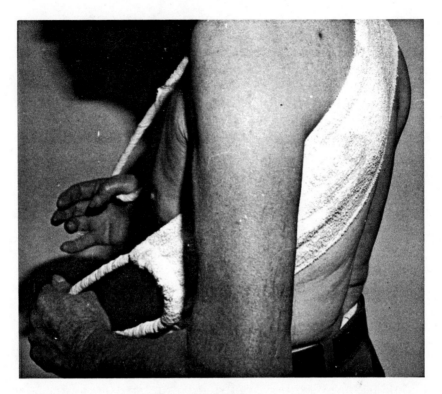

Figure 3-13.   Back dryer.

amount of elbow flexion and reaching ability to dry himself adequately.

Prevention of Decubitus Ulcers

As mentioned in the last chapter, people with spinal cord injury could develop *decubiti*, or pressure sores, resulting from sitting in the same position without moving for a long period of time. They are also sometimes referred to as decubitus ulcers. Since these open wounds can become infected, the disabled individual must stay alert to prevent this condition from occurring or, if necessary to seek treatment in the initial stages. Otherwise, serious complications may result, and in some cases skin grafts might need to be performed.

To keep decubitus ulcers under control, a spinal injured person should examine himself daily with a so-called *rear view mirror check*. To do this, use a hand mirror; look at your back and buttocks, inspecting for any signs of redness and pressure. Quadriplegics are not able to make the inspection themselves, so they ought to be certain their attendant assists in doing this task. Furthermore, someone with this disability should consider other precautions in preventing pressure sores, such as refraining from sitting or lying in one position too long, keeping clothing from wrinkling beneath him while sitting in a wheelchair, and wearing large enough shoes so his toes remain in proper alignment.

MANICURING YOUR NAILS

Clip your nails at least once a week so they will not break off. If you have impaired eyesight, tremors of the hands, or are incoordinated, let someone else do this for you. People with loss of sensation or poor circulation should guard against injury to the tissue surrounding their nails.

CLEANING YOUR FINGERNAILS. If you cannot use your upper extremities, make sure to have your fingernails cleaned daily to prevent an accumulation of dead skin. Remember, never allow the tissues to collect underneath your nails, because the area could become sensitive. Try soaking your hands in warm water and rub with a soft brush to loosen the dead skin; you could also apply a lotion or cream.

CARING FOR YOUR TOENAILS. If possible, cut your toenails soon after you bathe, since then they are less brittle and will not split as easily. A light toenail clipper or scissors with short blades works the best; however, if your nails are too thick, select a heavy-duty one.

ASSISTIVE DEVICES. Nail grooming requires fine dexterity and good hand coordination. For these reasons some disabled people find this task difficult. Special devices may help to make this job easier for those with hand limitations.

1. Sandpaper files. While some handicapped people file their nails with an emery board, others may find it easier to use sandpaper. One method for this is to tack or glue a strip of sandpaper to a narrow piece of wood, making a large homemade fingernail file. Or, a person with limited hand

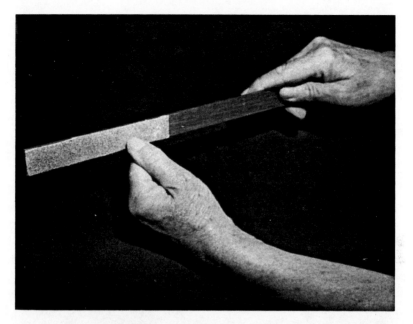

Figure 3-14. Hand-held nail file.

Figure 3-15. Mounted nail file.

use may want to fasten a larger piece of the sandpaper to a flat board and rub the nail over it.

2. Mounted clipper. Mount a large fingernail clipper on a piece of wood ¾ inch thick, approximately 5 inches wide and 10 inches long. Position it in the middle of the board near one end. Fasten the clipper down with a screw through a hole that is provided. Tack a small strip of wood ¼ inch by ¾ inch on each side of the clipper to keep it from shifting. You can rest your hand on the remaining portion of the board while clipping your nails. (see Fig. 3-16).

3. Cable nail clipper. This nail clipper is specially designed for someone with flaccid upper extremities. A large nail clipper is attached to a plywood base with three screws. A bicycle cable connects the clipper with a pedal for foot operation. Since no commercial source makes such a device,

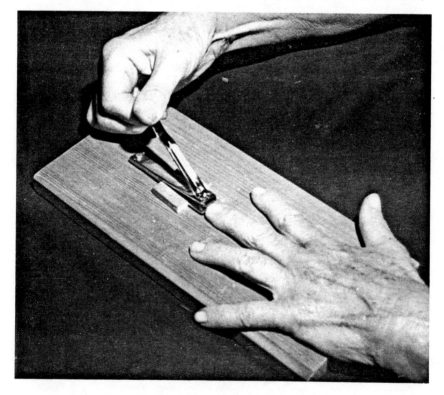

Figure 3-16.   Mounted clipper.

you may contact Project Threshold at the Rancho Los Amigos Rehabilitation Engineering Center for assistance in designing such an aid. (*See* the list of manufacturers, distributors, and resources at the end of the book.)

PROFESSIONAL MANICURE OR PEDICURE. If you are unable to use any of the clipping or filing methods described previously, why not consider going to a beauty training school and having a professional manicure or pedicure when needed.

GROOMING YOUR HAIR

To always look your best, comb and brush your hair often. Brushing stimulates scalp circulation and prevents dandruff from accumulating. However, for some disabled people hair care is not easy. Those in wheelchairs may find mirrors or standard dressing tables and bathroom vanities too high. Furthermore, individuals with impaired grasping ability are sometimes unable to hold a comb and hairbrush in the regular way. To solve these difficulties, disabled people use various aids.

ADJUSTABLE MIRRORS. A handicapped person could put an

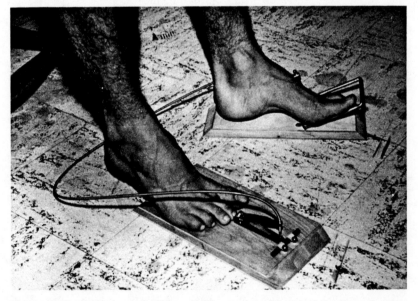

Figure 3-17. Bicycle nail clipper. Illustration furnished by Rancho Los Amigos Rehabilitation Engineering Center.

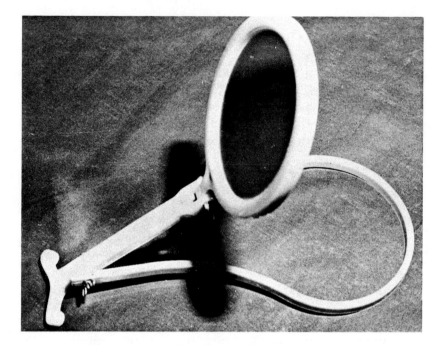

Figure 3-18. Adjustable mirror.

adjustable mirror in his lap, placed at a convenient level, or hang one around his neck to free both hands. If you choose a mirror that will fit around your neck, make certain you consider the weight. Remember, too, that some also swivel to any angle.

FINGER RING HAIRBRUSH. You can slide your finger into the handle of a finger ring hairbrush so that it fits securely in your hand. This brush is ideal for brushing or shampooing hair.

EXTENSION COMB. The 20 inch long extension comb has a lock setting at the joint to hold the unbreakable plastic comb in place. You can bend the shaft, and adjust it to the best combing angle. The handle may also be bent to fit any person's hand and may be padded with foam rubber if desired.

HAVING A NEAT SHAVE

Depending on the disability a person has, he could have difficulty shaving. Those with upper extremity weakness often find this daily living activity troublesome. If the person's forearm

Figure 3-19.   Finger ring brush. Illustration furnished by Cleo Living Aids.

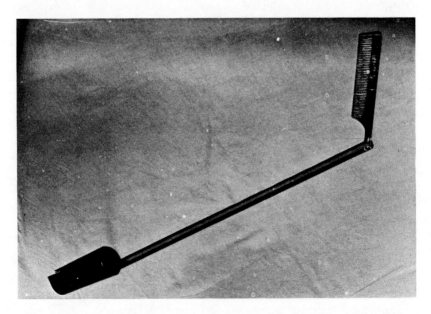

Figure 3-20.   Extension comb. Illustration furnished by Cleo Living Aids.

Figure 3-21.   Universal shaver holder. Illustration furnished by Help Yourself Aids.

is too weak or unstable, he might be able to prop his elbow on a flat surface for support. Many handicapped people must use an electric razor to eliminate the possibility of cutting themselves. However, if you are thinking about purchasing one, make certain it is not too heavy. Battery-powered shavers are also worth investigating, especially for those in wheelchairs who may live in houses where electrical outlets are inconvenient to reach. If you have a difficult time holding an electric shaver, you can purchase a universal electric shaver holder, which is designed to fit all popular brands of electric shavers, including Remington®, Sunbeam®, and Norelco® Dual Head and Triple Head. Two Velcro® straps hold it securely in place.

APPLYING COSMETICS

While many women with upper extremity limitations may want to use cosmetics, they could lack the fine motor dexterity and finger strength required to manipulate lipstick tubes or other cosmetics. Sometimes special aids and methods can be used to make this task easier.

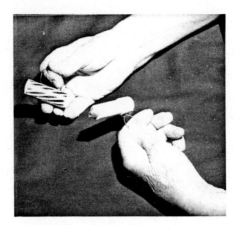

Figure 3-22.　Easy-to-use lipstick tube.

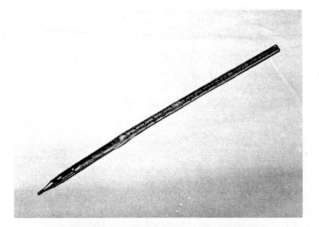

Figure 3-23.　Aluminum tubing mount.

Figure 3-24.　Powder puff holder.

LIPSTICK OR MASCARA TUBES. Depending on the disabilities, a person might be able to use lipstick or mascara tubes more conveniently if the tubes are built up with tape or foam rubber to provide better friction for grasping. Wrap a small piece of adhesive-backed tape or rubber around the top of the tube to make it simpler to remove. For someone who has difficulty pulling a tube apart, attach a loop of fabric to the bottom and the top tubes. You can then place one of your fingers or thumb in each loop and pull.

ALUMINUM TUBING MOUNT. If you have limited reaching ability, mount your lipstick in a piece of aluminum tubing secured with some tape. You can also apply mascara using the same method.

POWDERPUFF HOLDER. For some disabled people, this powder-puff holder will help extend their reach for applying cosmetics. You can make this device at home. Simply use a wing nut to fasten a clothespin to a narrow piece of wood. Then insert the powderpuff into the clothespin to hold it securely.

PREVENTING TOOTH DECAY

Some handicapped people are unable to brush their teeth without assistance. A few of the reasons for this include the following: the person's inability to reach his mouth due to joint contractures or upper limb weakness, the inability to grasp a standard toothbrush, and difficulty in squeezing toothpaste tubes. Others cannot rinse out their mouths or use dental floss.

Depending on your disability, you could possibly handle an electric toothbrush better than a standard one. The power action of the bristles enables some disabled people to take better care of their teeth. Although electric toothbrushes are heavier, they have a larger grasping area. In certain cases, people with upper extremity limitations can keep the elbow next to the side of their body for added support and control while still being able to reach all areas of the mouth.

Some individuals with physical impairments may prefer to use a standard toothbrush with a built-up handle. A piece of foam rubber tubing can be used to build up a toothbrush handle, but you can also purchase one with a 1½-inch diameter lightweight and durable rubber handle.

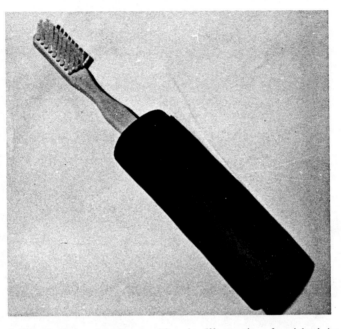

Figure 3-25. Built-up handle toothbrush. Illustration furnished by Help Yourself Aids.

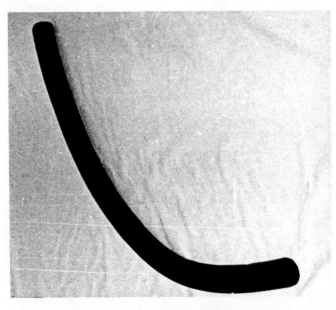

Figure 3-26. Foam rubber tubing. Illustration furnished by Help Yourself Aids.

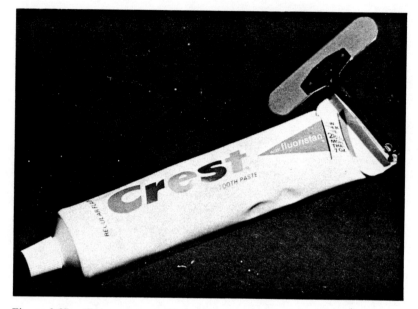

Figure 3-27.   Tube squeezer. Illustration furnished by Help Yourself Aids.

Figure 3-28.   Suction denture brush. Illustration furnished by Help Yourself Aids.

Those who have difficulty squeezing toothpaste out of a tube might want to try a tube squeezer that has a long handle and a large key. Just attach the key to the tube and turn it.

People who wear dentures need to clean them often. One device that will help some disabled individuals is a suction denture brush. You can use this aid with one hand, since the suction cups hold it in place while you cleanse the dentures. This prevents the possibility of bumping your teeth against the sink during cleaning.

CARING FOR YOUR EYEGLASSES

If you have restricted use of your arms or lack good coordination, you may be aware that cleaning your glasses can be a tedious task. To make this less frustrating and to avoid the possibility of breaking them, here is one way you can stabilize the glasses while washing and polishing the lenses.

You can have a carpenter or handyman make a simple device for little expense. Have him screw two switch protectors, opposite one another, to a piece of plywood 6 inches square. Fasten a hook

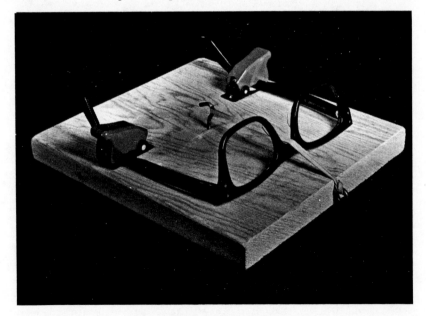

Figure 3-29.   Eyeglass holder.

in the center and one in the middle of the front edge. To use this aid, simply lift up both switch protectors, which will remain open while you insert the earpieces. Then stretch a rubber band over the bridge, hooking it over the two hooks to secure the glasses.

DRESSING GUIDELINES

Later, in Chapter 11, we will discuss some considerations you should think about when purchasing clothing. Ways of making the activity of dressing for handicapped people easier will be discussed here. Did you ever stop to think that this daily living task is somewhat complicated, requiring agility, balance, and a certain amount of dexterity? Five questions must be asked when analyzing and developing shortcuts and methods for disabled individuals.

1. What is the extent, degree, and location of the impairments—i.e. the ability to reach the back of the neck, waist, or feet?
2. Does the limitation cause a loss of strength, incoordination, or restricted motion?
3. Can the person pull on and take off clothes?
4. Is the individual's sitting balance impaired?
5. Will the person have the ability to reach, hoist buttocks, or arch his back?

Above all, it is important to sit in a comfortable position that allows for the most freedom of movement. Also, one should remember to lock the brakes of the wheelchair while sitting in it.

Buttoning Those Buttons

Although a person can wear clothes with other types of fastenings, he may sometimes wish to put on garments that have buttons. This kind of closure could be difficult to manage for someone with hand involvement or the inability to grasp the buttons securely. However, using a buttoner could make this task less frustrating. These devices have a stainless steel loop that is embedded in a plastic core of a wooden or plastic handle. The individual simply puts it through the buttonhole and over the button, pulling the button through to the other side.

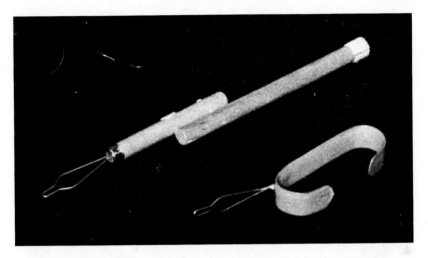

Figure 3-30.   Buttoners by Cleo Living Aids and Help Yourself Aids.

Putting On and Taking Off Your Upper Garments

People with upper extremity weakness causing difficulty in putting on and taking off shirts, blouses, sweaters, and coats can solve this problem by ducking the head, enabling them to pull the garment over their flexed neck. A second way is to support the weak arm on something, put it into the sleeve, then put the clothing onto this arm but not over the shoulder. After doing this, the person can use his weaker arm to steady the other one as he lifts the garment over his head. He then shifts his body until it falls into place.

To put on front-opening garments, the handicapped person should pull them over one shoulder, remembering to put the most involved limb through the sleeve first. Next, using lateral trunk motion, he should swing his clothing across to the other shoulder and place his arm into the sleeve. Another method to accomplish this is to lay a topcoat or overcoat over a chair or on a hanger and then to back into it before slipping one's arms into the sleeves.

For a handicapped person with restricted shoulder movement, removing clothing is also sometimes difficult. One way to make this easier is to slip garments off the shoulders. With the other hand or teeth one can pull on the sleeve of the least involved arm until the clothing slips down.

Difficulties with Lower Extremity Clothing

If someone has limited trunk motion or joint contractures, reaching the feet could be impossible. When people also have upper extremity weakness, they may be unable to pull on shorts, slacks, or trousers. Often an individual with this difficulty can use a utility stick to grab his pants and pull them within reach.

Some handicapped people can remove clothing while sitting if they raise the right side of their body using one hand and push clothes off over their buttocks with the other. They reverse the process for their left. After that, they can pull their trousers off by grasping the cuffs. Of course, crossing the legs reduces the reaching distance. However, an easier way is to just kick or push the garment off with the utility stick.

Managing Socks and Stockings

Just as with slacks, shirts, trousers, and coats, some disabled

Figure 3-31.   Utility stick. Illustration furnished by Help Yourself Aids.

people cannot bend down to pull up or fasten their hose, socks, or stockings. In addition, other limitations, such as swollen ankles, could also make this task difficult. Therefore, because of these various limitations, no single aid will work for all people. The utility stick discussed earlier can be used for pulling up footwear too, since it has a hook at one end for this purpose. Another helpful device is a stocking aid. To use it, a woman merely needs to place a stocking over the flexible plastic core. Then, she can insert her foot into the opening and pull. This brings the stocking over the heel of the foot onto the calf of her leg. Two clips fasten the hosiery to bring it within reach.

Getting In and Out of Your Shoes

Being unable to bend or having joint weakness can also interfere with someone's ability to put on and take off his shoes. If possible, when doing this task one should sit in a well-balanced and comfortable position. Often sitting in a chair with arms

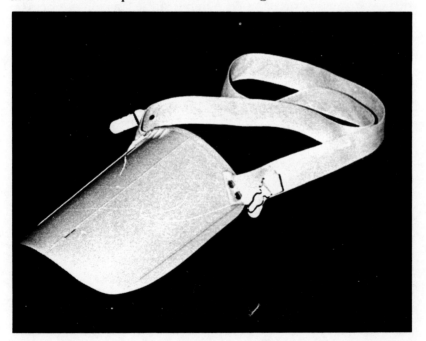

Figure 3-32. Stocking aid. Illustration furnished by Cleo Living Aids.

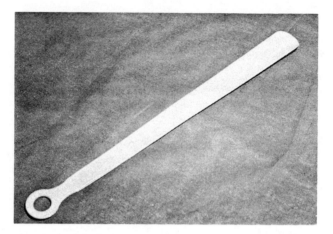

Figure 3-33.   Long-handled shoe horn by Cleo Living Aids and Help Yourself Aids.

rather than on the edge of your bed is better, since this gives more support. The armrest is also helpful if the individual begins to tire or starts to lose his balance. A handicapped person might also find it easier to cross his legs or brace one foot on a stool or chair when putting on or taking off shoes. Other devices may also be helpful.

LONG-HANDLED SHOEHORNS. Plastic or metal long-handled shoehorns measuring between 12 and 24 inches, are available from various mail-order houses. Some have a plastic covered hand grip with a curved hook for pulling up socks and other types of clothing.

ZIPPER SHOE FASTENING. A zipper shoe fastening enables a person to put on and take off shoes without undoing laces. They zip open, zip closed, easily and quickly.

ELASTIC SHOELACES. Putting elastic laces in shoes, enables someone to slip them on and off without tying or untying. These can be purchased from either Cleo Living Aids or Help Yourself Aids.

KNO—BOWS®. Kno-Bows are a one-handed shoelace fastener that can be used easily. The individual simply pinches them together and pulls on the knob to tighten his shoelaces. To loosen them he simply pushes the two sides of the Kno-Bows toward one another. This shoe fastening is ideal for those who lack the

Figure 3-34. Kno-Bows by Cleo Living Aids and Help Yourself Aids.

coordination to lace and tie their shoes, those who have arthritis, and those who have cardiac problems.

EATING WITH LESS EFFORT

Eating is a pleasurable experience, but for some severely disabled people who have one or more of the following limitations, the task could be quite complicated.

1. The inability to eat at a standard table height. Due to poor trunk balance or upper extremity involvement, some might need to eat in a specially designed place.
2. Limited rotation of the head and forearms that interfere with the positioning of utensils and the correct mouth approach.
3. Impaired grasp or hand funtioning.
4. Restricted or difficult mouth reach.
5. Lack of strength or coordination needed for self-feeding.

If you have any one of the above limitations, you may need special devices or some way of stabilizing your plate. Here are three ways of adapting conventional utensils and dishes for those with limited hand use: selecting utensils with larger than normal handles, building up standard flatware in some way, and using a cufflike device. In some cases those with poor wrist extension may want to use a splint or sling to assist themselves in eating.

Depending on an individual's disability, long-handled utensils can enable the person to lift his food easier. Those with an adjustable angle cut down the amount of motion for eating. A disabled person with two involved hands must find ways of stabilizing the plate and keeping food from falling off the edge. Special knives and various types of holders are also available. Following are some of the assistive devices some handicapped people use when eating.

BUILT-UP HANDLE UTENSILS. These built-up stainless steel utensils have rubberized handles, which can range from $1^5/_{16}$ to $1\frac{1}{2}$ inches in diameter. These oversized handles enable the disabled person to grasp his knife, fork, or spoon more easily.

Figure 3-35.   Built-up handle utensils. Illustration furnished by Cleo Living Aids.

HORIZONTAL PALM SELF-HANDLE UTENSILS. Horizontal palm self-handle utensils have a plastic-covered hand grip that is bendable for adjusting to fit an individual's hand.

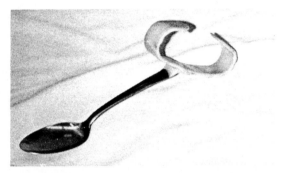

Figure 3-36. Horizontal palm self-handle utensils. Illustration furnished by Cleo Living Aids.

VERTICAL PALM SELF-HANDLE UTENSILS. The vertical palm self-handle utensils have handles that bend 90° so that a handicapped person's hand, which is then in a vertical position, can move more easily from the table to the mouth. These utensils with plastic-covered handles are also adjustable and will fit any individual's hand. They can be bent to make disabled people's eating activities less of an effort.

Figure 3-37. Vertical palm self-handle utensils. Illustration furnished by Cleo Living Aids.

EXTENSION FORK. The extension fork aids those with limited movement of the arms and shoulders. The length of this utensil is 15 inches when completely extended.

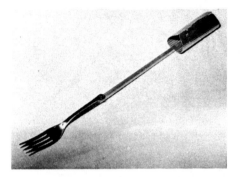

Figure 3-38.   Extension fork. Illustration furnished by Cleo Living Aids.

BENT SPOONS. Bent spoons have an offset design that makes them easier for some people with limited motion to use. They are available in right or left styles that provide an individual with a secure grasp.

Figure 3-39.   Any ordinary teaspoon or tablespoon can be bent as shown.

LEVEL SPOONS. Level spoons use a mechanical self-leveling device to help the person eat without spilling food. These stainless steel spoons can be purchased in various sizes with right or left functional grip or standard vinyl built-up handles. These are available from Cleo Living Aids.

SANDWICH HOLDER. A plastic sandwich holder is designed to grip a piece of bread. Consequently, it can extend some disabled people's reaches. The individual can also insert this aid into any utensil holder if so desired.

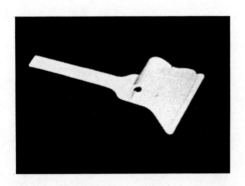

Figure 3-40.   Sandwich holder. Illustration furnished by Help Yourself Aids.

ADJUSTABLE SWIVEL UTENSILS. Adjustable swivel utensils have a swivel mechanism that keeps them level when the person has no wrist or finger motion. Two stops regulate the amount of swivel, and the flat handle can fit into a utensil holder. (This is made by Cleo Living Aids.)

LONG-HANDLED UTENSILS. People with a limitation of hand motions are sometimes able to eat more easily with long-handled utensils. They provide for greater comfort, and tightening a set screw changes the angle adjustment. Furthermore, they have a built-up vinyl hand grasp that helps the disabled individual to grip them firmly (made by Cleo Living Aids).

ROCKER KNIFE. A rocker knife has a sharp curved blade with a steel handle. Various types also have two or three prongs for picking up food.

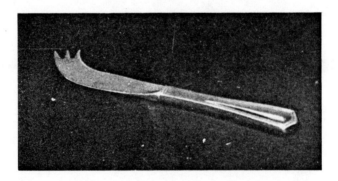

Figure 3-41.   Rocker knife. Illustration furnished by Cleo Living Aids.

FOOD GUARDS. Food guards are manufactured of molded polyethylene plastic or of stainless steel with electronic welding for maximum durability. It is possible to purchase one of two metal types that fit plates either between 9 and 11 inches or 6 and 8 inches. The lightweight plastic variety clips onto any size plate and is easy to clean.

Figure 3-42. Food guard. Available in plastic or metal by Cleo Living Aids and Help Yourself Aids.

ROUND SCOOP DISH. A round scoop dish with an 8-inch diameter has a low rim on one side and a higher one on the other. To make scooping food easier, the bottom is padded with nonskid rubber to assist in having better control when eating. You can purchase these dishes in various colors.

Figure 3-43. Scoop dish. Illustration furnished by Help Yourself Aids.

LITTLE OCTOPUS® SUCTION HOLDERS. Little Octopus suction holders have twenty-four tiny suction cups on both sides of the rubber pad. This holder has a double gripping feature that secures plates, bowls, and other items to flat surfaces. Each one is ⅛ inch thick and 3 inches in diameter.

Figure 3-44. Little Octopus suction holders. Illustration furnished by Help Yourself Aids.

TAKING A DRINK

When drinking, some people with hand and arm involvement can find it difficult or impossible to lift a cup or glass to their mouths. For instance, a quadriplegic who has little or no use of his upper extremities may only be able to drink through a straw. Other handicapped people need a way of holding their glasses steady. Individuals with either poor motor control or weak grasp may need a cup or glass having large handles so they can hold it more securely. Therefore, the following aids can be of assistance to some people with various disabilities.

BILATERAL GLASS HOLDER. The heavy-duty steel-handled bilateral glass holder is often recommended for disabled people with incoordination. This vinyl-covered holder has a clamp mounted near the top that adjusts it to fit any size glass.

Figure 3-45. Bilateral glass holder. Illustration furnished by Help Yourself Aids.

WONDER-FLO® DRINKING CUP. One can tip the 8-ounce Wonder-Flo® drinking cup and suck enough water at one time for a good swallow. After one stops sucking, the flow stops. Pushing the rubber button opposite the straw on top of the cup controls the amount of liquid that is released. This nylon-covered drinking cup can also be washed in the dishwasher safely.

Figure 3-46. Wonder-Flo drinking cup. Illustration furnished by Help Yourself Aids.

PLASTIC-HANDLED MUG. Plastic-handled mugs are often ideal for someone with upper extremity weakness, since they are designed to be grasped many ways. These 12-ounce mugs can be purchased in a variety of colors.

Figure 3-47.   Plastic-handled mug. Illustration furnished by Help Yourself Aids.

GLASS HOLDER. This glass holder attaches to various sizes of glasses and provides for a strong, firm handle. These are manufactured from stainless steel and are plastic covered. One thumb screw adjusts to hold any size glass.

Figure 3-48.   Glass holder by Cleo Living Aids and Help Yourself Aids.

BULLDOG STRAW CLIP. Hold your straw in place with a bulldog clip. Simply attach it to the side of the glass or cup and push a long plastic straw through the hole.

Figure 3-49.   Bulldog straw clip.

INSERT A STRAW. Punch a hole in the lid of any container and insert a bendable paper or plastic straw.

Figure 3-50.   Inserting a straw.

HIRING AND FIRING YOUR ATTENDANT

It was mentioned previously that some handicapped people need to hire attendants since they cannot perform all the daily living tasks themselves. For instance, Judy, a thirty-year-old quadriplegic and a counselor for a local mental health agency hired Diane, who arrives at 5 AM each morning to lift her out of the bed, dress her, groom her, prepare her breakfast, and drive her to work.

Many states help provide attendant care services for severely disabled individuals. However, there have been some problems. In 1977, Medicaid decided to no longer pay a person's attendant if the individual received more than a certain income. This meant that someone who did not earn enough to pay an attendant but still earned over a given amount, was not eligible for government funding. To continue to receive the service, the person would be required to quit work. Luckily, in a test case in October of that year on behalf of nine disabled people, a court ruled that the law was unfair.

Another difficulty that sometimes occurs is that, instead of giving the money to the disabled person to pay his attendant, the check is made out in both the employer's and the employee's names. In such circumstances, two signatures are needed before the check can be cashed. This sometimes poses a difficulty, since the attendant may think of himself as being an employee of the government rather than as having a personal interest in serving the individual who hired him.

Of course, this is not the case everywhere. The California attendant care program functions much the same as other programs; therefore, it will be examined. This state provides a Homemaker Chore Service through county welfare departments. There are basically two types of services. First, if the disabled person only needs assistance a few hours a week for such tasks as housekeeping or grocery shopping, the agency will send a chore provider to do this work for him. The second type of service is when an individual needs daily care amounting to more than twenty hours a week. If this is the case, the person's county welfare department gives a cash grant and the right to hire an attendant. To be eligible for this payment, the person must justify every hour of time someone is on duty. Therefore, when your attendant is working, you must plan to use his or her time wisely. For example, Judy has forty-five hours of attendant assistance, which she allocates this way:

Weekdays

Dressing, breakfast, and transportation to work	3 hours
Dinner	2 hours
Bedtime assistance	1 hour

Saturday

Dressing and breakfast	2 hours
Shopping and cleaning	3 hours
Lunch	1 hour
Dinner	2 hours
Bedtime assistance	1 hour

Sunday

Dressing and breakfast	2 hours
Lunch	1 hour
Dinner	2 hours
Bedtime assistance	1 hour

If possible, a handicapped person should hire at least two attendants to share the responsibility instead of just relying on one. For instance, one attendant might work the first few days of the week, and the other, the latter half. There are good reasons for doing this. First, sometimes the individual on whom a person is relying may be unable to assist him. In this case he has someone else capable of assuming the responsibility. Second, in certain instances disabled people must fire an attendant. By employing more than one, they will then have another person on whom to rely.

But what should be the relationship between you and the individual you hire? Remember that first and foremost you want to retain control over your life. In other words, be congenial and friendly but do not forget your major role, a manager and supervisor of your attendants. Therefore, be sure the person does the job in a way you want it done.

HIRING YOUR ATTENDANT. Finding good reliable attendants is often a difficult task. Here are some suggestions that may help. Talk to other disabled people in the community. Discuss with them how they have solved their attendant problems. Then consult various agencies that help disabled individuals. Perhaps they can assist you in locating someone. Often, high school, college, and university students are looking for part-time employment and are willing to assume this responsibility.

When it is time to hire your attendants, you should make a careful selection. There are some things you should look for during the initial interview and in the few weeks the person works for you. Keep in mind these guidelines:

1. When interviewing the person for the first time, ask yourself the following: Is your personality compatible with the person? In other words, does he like you and you like him?
2. Find out if the person has a current driver's license and if he has automobile insurance.
3. Make sure to get character references.
4. Be certain your attendant has time enough for the job.
5. After you hire the person, continually analyze his work habits. Does he follow your instructions or pretend to understand when he actually does not?
6. Keep noticing whether the person is on time and does his job efficiently. Responsibility is important. After all, you are depending on him for many of your basic needs.

FIRING YOUR ATTENDANT. Firing someone is never easy, but do not be too reluctant to do this, since your well-being and happiness depend partly on your attendant's competence. Therefore, in the event you feel you must dismiss the person, do not be too hasty or angry. Discuss your grievance with him more than once. Get his side of the story, then talk about what steps you and he might take to improve the situation. If this does not bring results, warn the person that he must improve his performance and give him a deadline. In cases where this does not help, you may have no other alternative than to fire your attendant.

Being able to take care of your personal hygiene needs is one of the most important aspects of learning to live independently. If you are unable to perform all the necessary tasks yourself, you have the responsibility to hire attendants to help you. However, above all, remember that others are more likely to relate to you in a positive way if you present a neat appearance and have a happy smile.

POINTS TO REMEMBER

1. *Disabled people should feel comfortable in bed.* Therefore, some of them must learn positioning skills, such as rolling over, sitting up, and moving forwards and backwards on a mattress.

2. *Many individuals confined to wheelchairs can learn transfer techniques.* These include transferring to a bed, to a toilet, or into a tub.

3. *Those with spinal cord injury often cannot control their urinary functions.* Consequently, they must learn proper catheterization techniques, the method of b.i.d. irrigation, and ways to avoid genitourinary complications.

4. *A person with loss of sensation in his rectum does not usually have enough strength to do a bowel movement normally.* In these cases, he must use digital stimulation, chemicals and agents, or enemas.

5. *Care for your skin properly.* Use good washing techniques. People with spinal cord injury must often inspect their bodies regularly for decubitus ulcers.

6. *Handicapped individuals sometimes need to devise special techniques for drying themselves.*

7. *Proper hair care is important to help stimulate the scalp and prevent dandruff.* Those with impaired grasping ability or upper extremity weakness might find the use of assistive devices helpful.

8. *Men with hand or arm involvement might need to devise special ways of shaving.* Depending on their disability they may or may not be able to manage a safety razor.

9. *Women with lack of fine dexterity and finger strength may have difficulty applying cosmetics.*

10. *People who have hand and arm involvement could find it difficult to brush their teeth.* Some reasons for this are the person's inability to reach his mouth, joint and upper limb weakness, and his inability to hold a toothbrush.

11. *Cleaning eyeglasses can be a tedious task for people with hand weakness or poor coordination.*

12. *A person with handicaps must use special dressing methods.* Often they can use aids to help them button buttons, put on

and take off upper extremity garments, manage lower limb clothing, pull the feet into and out of socks and stockings, fasten and then unfasten shoes.

13. *Someone's limitations may hinder his self-care skills of drinking and feeding himself.*

14. *Individuals with severe handicaps often hire attendants.* They should be aware of how to hire, supervise, and if necessary fire that person.

Chapter 4

DOING THINGS THE SIMPLE WAY

For all people simplifying housework is important, but for a physically disabled person, this often becomes crucial. In fact, the mere independence and quality of life may depend on how well an individual learns this technique. Sandy, a paraplegic with limited hand use, soon plans to marry but wonders how she will do the numerous household tasks. Jim, a student with cerebral palsy lives alone and must take care of his personal needs while attending school. If Sandy and Jim are to successfully manage their daily activities, they must learn to work with the least amount of effort. Two reasons why this is essential are the following: to reduce how long each job takes and to save energy while avoiding fatigue.

As has already been discussed, when any disabled person wants to become self-reliant, time is important. For example, unlocking a door takes only a few minutes for most people, but Jim must allow a longer time to accomplish this. Thus, for him to live independently, go to college, and participate in recreation, he must develop effective ways of doing his work. Since Sandy exerts a great amount of energy when pushing her wheelchair, she conserves her strength in every possible way. Because she tires easily, Sandy avoids becoming exhausted. In order to accomplish her many chores, she must find the least strenuous methods for doing them.

Other handicapped people face the same problems. This chapter explains seven ways they can make their work easier. Sandy and Jim will serve as examples of applying these suggestions.

ANALYZE YOUR DAILY TASKS

Before you begin your work each morning, stop and ask yourself, "What do I need to accomplish?" Take a few minutes and list the things you want to complete, and consider the time each will take. Are the jobs really important? Are they really necessary? Sandy asks herself these questions about cleaning. Prior to her automobile accident, she spent many hours dusting; every Monday and Wednesday morning she polished the coffee table in her living room. Of course Sandy wants to be a good housekeeper, but since her injury she finds cleaning difficult and decides to dust only once a week.

Plan your routine and consider when it is easiest for you to do a particular type of work. The period of the day people work better differs from one individual to another. There are professionals in the scientific and medical community who think that the human body is regulated by "biological clocks" that determine when a person can perform the best. Some people work efficiently in the mornings; others feel more alert at night. Therefore, schedule your activities so they correspond to the time when you usually accomplish the most. Sandy discovered how to organize her household duties this way. She does not like to vacuum. In the past she had left this until late afternoon. For Sandy, however, this is now a challenge that requires much effort. She has switched her vacuuming from the afternoon to the morning when she is more rested. She further decided that in the afternoon she should sit quietly in her wheelchair and do less strenuous work.

How do you know when to change tasks? Here are some ways to tell. Analyze how you feel at different times and plan accordingly. Observe when you do certain things better. Do not fight fatigue. If you are tired, quit what you are doing and come back to it later when you are more rested. Schedule only as much as your time comfortably allows. Often people try accomplishing many things in too short a period. This can lead to needless frustration. Remember, you are at your best when you are not under pressure. Finally, consider your health. If you feel you should rest in the afternoon, by all means do. Plan your housework so it is not a burden but a challenge you can manage in the easiest possible way.

FIND AN APPROPRIATE PLACE

Find a location that is comfortable, convenient, and easily accessible to perform a task. Months ago, Jim learned this because of his limited hand use. For most people, opening a letter is simple, but Jim's poor coordination makes it impossible to accomplish this in the usual way. He must first lay the letter down, and with his left hand holding it securely, Jim then uses a knife to open his mail. He finds that putting the letter on a table is the best way since this surface provides a firm base of support. Tearing then becomes less likely.

Finding the right place to accomplish a chore often takes careful thought. Of course, where you choose to do a certain job will depend on your disability and individual preference, but here are a few points to consider.

SELECT A COMFORTABLE LOCATION. Never try working somewhere that is not suited to your special needs. For instance, Jim does not open a jar on the table. Instead, he holds it securely between his knees and loosens the lid.

CHOOSE A SPOT THAT IS ACCESSIBLE. Before Sandy was injured, she did many of her household duties on the kitchen table. She still enjoys sitting at the table, but she had it modified. A friend removed the center brace so that she could wheel her chair closer. Now Sandy can still use this area without difficulty.

Height is another important consideration, especially for someone in a wheelchair. Kitchen countertops are about 36 inches high, and for most people this is adequate, but for a disabled person it may not be. When possible, never work on a surface higher than you can conveniently reach, because this may cause strain. These conditions can also bring about fatigue, so always take this into account.

CONSIDER SAFETY. Jim has problems with his balance and often falls, but he likes to stand in front of the sink and wash dishes. However, as a precaution he keeps a kitchen chair beside him so that he can grab it if he starts to lose his balance; he also keeps a rubber mat under his feet to reduce the likelihood of slipping.

SHOULD SOMEONE ELSE HELP?

Certain daily living skills could be difficult or impossible for some disabled people to accomplish alone, and they may need assistance. For instance, Sandy cannot hold her fork while she cuts meat. In order to get this done, she will need her husband's help. Following her accident, she was reluctant to ask for assistance. An example of her frustration became evident when she struggled unsuccessfully for twenty minutes to button her blouse, and then when she requested a friend to fasten it, she felt like a little child. One day, Sandy realized that this was a negative attitude and that she still had not accepted her disability. She then began thinking more positively about herself and became aware that she was still a useful person and that her disability did not diminish her worth. Everyone needs help to accomplish certain things throughout life. Some handicapped people need more aid than a nondisabled person, but this is no reason for them to feel helpless or a burden on others.

DO IT THE EASY WAY

Disabled people must sometimes do things differently than the able-bodied and must find ways to minimize the time and effort a job takes. On the other hand, they should try to do each task as well as possible. Accomplishing things easily while maintaining the highest quality performance takes some thought. Solving problems requires creativity—for instance, putting slacks on a hanger. Jim found this difficult, so he decided to fold them, lay them on the bed, and then slide the hanger to the center of the legs. When he picked the hanger up, his slacks were neatly in place.

Do not struggle and think that you must do household chores the same way someone else does if you are handicapped. Try to discover ways to make your work easier. While others may give you ideas to simplify your work, this is an individual matter, so stop wasting energy and start planning how to accomplish things the easy way.

DO THINGS SIMULTANEOUSLY

If possible, do more than one household chore at a time. You can often use this helpful hint in the kitchen. Sandy enjoys cooking, and takes pride in making stew and meat loaf. However, since her accident it now takes her longer, and she is limited in the minutes she can spend. Instead of completely relying on packaged foods, she still makes these dishes while having her cookware and ingredients out on the table. For instance, when Sandy makes a meat loaf, she molds two or three, bakes one, and puts the others in the freezer. By doing this, she can still have the fun of cooking without spending so many hours doing it.

IDEAS FOR CHANGING YOUR WORK HABITS

Home economists have developed ways to alter housework and make it easier: change your body position and range of motion, use different equipment, find a different work place, substitute raw materials, and modify the finished product. Sandy and Jim used these ideas in the following ways.

CHANGE BODY POSITION AND RANGE OF MOTION. Often it is important for people to position their bodies differently. The way you sit and use your limbs can make your work easier. While Sandy bakes bread she allows her arms to rest on the table when kneading dough, and it serves as a base of support. She also limits her range of motion, keeping her rolling pin and other utensils in a semicircle to reduce cross-back movements.

CHANGE EQUIPMENT AND ADAPT IT TO YOUR NEEDS. Select the right tools for the job and for your abilities. Often assistive devices are a great help. Throughout this book many will be presented that you can purchase from various suppliers, while others could be made at home. However, always remember to be resourceful, and if possible, purchase or create an aid that will help you with your household tasks.

CHANGE THE PLACE YOU WORK. Decide where to do a job easily. Some people think they must perform a particular daily activity in a certain place, but this is not always necessary. Be flexible and choose the best location in your house to accomplish it. Sandy was accustomed to taking a shower and dressing herself in the bathroom. This is no longer possible because she cannot stand. After experimenting, she decided the bedroom was more convenient. She can wheel her chair to the bed and transfer onto it. Because Sandy has weak trunk muscles, she can lie down, pull her slacks on, and lean against a pillow for support. Where you do a task becomes important. Even if the location is not essential in doing your work, it could be a factor in reducing physical strain.

CHANGE RAW MATERIALS. You can sometimes make your housework simpler by substituting other materials. Sandy saves time in cooking this way. In the past, she spent hours baking cakes. She still enjoys cooking, but her disability now makes this more difficult, so Sandy must find an easier way. While making a cake from scratch may taste better, using a mix has become more efficient for her. Where she combined nine ingredients to make her cake, by using a mix she only adds water and eggs. Fewer contents make this procedure faster and easier. Since Sandy lacks arm movement to stir the batter adequately, she has learned to use a mixer for this job.

CHANGE THE END PRODUCT. You can often alter the form of the result. Sandy learned this while preparing her favorite meal, macaroni and frankfurters. She cannot grate cheese for the casserole and decides to combine canned macaroni and vienna sausages to make the same delicious meal. Using two products to make one is especially helpful in cooking. In fact, the Campbell Soup Company publishes a cookbook, *Mealtime Manual for People with Disabilities and the Elderly*, that explains other ways you can prepare delicious foods easily.

MAKE YOUR BODY WORK EFFECTIVELY

Use your physical abilities to a good advantage. Do not rely completely on assistance from others or from adaptive equipment while neglecting to exercise your body. Inactive muscles grow weak and wither. To prevent this from happening to you, remain as active as possible, but strive to accomplish things in an effortless way. Here are four suggestions.

USE OTHER MUSCLE GROUPS. When one part of your body has been injured so it cannot perform a task, use another. Such compensation often helps you achieve greater independence. For instance, Jim has poor dexterity and is unable to grasp small objects, so he easily picks up a tiny medicine bottle another way. Jim extends his arms and rests them on a table near the bottle. Then he can slide his hands together and catch it between his wrists.

USE SMOOTH RATHER THAN JERKY MOVEMENT. Control your

actions and avoid quick movements when possible. You may need to concentrate closely, but try to eliminate unnecessary motions. When Jim picks up a glass, he tries not to tip it over when he brings his hands together carefully. This takes more time, but Jim plans his movements beforehand and tries to make each one as precise as he can.

USE GRAVITY TO THE BEST ADVANTAGE. Let gravity do your work when possible. Jim does this effectively while cooking. When chopping vegetables on the countertop, he also places a bowl in the sink. After he finishes, he slides his cutting board over to the sink, tips it up, and lets the pieces drop into the container below.

USE CASTERS AND MOMENTUM TO SIMPLIFY YOUR WORK. Causing something to move easily helps homemakers do the daily chores. Sandy applies this principle and had casters put on her wastebaskets so that she can roll them out of the house and dump the trash into a garbage can located at ground level. Often people exert themselves too much when moving objects. With casters this is not necessary, because once something is set in motion it develops impetus and keeps going. Actually, using so much effort sometimes can make the job even more difficult.

This chapter has presented several ideas that can help you save time and energy. People often have fixed work habits similar to those of their mothers or grandmothers. Frequently they do things in a certain way with no thought given to it beforehand. This can cause needless problems and frustration. So, organize your work, and start doing it the simple way.

POINTS TO REMEMBER

1. *Analyze your tasks.* Define the household jobs you must finish each day. Assign each duty a priority and make sure it is really necessary.
2. *Choose a good time.* Find out when you work the best and schedule your routine accordingly. Do not fight fatigue; always take care of your health.
3. *Select an appropriate work place.* Look for a comfortable, convenient, and easily accessible place to do each household task. Avoid physical strain when possible, and always keep safety in mind.

4. *Ask for help.* Someone else possibly can do a chore faster and easier than you, so do not be reluctant to ask for assistance when you need it.
5. *Find an easy way.* Perform your household duties the best way that you can but with the simplest method possible.
6. *Do tasks simultaneously.* Combine your jobs to save time and energy.
7. *Change your work habits five ways.* Alter your body position and range of motion, use adaptive equipment when needed, find another place to work, use different raw materials, or change the end product.
8. *Use your body efficiently.* Different muscle groups can compensate for impaired ones. Control jerky movements. Gravity helps simplify your work. Install casters and allow momentum to help you.

Chapter 5

PLANNING YOUR KITCHEN

E very day homemakers spend countless hours in the kitchen preparing and serving food, so their work place should be attractive and convenient. However, for people with physical limitations, this is not only desirable but necessary. Many times how well a handicapped person works in this area depends on careful planning. To help you understand important features in designing kitchens for disabled homemakers, a few of them will be examined in detail.

KEEP THE BASIC FLOOR DESIGNS IN MIND

One of the best ways to start thinking about an efficient kitchen is by understanding the three basic kitchen floor designs.

THE U DESIGN. Ideally plan your work area in a U shape to have the maximum amount of counter space. Remember to leave no more than 5 feet between each surface to reduce bodily movements. If you use a wheelchair, this will also allow you to turn in a complete circle. When possible, plan your kitchen so that the sink and range are on either side of you, which helps in making meal preparation easier.

THE L DESIGN. The L-designed kitchen is the second best choice. There is not as much counter space in this design as in the U-shaped kitchen. Therefore, plan to use it to good advantage. One advantage to this design, however, is that an L shape reduces your movement between work centers.

THE CORRIDOR DESIGN. Corridor arrangements usually give you the least amount of area for meal preparation, and you must also be constantly turning to use both surfaces opposite each other. When members of your family walk through the corridor

97

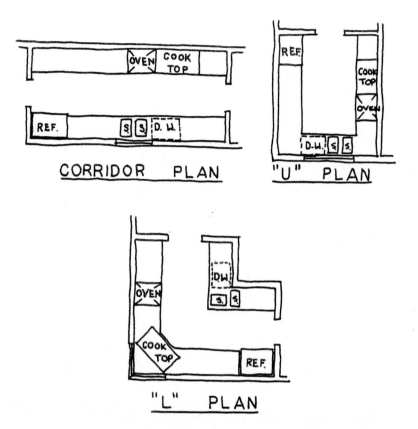

Figure 5-1. Basic kitchen counter designs.

while you are working, they probably will interfere with your kitchen routine. If you are ambulatory, be sure the counters are close together to reduce walking; this also makes reaching and turning easier. People confined to wheelchairs should make sure they allow enough room in the aisle to turn the chair comfortably.

CONSIDER YOUR DISABILITY

In determining the best kitchen layout to meet your needs, think about both your physical limitations and abilities. Keep the following two points in mind.

Your Mobility. Can you walk? Do you have good balance?

Must you use a wheelchair? Just as with other facets of daily life, the extent of your mobility has special implications in the kitchen. For instance, someone with poor balance may slip on wet floors. A person who could easily fall might also want to use a security strap while working at the kitchen sink (see Fig. 5-2). If you are handy with needle and thread, you can make one at home from a piece of unbleached muslin or other heavy material. Cut a strip to the desired length that will fit around your waist and still provide extra slack so you are able to move freely while working. The ideal width for this band is approximately 3 inches. Sew safety snap eyes at each end of the strap. To do this easily, fold the two corners of the material over each snap eye in a triangular design; then stitch over the eye to hold it firmly in place. Next, screw two hook eyes on the facing of your cabinet, so you can fasten the snap to them while working.

YOUR ABILITY TO BEND AND REACH. Figuring out how far you can bend or reach is quite simple. To find how far you can bend from a standing position, simply lean forward and then sideways, trying to touch the floor. Measure the distance with a yardstick. If you sit in a wheelchair, knowing how much you are able to bend

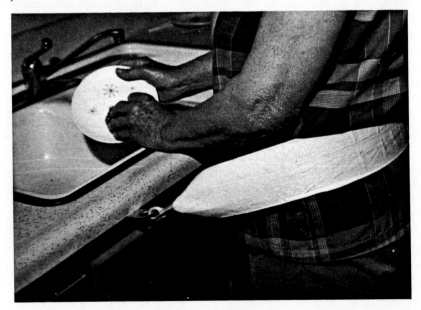

Figure 5-2.   Security strap.

is even more important. To determine this, lean over both sides of your chair and reach as far as you can on either side. Then take a measurement. Among other things, this helps ascertain your ability to use lower cabinet shelves. For some disabled people this presents no problem, while it may be impossible for others.

To discover how far you can reach, draw your work curve. Pin a large piece of paper to a wall. Stand or sit a foot away, extend your arm, and sketch a line. Be sure to reach as far as you can. When you have finished, take a yardstick and measure from the base of the curve you have drawn to the high point. This gives you the maximum distance you are able to reach easily.

THE WHEELCHAIR KITCHEN

If you use a wheelchair, think about the following specifications so that your kitchen area will be easily accessible.

COUNTERTOP SPACE. Consider three basic guidelines when designing your countertop. First, plan at least 1½ feet of counter on the door-opening side of your refrigerator. This space is handy for setting food that you plan to put in or take out of the refrigerator. Second, allow 2½ feet on the right and 2 feet on the left of the sink for ample work area. Finally, provide 2 feet of heat resistant counter on the right or left side of the range.

Remember also to allow enough space for a mixing and serving area. Your mixing center should be 3½ feet long near either the sink, refrigerator, or range. If possible, locate a serving center near where your family usually eats.

Obviously, you can use one countertop for more than one purpose but try never to have less than 10 lineal feet.

COUNTERTOP HEIGHT. Build your counter 31 inches high instead of the normal 36 inches, so that you are able to perform most kitchen tasks easily. This dimension enables you to wheel your chair underneath the surface without any obstructions.

COUNTERTOP DEPTH. Most counters are 24 inches in depth, but since the wheelchair homemaker generally uses only 16 inches, much of the back portion of this space is wasted, so arrange to use it for storage.

Using Your Sink

Did you know that homemakers spend much of their time in the kitchen at sinks? To make this place convenient and accessible for you, there are six things to consider.

SELECT A SHALLOW SINK. Make sure your sink is not too deep. Look for one in a kitchen that has sides no higher than 5½ inches. Here are some reasons why this is important. A shallow sink makes it possible to reach all areas while not having to strain and also to wheel your chair under the basin, still leaving adequate space for your knees.

Most homemakers like sinks that have more than one bowl. If this is your preference, be sure that at least one of them is shallow. One type is the Triple Concept® stainless steel sink, which has two oversized bowls measuring 15½ inches wide, 19 inches from front to back, and 7 inches deep. The center one is shallower, with dimensions of 5 inches deep, 9 inches wide, and 11 inches from front to back (see Fig. 5-3).

ADVANTAGE OF REAR DRAINS. Having a rear corner sink drain provides for more knee room beneath the cabinet and is safer. All hot pipes are then out of the way so that your legs will not accidently touch them while working from a wheelchair. For homemakers with no sensation in the lower part of the body, this is even more important because heat could severely burn them without their knowing it. To give added protection, insulate the bottom of your sink along with the hot water supply pipes. You could also insulate the trap and drain pipes.

CHECK THE FAUCETS. The long swing type of faucet with mesh aerators or a screen allowing water to spray rather than splash is preferable. Those having a single lever permit you to control both temperature and flow using one hand. Move the lever from side to side for hot or cold water; lift the handle up or down to regulate the volume. This type of faucet is the safest because you are able to adjust the temperature first before turning the tap on to avoid being scalded.

However, if you live in a house with two faucets on your sink, be sure they have long handles that are easier to grasp. Since some disabled people do not have much strength in their hands, the extra length provides greater leverage.

SIDE FAUCET SINKS MAKE REACHING EASIER. Some people can only extend their arms a short distance. Is this your problem? If it is, install a one-bowl sink sideways so that the controls are where you can reach them easily; place the faucet on either the right or

Figure 5-3.   Triple Concept stainless steel sink. Illustration furnished by American Standard U. S. Plumbing Products.

left, depending on which arm you use. Locate the controls on the side where you will not block the walking path of others as you work from your wheelchair.

CONSIDER THE SPRAY HOSE. Be sure the hose is long enough and has an easy-to-work thumb lever that permits filling pots on the counter, rather than lifting them from the sink. A thumb lever also makes washing and rinsing easier.

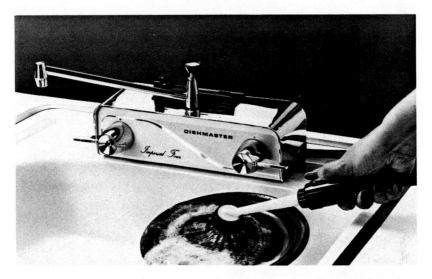

Figure 5-4. Dishmaster. Illustration furnished by Manville Manufacturing Company.

USING A DISHMASTER®. Some disabled homemakers may prefer to install a Dishmaster on their sink rather than a spray hose. This handy dishwasher has several advantages. It makes cleaning your dishes, electric utensils, pots and pans, fine china, and silverware easier. You can scrape, wash, and rinse with one effortless motion. Using the Dishmaster helps conserve your cupboard space, water, and detergent. You are also able to use it quickly and quietly.

If your physical limitations permit, you may be able to install this device yourself. Simply turn off the hot and cold water underneath the sink. Remove the present faucets, and replace them with the Dishmaster.

Your Dishwasher

Built-in dishwashers are convenient, but you must plan for them carefully. Since the standard machine is 36 inches high, it cannot fit under a 31-inch countertop. However, with one simple modification you can solve this problem. Just make a 5-inch raised offset in the countertop next to the sink and slide the dishwasher underneath.

No matter whether your machine is built-in or portable, choose one that you load from the front and not the top. The controls should also be in front, and make certain the racks slide out independently of each other. Then look to see if the machine has a self-clearing drain. Even though most models have this feature, check for it anyhow because it is difficult to unclog a drain from your wheelchair since you cannot usually reach it easily.

Make Your Cooking Center Convenient

Your cooking center consists of a range and oven. They can be a combination unit, or they can be built separately into your countertop and kitchen cabinets. Follow these guidelines in selecting your appliances.

BUILT-IN COOKING TOP. Choose a two, three, or four burner gas or electric cooking top that fits close or flush to your countertop. Although many are made this way, some types are recessed below your work level, making it necessary for homemakers to lift their pots and pans. Avoid installing this type. Select a staggered pattern of burners, making reaching the rear ones safer.

ELECTRICAL INSTALLATION. You must install a special 210-volt circuit for your electric range.

COMBINED COOKING TOPS AND OVENS. Choose a combination cooking top and oven with a side-opening rather than a down-dropping door for greater accessibility. On the other hand, a drop-down door serves as a shelf to slide food in and out of the oven. However, if you have an electric model, you can arrange to have both of these features by installing a burnproof shelf under the sliding door. This is not possible with a gas model since flames are at the bottom.

BURNER SWITCH KNOBS. To avoid reaching over the heated areas, select a range top with burner knobs located in the front, not on a back panel.

REMOTE CONTROLS. You can sometimes purchase remote push-button units on a long flexible cable that may be installed anywhere, making it convenient for you to regulate your stove from a wheelchair. Some provide as many as five settings and have a light indicator for each burner. Easy-to-push buttons make cooking easier for someone who has difficulty turning knobs.

SEPARATE OVEN. Since you can install a built-in oven at any height, make sure you will be able to reach it from your wheelchair. To accomplish this easily, simply lower the unit and plan for the most used oven shelf to be level with your countertop. Although the unit may be located anywhere in the kitchen, never put it near the refrigerator due to the warmth, and be sure your cooking top is heat resistant if placed next to this unit. If possible, you should choose an oven with a side-opening rather than a drop-down door for two reasons—so that you will not have to reach over it, risking the possibility of being burned, and so that you can wheel your chair closer to the shelves, making your work easier.

On some ovens the broiler is underneath, while others have it along the side. There is one big problem with those below the unit. Depending on your reaching ability, you might not be able to retrieve things from a bent over position.

Keep in mind that you can also purchase ovens that clean themselves, but because of the extreme heat, make certain they are vented. When you buy an oven without the self-cleaning feature, look for one with a removable door, which makes the chore easier.

Be Sure Your Refrigerator Is Handy

In buying a refrigerator make sure you will be able to use it conveniently. Some of them on the market today are designed poorly for people in wheelchairs, and you could not reach the top shelves or even the rear of the lower ones. On other models the freezer may be out of reach. Use these guidelines in buying your refrigerator.

CHECK THE SHELVES. Select one with slide or swing out shelves, so you can reach food without straining to obtain it from the back of the box.

CHECK THE DOOR SWING. Since refrigerator doors can swing either left or right, choose the direction according to which arm you use for reaching. The opening edge should face the countertop.

CHECK THE FREEZER COMPARTMENT. So you can use your freezer easily, the compartment must be alongside your refrigerator or at the top; never on the bottom, since it may not be accessible. The side-by-side models have a vertical freezer next to the refrigerator. This type has two doors that open from the middle, which is also handy.

CHECK FOR AN ICE CUBE MAKER. An automatic ice maker

eliminates the job of carrying water-filled trays from the sink to the freezer. Even for the disabled who use crutches or have poor hand coordination, this is an important consideration. However, one must have special plumbing connections that attach to cold water piping. Some refrigerators also have a cold water and ice dispenser on the outside so that one does not need to open the door.

CHECK TO SEE WHETHER THE REFRIGERATOR IS FROST FREE. Since the task of defrosting is laborious and often impossible for some disabled homemakers, select a model that is frost free. Although they are somewhat more expensive to operate, you can save endless hours of difficult and tedious work.

You Cannot Always Remodel a Kitchen to Accommodate Your Wheelchair

Whenever possible, you should design or remodel a kitchen to make your work easier. However, sometimes you cannot make alterations, especially if you rent. Depending on the cost and whether or not the alterations will damage the premises for future tenants, some landlords consent to making slight modifications; but major ones such as lowering the countertops, sink, or range usually are not permitted. So, if you are renting, what can you do to make your kitchen more convenient? Here are a few suggestions.

MAKE SPACE FOR YOUR LEGS. Provide room for your legs under the sink. First, remove the footrests from your wheelchair, allowing you to move closer to the counter. Second, ask your landlord if you can take the cabinet doors off under the sink. To do this, just take the center pins out of the hinges. Besides giving additional space for your legs, you have more room for turning your wheelchair around. As indicated earlier, do not forget to insulate the hot drain pipes. Finally, if you do not like the appearance of doorless cabinets, hang some type of pull curtain over the openings.

MODIFY YOUR SINK. If your sink is too deep, put a simply made slanted rack on the bottom to raise the height. When you are short of counter space, put a board over your sink with 1-inch by 1-inch strips of wood fastened underneath to hold it in place.

FIND A DIFFERENT WORK PLACE. When the countertop is too

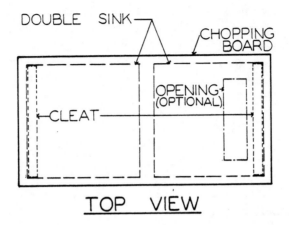

TOP VIEW

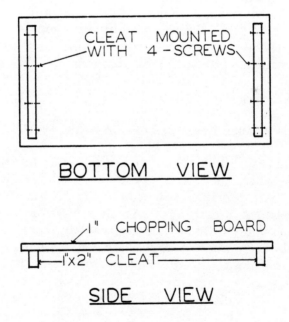

BOTTOM VIEW

SIDE VIEW

Figure 5-5. Slanted rack.

high, do your kitchen tasks somewhere else. Use your kitchen or dining room table, which has a lower surface. A fold-down table hinged to a wall, the drop-leaf variety, or a folding type such as a card table would also serve this purpose. You can also work on a slide-out breadboard. If your cabinet does not have one, make it by simply laying a piece of plywood over the drawer to match your height when sitting.

PLANNING A KITCHEN FOR THE AMBULATORY HOMEMAKER

Up to this point the chapter has concentrated on homemakers confined to wheelchairs; however, disabled people who are ambulatory may also have functional limitations. These can include those who wear braces, use crutches, or must work one handed, as well as others. Fortunately, in planning a kitchen for these handicapped people, there is no need to plan for each disability individually. Obviously shorter homemakers would need a lower work surface. Keep in mind, too, that many of the principles discussed concerning planning kitchens for those in wheelchairs are also applicable to the disabled homemaker who is able to walk. This section presents some other special considerations.

To Reduce Your Walking Know the Work Triangle

If you have difficulty and use extra energy while walking from place to place, you should use the work triangle to help gauge the flow of your work. Of course, you should leave enough room between work areas to perform all kitchen tasks comfortably; however, you should not waste space that requires extra steps. If possible, keep your sink, range, and main work surface near each other. The following are the recommended distances for the kitchen work center, as measured from the front of each appliance.

Refrigerator to sink	4 to 7 feet
Sink to range	4 to 6 feet
Range to refrigerator	4 to 9 feet

Furthermore, as was stated earlier, the U and L are the most convenient kitchen shapes, with the sink located in the center of one countertop, also close to the range.

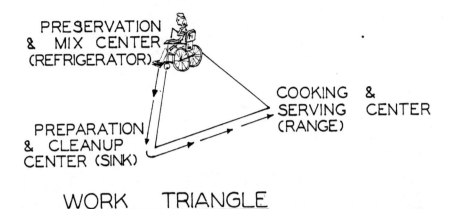

Figure 5-6. Work triangle.

Have a Continuous Work Surface

Just as with the homemaker in a wheelchair, some people who are ambulatory have difficulty lifting and carrying hot, heavy pans and spillable things. This is even more true for those with hand and arm impairment. Consequently, it is important that all kitchen countertops be on one level, to push and slide rather than carry things from place to place.

Sit Down and Work

Even though disabled people can walk, they may become overly tired or feel pain in the lower extremities as a result of prolonged standing. Consequently, some handicapped home-makers find it necessary to sit when performing cooking tasks. If this is your case, plan your kitchen so you are able to work while sitting comfortably in a central countertop location next to the sink and, if possible, within easy reach of your stove. Do not forget to provide for kneehole space underneath your sink and perhaps beneath the surface unit.

To sit at the normal 36-inch counter most people need a 24 inch high sturdy stool. However, these dimensions will of course depend on a person's height. Often it is possible to purchase stools with casters that allow movement between work areas without standing. Another important feature to look for is a swivel seat to allow turning from side to side or completely around without getting up from the seat. Make certain that the seat you choose has a comfortable back for resting against when you decide to take a break from your kitchen routine. Whether or not you choose a stool with arms will depend upon your disability. Some people who are overweight or who have upper extremity limitations work better if the one they select has no arm rests. Generally speaking, sturdy arms at the proper height provide support for lowering into and getting up from the chair. Finally, most individuals sitting on a 24 inch high seat will need a footrest. Those with no impairments to their lower limbs can usually put their legs on the bottom rung, but others that have some leg involvement may need to place a support at the proper height. Sometimes one can also use a wooden bench or build a shelf at the back of an open kneehole space.

Figure 5-7. Bar stool.

Check the Appliances

Some people may think that an ambulatory homemaker can always use standard appliances. This is not necessarily true. For individuals with certain handicaps, some features are often difficult or even impossible to manage. For instance, a handicapped person without good balance and agility often cannot use a very low, below-the-oven broiler on some gas ranges. A solution to this problem could be to use a portable electric broiler instead.

Another difficulty that often arises for ambulatory homemakers is having an oven door that may be too heavy for a person who lacks strength in the arms. To remedy this problem, often a serviceman can readjust the springs. If this is not possible, it may be necessary to use a portable oven.

PLAN FOR GOOD LIGHTING

All well-designed kitchens should have good and ample lighting, but too much from one source often causes glare and shadows on a person's work. To avoid this happening to you, locate a spot or strip light over each of your work areas. If you touch the fixtures frequently, install cool fluorescent bulbs, which are cheaper to operate and give off rays more comfortable to your eyes. Of course, window lighting is desirable, so always try to have at least one window in your kitchen.

HAVE ADEQUATE VENTILATION

An exhaust fan in your kitchen clears the air of greasy or smokey fumes and will keep your kitchen cool. Remember that vents, such as one over the range with a fan, purifies the air making cooking more enjoyable.

Designing your kitchen so you can use it conveniently takes careful thought, so give special attention to this area when planning a new home or remodeling an old one.

POINTS TO REMEMBER

1. *Consider your disability.* Think about your mobility. Measure how far you can bend; draw a work curve.

2. *Remember the basic kitchen shapes.* They are the U, the L, and the corridor design. Decide which one is best for you.

3. *Wheelchair dimensions.* Be sure to comply with the specifications for countertop space, height, and depth.

4. *Sink considerations.* People confined to wheelchairs need shallow sinks, long-handled faucets with aerators, and spray hoses. A sink installed sideways may also have advantages. Some may also find a Dishmaster helpful.

5. *Plan for a dishwasher.* With a 31 inch high counter make a 5-inch offset for the machine. Select a front loader with controls also in the front; look for slide-out racks and self-cleaning drains.

6. *Make your cooking center convenient.* Keep these features in mind.

    a. Built-in cooktops with two, three, or four burners should be level with the countertop. Choose one with a staggered pattern.

    b. Combined cooktop and oven. Ovens having a side-opening door are more accessible.

    c. Burner switches are more convenient on the oven front.

    d. Remote controls are available.

    e. Cooktop requires a 210-volt circuit.

    f. Separate ovens can be built in at any height. Side-openings ones are manufactured. You can purchase them with broilers and self-cleaning units.

7. *Have a handy refrigerator.* Inspect the shelves, door, freezer, and ice maker. Be sure the unit is frost-free.

8. *You cannot always remodel.* Make space for your legs and modify the sink without much structural modification. Find a different work place.

9. *Special planning for the ambulatory homemaker.* Those who wear braces, use crutches, work one handed, or have other physical impairments may need to think about their disability when designing a kitchen.

10. *Know the work triangle.* Build your kitchen according to the recommended distances from each service center to the front of appliances.

11. *Have a continuous work surface.* All countertops should be on the same level.
12. *Some homemakers need to sit while working.* Most people can use a 24 inch high stool to sit at the countertop as they do household tasks.
13. *Check the appliances.* It does not always follow that since a person is not confined to a wheelchair he can use standard appliances.
14. *Plan for good lighting.* Avoid glare and shadows. Use fluorescent bulbs and have good window lighting.
15. *Provide ventilation.* Install exhaust fans and vent all appliances adequately.

Chapter 6

COOKING MADE EASY

E ven though you have severe physical handicaps, you may be able to prepare a meal. Thousands of disabled people are doing it, including many with 'upper extremity impairments. However, depending on your limitations, it might be necessary to alter some of the procedures or use special devices. Therefore, this chapter will present various techniques and aids people with different disabilities often find useful when cooking.

BASIC COOKING ACTIVITIES

Carrying Without Spilling

As mentioned earlier, some handicapped individuals have problems carrying things and may spill liquids while transporting them from place to place. Those with certain disabilities—including people with hemiplegia, upper extremity weakness, incoordination, and arthritis—might find this task especially difficult. Others who use crutches or who are confined to wheelchairs may also have this problem. Consequently, a good rule to remember is *safety first.* Always analyze each job carefully before doing it. If you plan to move liquids, do not forget that it is easier to fill a pot or pan half full to lessen the weight and to avoid possible spills. Should you need more water, you can always use a glass, cup, or pitcher to add it later. Another thing to remember is to plan in advance how you will lift everything. This will help eliminate or reduce the possibility of accidents. Finally, never pick up cookware unless you are sure you can do it safely. There are also many ways handicapped people can make carrying easier.

SERVING CARTS. People who are ambulatory can use metal serving carts on casters to avoid carrying things and to minimize the chance of spillage. Since you should slide rather than carry items, try to purchase a cart that will be level with your countertop or table. To provide for better control, grip, and forearm support, you can also build up the handles with foam rubber.

TABLE ON WHEELS. If you know a handyman, why not have him build you a table on wheels (see Fig. 6-2). One convenient feature of this design is that it has an adjustable pull-out tray. Be sure also that you have someone nail a piece of quarter round around the edge of the tray to keep things from sliding off. Have the top covered with laminated plastic or aluminum sheeting for effortless care. Plans are available from the Occupational Therapy Service, Institute of Rehabilitation Medicine (*see* Appendix for address).

LAPBOARDS. An indispensible aid to help wheelchair home-makers in the kitchen is a lapboard. You can have one custom-built for yourself. It is simple to make and inexpensive too. Build it of stained or varnished plywood to slip over your wheelchair's armrests with brackets underneath to hold it and a wood strip for support (see Fig. 6-3). Marilyn has one measuring 23½ inches deep, 25¾ inches across, 18¾ inches from the peak of the cutout to the end of the board, and 15" wide for the cutout. Of course, the size of your chair, the amount of space you want, and the room you need for your abdomen will help determine the dimensions of the board. Some people also desire to have an edging. Like the table on wheels, you may use three-quarter round strips. Additionally, you might wish to cover the top with laminated plastic. Then you can set hot dishes or a cup of coffee on the surface. Also, when having your chair measured for a lapboard, be sure to sit in the one you use most often, since wheelchairs have varied dimensions.

Stabilizing

Some handicapped homemakers, particularly those who use only one hand or who frequently make jerky motions, might need

Figure 6-1.   Metal serving cart. Illustration furnished by Cosco Home Products.

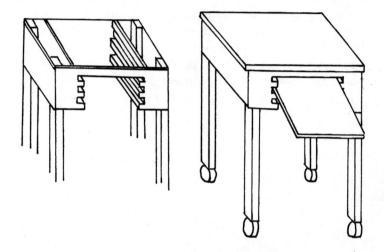

Figure 6-2. Table on wheels. From *Aids to Independent Living* by E. Lowman and J. L. Klinger. Copyright 1969. Used with permission of the McGraw-Hill Book Company.

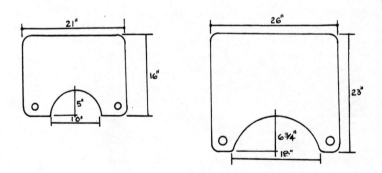

Figure 6-3. Lapboard.

to stabilize food, dishes, and pans. To accomplish this, they should develop special work habits and employ different techniques.

USING A CUTTING BOARD. A cutting board with two stainless steel nails can hold meat, fruits, and vegetables in place while someone peels, slices, or cuts them. It is easy to make one of a ¾-inch by 5½-inch piece of plywood. Attach a ¾-inch by 1-inch by 4½-inch brace to the underneath side of one end, allowing it to hook over the edge of your work surface. Then drive a 3-inch nail in place from the bottom to the top to hold the food (see Fig. 6-4).

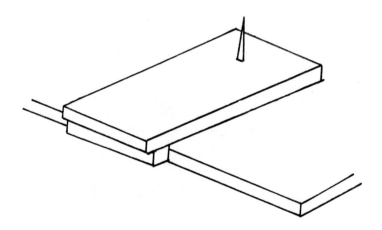

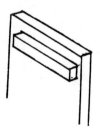

Figure 6-4. Cutting board.

SECURING A GLASS. There are many methods of stabilizing a glass. As was discussed in Chapter 3, you can put an octopus pad under any container on a countertop or table to hold it in place.

Mark, a college student with cerebral palsy, uses another method when mixing orange juice. He simply puts a glass into a much larger cup, which will hold it stationary while he stirs (see Fig. 6-5).

HOLDING BOWLS, DISHES, OR PANS STEADY. To secure a bowl, dish, or pan, you may find one of the following methods handy. A suction stand for stabilizing is often convenient. Set a suction cup on a flat surface and place the stand on it. By pushing down in the middle with your fist, the cup will adhere firmly to a surface. You can then place a bowl, pan, or dish inside the stand (see Fig. 6-6).

Figure 6-5. Glass stabilizer.

Figure 6-6.   Suction stand. Suction cups by J. A. Preston Corporation.

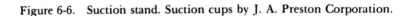

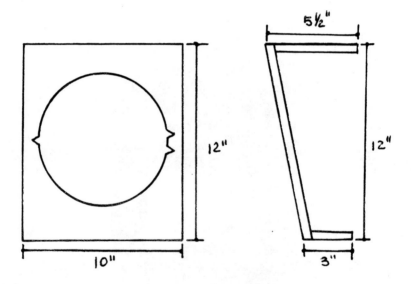

Figure 6-7.   Bowl holder.

A bowl can also be secured for mixing or stirring with a holder constructed of some pieces of wood (see Fig. 6-7). Cut a hole in a 10-inch by 12-inch piece of plywood to fit the size of your bowl. For a base, attach a board 5 inches high to the backside and one 3 inches high in front. Note that the top will slope to make your work easier.

Figure 6-8.   Wooden pan stabilizer.

You can also place a wet towel or dish cloth under bowls or pans to keep them from slipping or sliding. Sometimes, this method does not work as well as the methods described previously.

Some disabled people can stabilize a pan with another device built of ½-inch plywood. The handle of the pan fits into a vertically notched piece of wood 2½ inches wide by 5½ inches tall, which is glued and nailed with small finish nails to a 4 inch by 5 inch rectangular base covered with laminated plastic and glued to a foam rubber pad, which creates friction so it will not move.

HOLDING BREAD. Some handicapped people may need to use a special holder to secure bread. Like many other devices already discussed, you can have this one custom made from a rectangular piece of plywood 6 inches by 10 inches that is 1-inch thick. Cover this holder with laminated plastic and place a stainless steel nail in each of the four corners to hold the bread. You can also make a bread holder on a 7 inch by 9 inch breadboard. Simply tack two wooden strips ⅜ inch high and ⅜ inch wide, forming an L shape in one corner to place your bread for spreading (see Fig. 6-10).

ANCHORING A PACKAGE OR BOX OF FOOD. A disabled person could need to secure a box or packet of food while trying to open it. If you require assistance with this task, here are some ideas you could try: use a brick and lay it on one end of the food package while unfastening the other end or hold the package between your legs during the process.

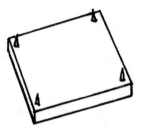

Figure 6-9.   Bread holder.

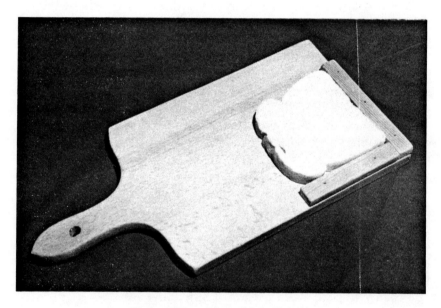

Figure 6-10.   Adapted breadboard.

Opening Containers

Opening containers can present special difficulties for those with joint impairments, hand involvement, or upper extremity weakness. Therefore, it is a good idea to find ways of accomplishing this in the easiest possible manner.

For many disabled homemakers, particularly those with arthritis, unscrewing certain types of containers might cause stress on the joints and aggravate the condition over a long period of time. This is especially true when twisting jar lids on and off, since a person sometimes must apply a great deal of pressure to release the cap.

UNSCREWING JARS. To minimize placing too much strain on your hands and fingers, you may want to try these five ways of unscrewing a jar.

1. Hot water. When opening a jar for the first time, pour hot water over the lid to help loosen it.
2. Tap the cap. Tapping the cap with the handle of a knife after you have rinsed it may assist you in freeing the lid.
3. Use a drawer. Place the bottom of the jar inside a drawer, close it to secure the jar, then lean against it so the base of the container will remain steady as you attempt to unscrew the lid (see Fig. 6-11).
4. Hold with pliers. Grasp the cap with a pair of pliers, which provides for more leverage as you attempt to twist off the cap.
5. Zim® jar opener. The Zim jar opener with metal teeth may be fastened to the wall and will grip the lids of sealed jars ½ to 3⅞ inches in diameter. The aid is ideal for homemakers who have a lack of strength in their hands. Merely insert a container into this jar opener, and give it a slight twist. With this device you are able to open anything with a screw, pry-up, friction, vacuum, or crown cap (see Fig. 6-12).

LOOSENING BOTTLE TOPS. Besides using the Zim jar opener or a pair of pliers to unfasten a jar lid, you can also use either to help you unscrew bottle tops. Another device that may assist you is the Bonny Top-Off® jar opener, which you can use for small bottle caps. Just place it on the cap and turn. You will be able to apply greater leverage. However, the pressure you are able to exert

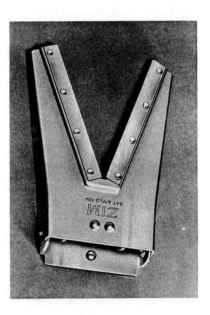

Figure 6-12.   Zim jar opener. Illustration furnished by Zim Manufacturing Company.

Figure 6-11.   Jar in a drawer.

decreases with a larger top size due to the opener's having a short handle.

OPENING CANS. Basically there are two ways to open cans: using an electric or a manual opener.

Electric models. Some handicapped people with hand and arm limitations find using an electric can opener easy and convenient to use, but there are some things to consider when you are thinking about purchasing one. First, whenever possible before buying, have the store clerk demonstrate each machine. Make certain the model you select cuts the lid off completely and leaves a smooth surface to avoid the possibility of cutting yourself when you handle the container. Then check to see how each machine holds the lid after it has been cut. On some models a magnet will hold it in place. Can you handle the top easily with your fingers? Look to see how the can is supported when it is being cut. Must you hold it, or does the can sit on a platform or other work surface? Be sure that the controls work easily. This

Figure 6-13.   Top-Off jar opener. Illustration furnished by Bonny Products.

is important for those with hand or arm weakness, since a machine that requires too much pressure to operate would be impractical. Large levers, a sliding bar, or big knobs are often easier to manage. Those with arthritis should choose a model that allows them to use the heel of their hand or the palm for controlling the machine. Next ask yourself these questions. How much does the machine weigh? Can I lift it? Sometimes a homemaker has little counter space and must slide it from the front to the back of the work surface when the opener is not in use. For those who do not have good coordination, a well-built, sturdy unit with a large base for stabilizing the machine is extremely important. Finally, is the model safe and easy to clean? Remember, you should be able to see the blades, but make sure they are in a place where you are unlikely to cut yourself. After you have finished using it, you also should be able to wash and wipe it dry without much effort.

One can opener that may be convenient for some handicapped people to use is the Hamilton Beach Insta-Clean® model 831 can

Figure 6-14. Insta-Clean model 831. Illustration furnished by Hamilton Beach.

opener/knife sharpener. A safety feature of this product is an automatic shutoff. Furthermore, for easy cleaning this model has a detachable cutting unit. To avoid the possibility of getting cut, the unit also has a magnetic lid lifter to hold the lid that has been cut until you are ready to remove it.

Manual types. There could be some types of cans you might not be able to open with an electric opener. In this case you might choose to do it manually. Three ways that people with various disabilities accomplish this in certain situations are by using an easy-to-turn key, a jumbo-handled can opener, and a knife or other blunt object to open a pull-tab on a beverage can.

Depending on the severity of the disability, a handicapped person might be able to use an oversized easy-to-turn key in place of the smaller one that comes with most vacuum cans and that is often difficult to grasp and to manage for someone with hand limitations. This opener is 6½ inches long and is reusable,

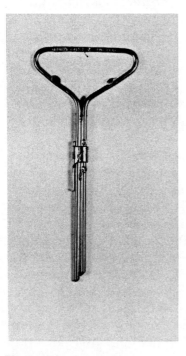

Figure 6-15. Oversized easy-to-turn key. Illustration furnished by Zim Manufacturing Company.

Figure 6-16. Jumbo-handled can opener.

since you simply slide the key off once the process is completed. Using this key makes opening cans easier.

Those with hand and finger involvement could also perhaps grasp a jumbo-handled can opener with a large built-up handle easier than the regular kind. These kinds are especially useful for puncturing cans containing milk or other liquids.

Pull tops on many beverage containers may also be difficult or impossible to manage for individuals whose fingers are stiff or lack good manual dexterity. One way to help solve this problem is to place a blade of a table knife or other similar object underneath the tab and pry it upwards.

Cutting, Peeling, Dicing, and Grating

The basic tool in the cutting process is your knife. It should be kept sharp in order to cut meat with less pressure and to prevent it from slipping. Remember also that practicing good safety habits is important when using one: cutting with the blade turned away from your body, being sure that your free hand is out of the range of the blade action, and if you must carry a knife being sure the point is downward. How you carry it is a factor if you have balance problems and may sometimes fall, since you will be less likely to injure yourself. Some of the specific types of equipment people might use in their cutting tasks are the following:

ELECTRIC KNIVES. Many handicapped homemakers find that using an electric knife is sometimes extremely helpful for dicing meats, fruits, and vegetables and for shredding salad ingredients. However, do not try using your knife to cut frozen foods or bones, since it will dull the blades. Before you purchase any model, consider your impairments. Do you have good grasping ability? Can you at least hold a knife using both hands? Do you have good perception? The latter point is extremely important because you can cut yourself easier with an electric knife than a standard one since the blades move. If you decide your limitations will not prevent you from using an electric knife safely, examine the unit carefully before you buy. Note the following points.

1. Check the weight. Make sure that holding an electric knife will not be too strenuous. So that you will be certain,

pick it up in the store and hold it a few seconds to see how it feels. Do this with several models to get an idea of how they would feel if you were cutting with them. Remember too that you can periodically stop and rest a while during the cutting process. Also, some people place their elbows on the counter for additional support.

2. Check the handle design. Electric knives with smaller grip-sized handles work well for someone with normal grasping ability, but for homemakers-with limited gripping strength, those with a hole in the handle are preferable since the person can slip the hand into them. Make sure the handle's length is not awkward to use.

3. Check the controls. First, look to see that you can reach and turn the on-and-off switch which controls the movements of the blades. Make certain also that it is in a place where you are not likely to hit the switch and start the knife accidently. Then examine the blade release mechanism. If possible, choose a model with one located in a position that you can reach easily, while avoiding the possibility of turning the knife on at the same time. Finally, remember, too, that when taking the blade out point it downward, release the blade, then shake the knife until it slips out part of the way.

An electric knife that has some of these features is the General Electric Electric Slicing Knife® (Model EK-9). This model is small, has a contoured plastic handle, and is easy to grip for people with the normal use of one hand. It has a safety device to prevent the knife from accidentally starting if it is dropped. A spring-loaded switch bar under the blade, which you only need to press lightly, starts the blade action.

Figure 6-17. Electric Slicing Knife (Model EK-9). Illustration furnished by General Electric.

Besides keeping in mind a few things when you are thinking about purchasing an electric knife, you should also learn how to use one properly. To help you do this, here are some guidelines.

1. Remember to hold the knife in a vertical position at a right angle to the table.
2. Stabilize what you are slicing on a cutting board, or use a fork when appropriate.
3. To begin cutting, make a start with the point of the knife. Keep the point at right angles to the table. Use one hand to move the knife back and forth in a sawlike motion to slice your food.

SLICER. If a disabled person has difficulty slicing, a handy appliance is the Waring Thin Slicer®. This unit performs all types of tasks from cutting food wafer thin to extra thick. It slices cold cuts, cheese, bread, roast beef, ham, turkey, and fruits and vegetables. In fact, because of its right-hand drive, it cuts just as commerical machines do. It disassembles for easy cleaning, has a low speed, high torque motor for safety, is

Figure 6-18. Thin Slicer. Illustration furnished by Waring Products Division.

compact, and folds easy for storage.

BLENDERS. Blenders are very useful for many disabled home-makers, especially those with hand and arm weakness, poor coordination, or arthritis, since this appliance can accomplish some mixing, chopping, and grating tasks, which take only a few seconds. However, just as with electric openers and electric knives, you must check the features carefully before you buy one.

1. Examine the base height. So that you will be able to add food to the container with ease, buy a blender with a low base. This is particularly important for homemakers confined to a wheelchair since they will have to fill the container from a sitting position.
2. Examine the container. To avoid added weight and the possibility of breakage, purchase a model with a container made of high impact, heat-resistant plastic. For those people with impaired hand functioning, a handle on the side of the container is a valuable feature.
3. Examine the controls. For homemakers with hand involvement, a slide bar or push buttons are simpler to operate than dials.

Hamilton Beach manufactures two blenders, the Fourteen Speed® Model 662 blender and the Seven Speed Plus® Model 697 blender, both of which have some of the features just described. Model 662 has a hi-low selector switch that provides for dual mixing speeds. The container, which holds 44 ounces of liquid, is shatterproof. This blender has stainless steel cutting blades for easy cleaning. Because of the push-button controls, less effort is required to operate this appliance for people with hand limitations. Model 697 also has push-button controls with a 44-ounce shatterproof container, along with 48-, 16-, and 12-ounce containers that are interchangeable, depending on the individual need (see Fig. 6-19 and 6-20).

FOOD PROCESSORS. Some disabled people may prefer to purchase a food processor rather than a blender. Waring Products manufactures the Waring Food Processor II®. This unit, which operates with a single switch, comes with three cutting blades for either cutting, medium shredding, or medium slicing. One

Figure 6-19.   Fourteen Speed Blender model 662. Illustration furnished by Hamilton Beach.

Figure 6-20.   Seven Speed Plus Blender model 697. Illustration furnished by Hamilton Beach.

Figure 6-21.   Food Processor II. Illustration furnished by Waring Products Division.

important safety feature is dynamic braking action, which enables the blades to stop promptly once the machine is turned off.

SCISSORS. A pair of scissors with long, sharp blades is often easier to manage than a knife when cutting pizza, bread, and chives, as well as other foods.

PEELER. Using a peeler is many times safer than working with a paring knife for people who lack coordination. Furthermore, peelers with wooden handles are often easier to hold for those with impairments (see Fig. 6-22).

OPEN-HANDLE KNIFE. The lightweight knife has a big, open handle so that some handicapped people with a weak grasp can control it with one or two hands while cutting. This knife is recommended for use by those with severe upper extremity weakness, especially a quadriplegic injured at the C6 or C7 level (sometimes the C5 or C6 level). Those with myogenic disorders such as multiple sclerosis or muscular dystrophy may also be able to use this knife successfully. However, according to some

Figure 6-22.   Peeler. Illustration furnished by Bonny Products.

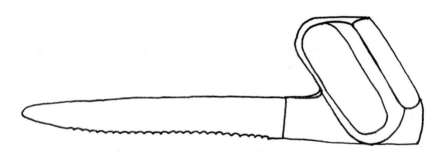

Figure 6-23.   Open-handle knife.

rehabilitation experts, this implement is not practical for people with poor coordination (Available from Unique Efficiency).

ONE-HANDED FOOD CHOPPER. A person with the use of only one hand can operate this chopping device by pressing the plunger downward, which rotates six blades inside the container for quick, easy chopping.

CHEESE CUTTER. Some disabled individuals with lack of

Figure 6-24. One-handed food chopper. Illustration furnished by Cleo Living Aids.

Figure 6-25.   Cheese cutter.

proper coordination may be able to use a homemade cheese cutter. To make this device, simply purchase a single-blade chopper and then build up the handle by wrapping with cloth or using foam rubber or other suitable material.

GRATERS. One can purchase different types of graters or adapt them so that those with physical limitations are able to use them easily. The following are two types that may prove practical for people with various hand impairments.

Those with the use of only one hand might want to set the grater on a wooden base edged with quarter round to hold it in place. Then position this kitchen device so that you are able to shred the food away from your body.

The Stay-Put® Grater has suction cups that hold it securely to surfaces. Three interchangeable plastic plates clip onto the stand for shredding and grating. Cleanup is minimized because of a bin

Figure 6-26.   Stay-Put grater. Illustration furnished by Help Yourself Aids.

that catches the food after it has been grated. Another grater is a
plastic Continental Grater 'n Bowl®, 8 inches in diameter with an
attachment that has sections for grating and shredding. The
bowl, made of high impact styrene, is stabilized by a nonslip base.
Individuals with poor coordination or upper extremity weakness
may be able to grasp the large easy-to-grip handle without much
effort.

ELECTRIC GRINDERS. An electric grinder is often useful to a
disabled person who is on a special diet and must only eat very
lean meat. Some other homemakers who like to prepare meals
from scratch but due to physical limitations who find cutting
meat or vegetables too time-consuming and difficult also prefer
using an electric grinder. However, if you decide to buy one,
consider these two points before making a purchase:

   1. The operating switch. Check to make certain that you
      can operate the on-and-off switch without difficulty.

Figure 6-27. Continental Grater 'n Bowl. Illustration furnished by Hutzler Manufacturing Company.

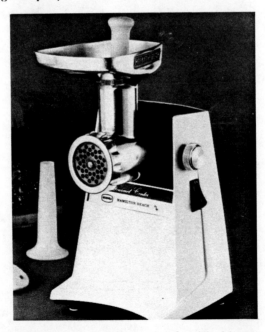

Figure 6-28. Food Converter Set. Illustration furnished by Hamilton Beach.

2. Handling the hopper. Be sure that you can put the hopper on and remove it from the unit.

One electric grinder that works well for some handicapped people is the Hamilton Beach Food Converter Set® (Model 168). It has push-button controls, which do not take much effort to operate. You must be able to lift the hopper into position, but it releases with an ejector button. You can handle all the unit's parts with one good functional hand or two weaker ones.

Pouring Liquids

Pouring liquids from containers often presents difficulties for people with various handicaps. For instance, those with arthritis or upper extremity weakness may find lifting containers quite a strenuous task. Anyone with cerebral palsy or Parkinson's disease might also have a lack of coordination or tremors and could splash or spill the liquid during the pouring process.

Sometimes choosing a lighter weight container might make this task less difficult. One example of this is when purchasing milk. Even though buying a half gallon will probably save money, the quart size is often not so bulky to handle. Below are some ways of pouring liquids that individuals with hand limitations might use.

JUICE POURER. Place a can or carton into the pourer and tighten the butterfly nut so that it will remain stationary.

Figure 6-29.   Juice pourer. Adapted from Elizabeth May, Neva Waggnor, and Eleanor May, *Homemaking for the Handicapped*, Dodd, Mead & Company, 1966, p. 128.

Adjust the chain to limit the pouring level and to prevent any spilling. Put your glass in a suction cup so it will not tip, and set it in position. Then using one hand, loosen the butterfly nut and start pouring.

BOWL HOLDER. This bowl holder is especially convenient for the homemaker with the use of only one hand. The stand holds a stainless steel bowl for mixing, which can also be tilted for pouring. Cleaning is also simplified since the 3-quart bowl can be lifted from the holder when necessary.

Figure 6-30.   Bowl holder. Illustration furnished by Help Yourself Aids.

KETTLE STAND. Since pouring hot liquids is sometimes hazardous for the disabled homemaker, a kettle or an electric hot pot, which we will discuss later in this chapter, may be positioned on a special stand so that a person is able to tilt it and pour hot liquids.

Figure 6-31.   Kettle stand. Adapted from Sydney Foott, *Handicapped at Home,* the Design Center, London, England, p. 26.

MILK CARTON HOLDERS. Quart, half-gallon, or gallon milk containers can slip into different-size holders that have handles which enable those with hand limitations to grasp the container more easily.

Figure 6-32.   Milk carton holder. Illustration furnished by Hutzler Manufacturing Company.

PITCHER. If possible, the handicapped person might have someone else put the liquid into a pitcher, which may be more convenient to use since the durable pitcher has a handle designed for easy lifting. The white three-position lid turns for free pouring, pouring with an ice guard, and for closing.

Figure 6-33.   Plastic pitcher. Illustration furnished by Rubbermaid, Inc.

CARAFES. Putting liquids in a carafe also has some advantages for handicapped individuals since it, too, has a lid to prevent spilling or splashing.

Figure 6-34.   Carafe.

GRIP 'N MIX® BOWLS. Grip 'n Mix bowls have large contoured handles that provide for a firm grip when mixing or pouring. These have spouts to allow no-drip pouring. Soft rubber rings on the base keep them from slipping when in use. They can be purchased in 1½- and 3-quart sizes.

Figure 6-35.   Grip 'n Mix Bowls. Illustration furnished by Rubbermaid, Inc.

PAN STRAINER. A pan strainer is very useful for the one-handed cook. Since the strainer is positioned on the top of the pan parallel to the handle, it is easy to use. The handle is spring loaded and designed to enable the homemaker to grip it securely.

Figure 6-36.   Pan strainer. Illustration furnished by Help Yourself Aids.

Beating, Mixing, and Stirring

You can make beating, mixing, and stirring easier if you remember a few basic principles. First, always tip your bowl or container so mixing will take less effort, and keep in mind, too, that moving your spoon back and forth across the bowl instead of in a circular motion often speeds the task. Second, if you plan to coat meat or fish, put the ingredients in a plastic or paper bag; place the food inside and shake it. Finally, another helpful idea is to use a ladle or cup to transfer batter from one container to another, thus avoiding lifting. In addition to these suggestions, you may find the following aids and appliances useful.

ELECTRIC MIXERS.   An electric mixer can solve the problem of mixing or stirring for a homemaker with upper extremity limitations who enjoys cooking but finds these tasks too time-consuming, difficult, or overtiring. There are basically two types of electric mixers: the portable hand-held variety, and the standard counter model. The one you choose will depend on how much you intend to use it and the degree of impairment you have in your hands and arms. If you only plan to use the appliance occasionally for such cooking tasks as mashing potatoes, a portable hand model will probably meet your needs, providing you can grasp it securely and hold it firmly, using one or both hands. Homemakers confined to wheelchairs often find portables convenient, since they can put the bowl on a lapboard, hold the mixer with one hand, and do the work. However, if you have many cooking activities that require mixing, you may prefer a standard counter model. This type is even more important for someone with poor coordination or extensive upper extremity weakness to avoid lifting. The following are a few guidelines for purchasing both types.

Portable mixers. First, inspect the handle weight, and while you are still in the store, hold the appliance as though you were using it. Ask yourself, "Will I be able to use this model with ease?" Remember also that very lightweight mixers do not have as much power for mixing as heavier ones. To solve this problem, you might want to choose a model light enough so that you can still manage it without too much difficulty but heavy enough to mix most things.

Second, examine the handle design. Make sure it is comfortable for you to hold. If you have a weak grasp, you may want to choose a mixer with an enclosed handle that will be less likely to slip from your hand.

Third, look to see that the heel rest is stable so that you can place the beaters on it. Be sure the beaters are also high enough and located over the bowl to avoid food dripping on your countertop or table below.

Fourth, make sure the controls are not too difficult for you to turn on and off. Be certain you can eject the beaters from the mixer without too much effort. If you have arthritis, select a portable mixer that you will be able to operate with the side of your hand so that you will not have to exert too much pressure on your thumb.

Finally, if at all possible, buy a mixer that has no center shaft, since it will be easier to clean.

The Waring Delux 12 Speed Hand Mixer® has features that enable disabled people to use this appliance with a minimum amount of effort. A wide open handle makes it easy for a person with hand limitations to grasp. The Delux 12 Speed Hand Mixer also has a convenient three-point heel rest so that you can set it on your countertop or table and the beaters will drip into the mixing bowl. A push-button ejector allows for quick removal of the beaters. This appliance can be purchased from the Waring Products Division.

Standard counter models. When buying a standard counter mixer, check the same features as you would for a portable mixer as well as three additional ones.

1. *Make sure the mixer is compact.* This becomes important because you may want to store the appliance when it is not in use. If you want to push it to the back of the counter, make certain that the mixer is light enough so you can. Homemakers sometimes plan to detach these units from their stands, but even when this is possible, the motor and beaters will usually be heavy to lift.

2. *Examine the bowls.* Those made of stainless steel rather than glass or ceramic are much easier to use. Often they are sold as optional equipment, but be sure to consider them since they will make your work less of an effort.

3. *Check the motor-beater handle.* Does it tilt back? Look for this feature since it makes putting ingredients into the bowl less frustrating.

The Sunbeam Mixmaster® (Model 42 W) has some of these design considerations. You can operate the Mixmaster with only one well-functioning hand, or if your upper limbs are too weak, you may be able to use the heel of both hands. In fact, even some amputees with a prosthetic device can grab the controls easily.

Figure 6-37.   Mixmaster. Illustration furnished by Sunbeam Corporation.

WIRE WHISK. Some disabled homemakers may prefer to use a wire whisk instead of an electric mixer for lighter stirring tasks, since sometimes the latter weighs too much. Whisks with large wooden handles may also be easier for individuals with incoordination or a weak grasp. The wire whisk often does a better job than heavier types of beaters, but in order to use it, you must have good upper arm and shoulder movement.

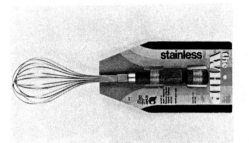

Figure 6-38. The Whip®. Illustration furnished by Bonny Products.

PRESTO WHIP®. By applying a downward pressure and then a spring release action you can use a presto whip with one or two hands. It has flexible stainless steel coils that enable a person to whip many substances thoroughly.

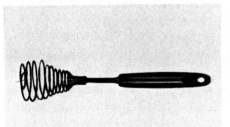

Figure 6-39. Presto Whip. Illustration furnished by Ecko Housewares Company.

SLANTED-HANDLE EGG BEATER. Egg beaters with slanted handles and ball-bearing mechanisms are much easier to use for some homemakers with limited forearm and wrist mobility. In order to operate the standard rotary beater, the person must have good functioning hands, and it may be necessary for the user to place the bowl and beater on a lower surface to reduce the power needed for completing the task.

Figure 6-40.   Slanted-handle egg beater. Illustration furnished by Ecko Housewares Company.

Breaking An Egg

People with hand limitations sometimes find breaking an egg difficult. If this is your problem, you might want to try a new method. One of the following four ways may make this simpler to accomplish. Try them and see which one works best for you.

BREAKING AN EGG WITH YOUR FINGERTIPS. To do this, pick up the egg, grasping one end with your thumb and forefinger and the other end with your thumb and second finger. Then hit the egg on the side of the bowl, so it breaks between your first and second finger. Now, quickly put the egg over the center of the bowl, and pull your forefinger and second finger apart in opposite directions, creating a slight pressure so the shell breaks, which allows the white and the yolk to slip out easily.

DROPPING THE EGG. Since some disabled people with severe

hand involvement are unable to crack an egg against the side of a bowl, they may be able to simply drop it into a dish. When doing this, center your hand over the container, level with the rim, and let the egg fall. Then, with a utensil, pick up the shells.

USING AN EGG SEPARATOR. Sometimes when cooking, the homemaker may want to separate the white from the yolk of an egg. You can do this easily with an inexpensive egg separator. When using one, break an egg in either of the two ways just described, but let it fall into an egg separator that you place over the container. The yolk stays in a small cup, while the white drains through slits into the bowl below.

Figure 6-41.   Egg separator. Illustration furnished by Ecko Housewares Company.

SETTING IT UPRIGHT.   If you want to break an egg that you intend to separate, you can lay it in an egg carton with the pointed end facing up. Chip off a little piece of the shell; then turn the egg over and let the white drip through the slit into the container. The yolk will remain in the shell since it is too large to pass through the small opening.

HINTS ON COOKING FOOD

In the previous chapter some methods of making the cooking center a convenient place for you to work were presented. Besides designing this place so it will be handy for you to use, there are other considerations you should think about when using a range or oven.

Light Gas Appliances Safely

While many homemakers cook with electricity, others prefer to use gas appliances. It is best for people with hand limitations to have cooking units with an automatic pilot light, but if your oven or range does not have one, here is how you can light it safely if you have the use of only one hand or have poor coordination. Lay a match on your nonautomatic gas burner's jet before turning it on. When using this method, your fingers never come into contact with the flame, and gas will not accumulate, thus avoiding the possibility of an explosion.

If you must hand light the gas jets, you can use long fireside matches. These are much safer since they will keep your hands away from the flame.

Advice on Ranges and Ovens

Working around a heated gas or electric range is potentially dangerous for anyone. This can be even more hazardous for a disabled person, particularly those with upper extremity weakness or lack of coordination. You should take the utmost care to keep from burning yourself. Depending on your limitations, you might find it safer and easier to cook with other types of appliances, which we will discuss later in this chapter, such as a

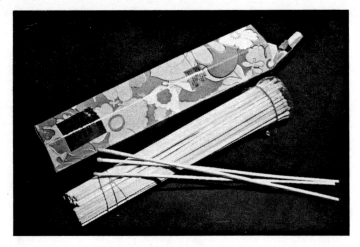

Figure 6-42.   Fireside matches.

microwave oven, table range, electric skillet, and different kinds of electric broilers. However, if you wish to use a standard range, here are some tips. First, never put anything on a heated burner. Instead, place your food on it and then start the range. This is important for persons with hand involvement, since they may have jerky motions and could get burned more easily. Another point to remember is that if you have difficulty putting things into the oven, do not preheat it no matter what the recipe indicates. Just put the food inside and then turn on the controls. After your meal has finished cooking, wait until the oven is cool before removing your pot, pan, or dish. In addition to these ideas, some other cooking aids may also be useful to certain handicapped homemakers.

COOKWARE WITH HEAT-RESISTANT HANDLES. Some pots and pans have heat-resistant handles that are made of wood.

ALUMINUM FOIL DISHES. You may want to cook in aluminum foil dishes, which are lighter in weight and are disposable.

LONG-HANDLED KITCHEN TOOLS. Long-handled tools, such as tongs, skewers, turners, forks, and basting brushes help to extend a person's reach. Some measure from 14 to 23½ inches long (see Fig. 6-43).

OVEN MITTS. Oven mitts will protect you from burning yourself when putting your hand into the oven or grabbing a hot pan (see Fig. 6-44).

Using a Microwave

For some handicapped people, cooking with a microwave oven has distinct advantages to other forms of cooking. First of all, these appliances are much safer. Unlike a range or oven, the food cooks, but the container does not get hot. Therefore, you are able to remove it from the oven without getting burned. A person also does not have to be concerned about burning his food since he can set a timer, which automatically shuts the oven off. This feature is very helpful for some disabled people. For instance, Mary Ellen ruined many meals because she put something into the oven, left the kitchen, and could not return to the kitchen when planned due to sporadic attacks of severe leg pains, which immobilized her for a while. Consequently, on many occasions

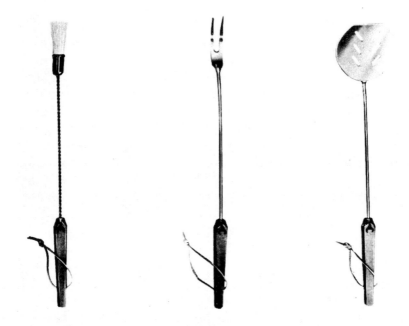

Figure 6-43.   Long-handled kitchen tools. Illustration furnished by Ecko Housewares Company.

Figure 6-44.   Oven mitts. Illustration furnished by Benhar Products.

she smelled food burning and knew she could not feed her family the meal. Mary Ellen no longer has this problem because she has a microwave.

Cooking in a microwave oven can eliminate lifting heavy pots and pans since you can cook your food in lighter weight glass or ceramic containers. Therefore, a disabled person, especially one with upper extremity weakness or lack of coordination, can often lift and hold the utensils more easily. (It is also a good idea to cook and serve food in the same dish to save time and effort when it comes to kitchen cleanup.)

Someone who, because of physical limitations, must rely on others for a major portion of his meal preparation might also find a microwave oven helpful since he can have another person cook the food, wrap, and freeze it in single serving portions that may be reheated. A disabled person might also wish to purchase convenience foods, such as T.V. dinners, boil-in-the-bag foods, casseroles, entrees, vegetables, pies, cookies, and breads, which can almost always be cooked in the container.

Before you use a microwave, you should consider a few things. According to an article in the June 1978 issue of *On Your Own*, a newsletter that is published by the University of Alabama which gives advice to handicapped homemakers, there are twelve points you should remember about microwave cooking:

1. Before using any microwave oven, read and follow the directions carefully. Operate the oven only when something is inside to avoid damage to the magnetron tubes.

2. Microwave energy is reflected by metal and absorbed by glass, plastic, and paper. For this reason you should cook in glass or paper, not in metal containers. You will find an assortment of microwave cookware in your hardware store.

3. One of the principles to keep in mind when cooking with microwave is not to overcook. Until you are accustomed to the length of time required for certain foods it is best to underestimate how long to cook something. If it is not done, you can always put it back in the oven for an additional few seconds.

4. Foods containing moisture cook more rapidly than dry foods. For example, meats cooked with sauce are ready sooner.

5. When time permits, let food stand a few minutes before

serving. This allows the microwaves to distribute the heat more easily.

6. Covering a dish helps to shorten the cooking time and in some cases prevents spattering. Plastic wrap can be used to cover plates of food for reheating. However, if a tight seal is formed, punch a few holes in the top to prevent spattering. Cooking bags are acceptable for microwave cooking if the bag is slashed for venting and metal ties are replaced with string or a rubber band.

7. You will be able to shorten the cooking time and the heat will be more evenly distributed, if smaller rather than larger quantities are prepared.

8. Because microwaves heat from the perimeter of the food to the inside, foods will be more evenly cooked if you turn the dish and stir liquids. Arrange solid foods such as chicken legs so that thicker pieces are toward the outer edge to insure a quicker cooking time.

9. Microwave cooking does not always produce the brown appearance preferred on certain foods. Some of the following toppings may be used to give a brown appearance: seasoned bread crumbs or crackers, croutons, dry onion soup mix, dry brown gravy mix, Worcestershire sauce, or brown seasoned powders.

10. Be careful not to underestimate the appropriate size of container for such foods as soups, casseroles, and sauces. Remember as these foods cook, their volume expands.

11. In cooking the more tender cuts of meats use the high power settings, and for less tender cuts use a lower one.

12. You can remove many types of food cooked in a microwave oven without the aid of pot holders. Only food cooked for a long period of time will transfer the heat from the food to the utensil.

But what model by what manufacturer should you buy? Consult the article "Microwave Ovens" in the June 1976 issue of *Consumer Reports*, which gives the results of testing done on sixteen different models. One of these, the Tappan Tap 'n Touch®, is recommended for physically disabled people. It has an easy-to-read front panel that automatically controls all cooking functions. A digital readout keeps account of cooking time and shuts the oven off when the food is finished cooking. It has a browning element and a three-way tray for browning flexibility.

Figure 6-45. Tap 'n Touch. Illustration furnished by Tappan Appliances.

Preparing Meals on a Table Range

If you are confined to a wheelchair and live in a place where your cooktop is too high for you to reach, one possible solution is to prepare some of your meals on a table range, more commonly known as an electric hot plate. You can put this appliance on your kitchen table or any surface that is a height you can work at conveniently. However, before you purchase one, check these features.

HEIGHT. Be sure to buy a low profile model so that you will not need to transfer pots and pans too great a distance back and forth from the burners to your work surface.

THE COOKING ELEMENT. Select a model with a tubular cooking element that lifts up for easy cleaning. Remember that units with exposed wire coils are dangerous.

Figure 6-46.   Double Burner table range. Illustration furnished by Hamilton Beach.

CONTROLS.   Depending on your limitations, choose table ranges with either a rocker switch on top of the unit or easy-to-turn knobs located in front of the unit. Some people with incoordination or upper extremity weakness may be able to turn on the range with a rocker switch by hitting it lightly with the fist. If you select one with knobs, make certain that the range has three settings, high, medium, and low so that you will have a variety with which to work (see Fig. 6-46).

One model that also has some of these features is the Double Burner Table Range® by Dominion. It has a rocker control switch located on the top of the unit with two heating elements—one of 550 watts and one of 1100 watts.

Advantages of Electric Skillets

Electric skillets often have some advantages for disabled homemakers. Frequently, handicapped people use one to prepare their breakfasts as well as their dinners since it is possible to cook entire meals in these appliances. Electric skillets can have appealing features for certain individuals with physical limitations. One feature is that when cooking with this appliance, the homemaker need not be concerned about reaching over hot burners. You can also set this appliance on your kitchen or dining room table and eliminate the problem of carrying food from the range to your serving center. But what are some of the things to consider as you think about purchasing an electric skillet?

SELECT A SQUARE LIGHTWEIGHT SKILLET. The easiest skillet to handle is a square one with sides several inches high. Purchase the lightest model but one with thick enough sides to cook food evenly. You may not need to lift it depending on your situation. Some alternatives are: sliding it out of the way when it is not in use and having another member of the family lift the skillet for you.

SELECT AN ALUMINUM OR STAINLESS STEEL SKILLET. Aluminum or stainless steel is lighter in weight than many metals used in cookware. Furthermore, try to purchase a model that has a Teflon II® finish inside for easy cleaning, since the food will not stick to the bottom of the inner walls.

SELECT A SKILLET WITH A HEAT-RESISTANT HANDLE. A heat-resistant handle should be located in a place that enables you to move the skillet easily and safely. People with various disabilities may choose a different handle design depending on their limitations. For instance, a person with only one hand might prefer a single handle, whereas those with weakness in both extremities should purchase one that has two handles so they can grasp it easily. Choose a model that also has a baffle which will protect your fingers from coming into contact with the hot metal as you lift the appliance.

SELECT A SKILLET WITH EASY-TO-OPERATE CONTROLS. Under-the-handle controls are often difficult to manage. If possible, purchase a unit with large knobs having easy-to-grasp, ridged edges. Make sure there is a baffle behind the controls to prevent you from burning yourself. Be certain, too, that you can read the temperature indicator and that the model has a signal light to show when it is heated to the proper temperature.

SELECT A SKILLET WITH A WELL-DESIGNED COVER. Be certain

Figure 6-47. Tri-Pan Fry Pan®. Illustration furnished by Nesco Products, Inc.

the handle on the cover is large enough and placed in a position so that you can grab it easily without worrying about burning yourself when lifting the lid. Remember, also, that you are able sometimes to build up the handle by fastening a piece of foam around this knob. In addition, choose an electric skillet with a high-domed cover that allows you to use it for either baking or cooking large pieces of meat. You can sometimes purchase a high broiler lid as an option with the skillet you buy.

Home economists working with the physically disabled often suggest purchasing the Tri-Pan Fry Pan® (Model B3039). This versatile appliance has an open handle designed with a baffle to keep your hands from touching the hot pan. Because of a tilt mechanism at the front of the pan, you can also raise it so that fat will run to all four corners. You can use the warming tray underneath for heating bread and rolls.

The Convenience of Portable Broiler Ovens

Some handicapped homemakers find it difficult or impossible to use a standard oven, which may be too high for them to reach. Instead they use a portable broiler oven. One good hint to remember, especially for those with upper extremity impairments, is to have an area in front of the broiler where you can set the food before lifting it into the broiler.

When purchasing this appliance, also be sure it has adequate safety features. Unfortunately, many lack on-and-off switches. Make certain the one you purchase does have this feature. Most importantly, decide how you will use your broiler. Will you use it for heating and broiling on rare occasions or rely on it as a substitute oven? Your decision could determine the price and quality of appliance you wish to buy. Basically there are two types: the countertop ovens, and open broilers.

COUNTERTOP OVENS. Shop carefully when you are looking for a countertop oven. To help you make your choice, the following are a few points to consider.

Inspect the element. All broilers have a heating element at either the top or bottom of the appliance. Select a unit with a more durable tubular element instead of the wire or coil type. Choose an element also that does not merely go around the perimeter of the broiler, but one that forms a cross in the center of the oven. Remember, too, that you should be able to remove the element for cleaning.

Inspect the interior. Ask yourself, "Will my pans fit into the oven, and will they slide in and out effortlessly?" Since there is often spattering as you broil, select an appliance with a smooth lining, which you can clean with the least amount of work.

Inspect the rack and rack supports. Make sure the racks are heavy enough so that they will not warp under intense heat. However, be certain they are light enough so that you can lift them without too much strain. Do not forget also to purchase a broiler with slotted rather than open wire racks, since there is less chance of grease flaring up. Check to see that the supports will hold the rack up when you pull them two-thirds of the way out. Then test to see whether you can pull the racks out without pulling the broiler off the counter or table.

Inspect the broiling pan. Buy a broiler with a deep broiling pan to hold a substantial amount of fatty liquids without spilling when you remove it from the oven.

Inspect the controls. You should be able to set the thermostatic control between 250° and 450°. Look also to see that the knobs are large enough for you to turn and that you are able to operate them without having to touch the hot metal on the outside of the broiler. Depending on your disability, a push-button model may be easier for you to use. Some of these models have three buttons labeled *bake, broil,* and *off.* Still other units have switches. If you wish to buy this type, check to see that you are able to switch from bake to broil without pulling the plug and having to plug the switch into a different outlet. An electric timer is also a convenient feature since it will turn the broiler off at a preset time. If you tend to be forgetful, an electric timer can help you avoid the possibility of burning your meal. Also, look for a broiler that has a signal light to indicate when the preheated temperature in the oven has been reached so that you can put your food inside.

Inspect the door. Be sure you can open the door without too much effort. Sometimes these appliances have large handles that are easy to grasp. This is an especially good feature for some people with upper extremity impairments. Make certain, too, that you can grab the handle without touching the hot metal on the outside of the broiler. You might also consider looking for a door made of heat-resistant material. Ask the store clerk which models have this feature. In any case, always use a pot holder when opening and closing the door. Check to see that the door stays on its hinges when you move it. On some broilers you may not be able to maneuver the door skillfully without undue effort, so check this.

Inspect the insulation. Of course, there is no way to look between the sidewalls of a broiler and check to see how much insulation a particular unit has, but there are two guidelines you can follow. First, ask the salesman the amount of and the type of insulation in the sidewalls of the broiler. Second, examine the door. Make sure it fits snugly to keep in the heat.

Inspect the power output. Before purchasing any broiler, be sure the wiring system in your house will accommodate the electrical demand the broiler requires. In other words, although these appliances are 120 volts, they can range from 1300 to 1650 watts. Therefore, make certain your home's electrical system will allow you to use a broiler safely.

The Farberware Turbo Oven® (Model 460R) and the Toastmaster Push-Button Oven Broiler® (Model 5242) are two ovens that have some advantages for handicapped people. The Turbo Oven has a side-opening door with a long handle, which insures safety and provides for convenience. Turbo cooking, which circulates air continuously around food, allows you to roast meat

Figure 6-48. Turbo Oven. Illustration furnished by Farberware.

Figure 6-49. Push-Button Oven Broiler. Illustration furnished by Toast-master.

on all sides without turning it. The outside walls of the oven always remain cool, so you can touch them and never burn yourself. Furthermore, this oven never exhausts hot air into the kitchen and is self-cleaning. Toastmaster's Push-Button Oven Broiler® (Model 5242) has three handy push buttons for baking, roasting, and broiling. This appliance has a catalytic porcelain interior with a continuous cleaning feature. You can select the correct temperature conveniently because of the color-coded push-button controls. The single shelf with top and bottom supports slides out easily without tipping.

OPEN MODELS.   The open broilers have a rack that lies over a tubular heating element. Any drippings fall into a stainless steel or aluminum drip pan containing water. There is no spattering or smoking, as the drippings do not hit a hot surface.

This type of broiler is particularly easy to manage for those with some loss of sensation, upper extremity weakness, or hand and arm involvement since the disabled person has no need to lift a heavy door, dripping pans, or racks. However, before you buy an open broiler, there are two things to keep in mind.

Examine the rack design. Make sure you can adjust the racks in two or more positions, which will enable you to cook different foods.

Examine how the broiler is disassembled. Select a broiler with a detachable heating element to make cleaning simpler.

One open broiler that some disabled people can use handily is the Farberware Open Hearth® Broiler. This stainless steel unit has a cooling cone to keep it free of smoke and spatter. However, a disadvantage of this model is that it does not have an on-and-off switch. To solve the problem, you can have the appliance cord spliced and a switch attached (see Fig. 6-50).

The Benefits of Hot Pots

As mentioned before, some disabled people have difficulty using a standard range. In addition, boiling water in a teapot or kettle is sometimes even more hazardous. Therefore, besides the kettle stand described earlier, another possible solution might be to use a hot pot, sometimes known as a liquid heater. Often these appliances are safer since one does not work over a flame. Most electric hot pots bring a cup of water to boil in one and one-half

Figure 6-50.   Open Hearth broiler. Illustration furnished by Farberware.

minutes, and some of these hot pots boil as many as six cups of water. In addition to boiling water, one can make coffee and heat soup, sauces, and vegetables. Unfortunately, not all hot pots meet the Underwriter's Laboratories standards for safety, so to select a hot pot with care, try to locate one following these guidelines.

1. Check the temperature control. Select a hot pot with settings that range from warm to boil. Be certain that you can move the control lever between the settings quickly so that the liquids inside will not boil over.

2. Check the handle design. Before you purchase a hot pot, hold it in your hand. Make sure your fingers will not touch the hot metal. The safest handle is one made of non–heat-conducting material with a baffle along the inside of the handle.

3. Check the construction. Be certain the base of the hot pot is stationary and that it does not become too hot, causing the possibility of burning your counter or table. If possible, choose one with a base of Bakelite® or another heat-resistant material. Remember, too, that a hot pot lined with a Teflon coating is easier to clean.

4. Check the cover. Even though a cover on a hot pot is not always necessary, it can often be helpful, especially for quick heating and simmering.

5. Check the plug location. Always try putting the plug into

Figure 6-51.   Poly Insta-Hot. Illustration furnished by Regal Ware, Inc.

the socket of the hot pot before purchasing it. On some models it could be in a place where it would be difficult for you to use.

One convenient hot pot is the Regal Poly Insta-Hot® (Model K7426), which holds up to six cups of liquid. You can use this appliance for warming soups, sauces, and baby bottles. The Poly Insta-Hot heats liquids at the rate of one cup per 75 seconds at the top temperature. This appliance has a temperature selector that can be set anywhere between 100° and 205°F, and control markings indicate warm and hot settings. The handle is built far enough away from the unit so a disabled individual's fingers will not touch the hot metal.

CLEANING UP AFTER YOUR MEAL

Earlier in this chapter how to carry things was discussed. Some of these ideas are helpful in cleaning the table, including using a metal cart, a table on wheels, or a lapboard if you are confined to a wheelchair. Listed below are also six other points you should consider.

1. Use plastic dishes, lightweight cookware, or disposable foil pans so that you do not have heavy items to handle.

2. When preparing a meal, you may want to use wax paper or paper towels to keep the work surface clean.

3. Work with the fewest utensils possible.

4. Soak dishes immediately after using them to help eliminate scouring. Remember, too, that hot water softens sugar and grease, while cold water loosens starchy foods, eggs, and milk.

5. Organize your sink area to create an easy flow of work when washing, rinsing, and stacking dishes. Furthermore, be sure if you have a two-compartment sink that you have your drain rack near the compartment where you rinse the dishes.

6. To conserve energy, air dry most of your dishes. For best results use a liquid or powdered detergent that will rinse off completely. Do not forget that only sterling, silver-plated, and cast-iron utensils need to be hand dried.

PORTABLE DISHWASHER. Since some chairbound homemakers do not have a built-in dishwasher, they may want to purchase a portable front-loading one. This kind has push-button controls, which are easy to operate (see Fig. 6-52).

DELUXE SUCTION® BOTTLE BRUSH. If you wash your dishes in the sink, you may want to use a Deluxe Suction Bottle Brush to get glasses, plates, and bottles sparkling clean. A large, 6 inch diameter suction cup secures this brush to the bottom of the sink and enables a person with the use of only one hand to wash dishes. The brushes, which are 7 inches tall, are made of nylon for long-lasting wear (see Fig. 6-53).

SPONGE-HEAD DISH MOP. A dish mop with a sponge may be handy for some handicapped people to use when scrubbing plates or washing the inside of glasses (see Fig. 6-54).

Every day many homemakers prepare breakfast, lunch, and dinner, but for some disabled people this can be a difficult task. Hopefully, the ideas discussed in this chapter will help you to simplify your daily mealtime routine.

POINTS TO REMEMBER

1. *Be careful when carrying foods or liquids.* Remember safety first. Depending on your disability, you might want to try using a metal cart, a table on wheels, or a lapboard.

Figure 6-52.   Portable dishwasher. Illustration furnished by Hobart Corporation.

2. *Some amputees, people with upper extremity weakness, or people who lack proper coordination may need to stabilize their food or utensils.* These individuals might want to use a cutting board, a wooden device to hold pan handles securely while cooking, a wet cloth to anchor kitchen cookware, or a bread holder. Others must use special ways to open boxes or food packages, such as using a brick to lay on one end while opening the other or holding the package between the legs during the process.

3. *Opening containers can be tedious for some disabled people with hand limitations.* Some methods to make this task easier include the following: pouring hot water over a jar lid, closing a drawer on a jar to secure it, grasping the lid of a jar or bottle with a pair of pliers, using a Zim jar opener, or

Figure 6-53. Deluxe Suction bottle brush. Illustration furnished by Cleo Living Aids and Help Yourself Aids.

Figure 6-54. Sponge-head dish mop. Illustration furnished by Empire Brush, Inc.

opening a bottle with a Top-Off vise bottle opener. Either electric or special manual can openers,such as Easy-to-Turn key, and those with jumbo handles work well for some handicapped people.

4. *Some disabled individuals need to devise special methods to cut,peel, dice, and grate food.* Electric knives and thin slicers are often useful to handicapped people for cutting purposes. Blenders also make dicing easier. Other aids include peelers, and a One-Handed Food Chopper. For grating, you could use a Stay-Put Grater or one that fits into a holder. Individuals who must have special diets often find a food converter very helpful.

5. *A handicapped person might use various ways to pour liquids.*Use a juice pourer, bowl and holder, kettle stands, milk carton holder, plastic pitchers, carafes, Grip 'n Mix Bowls, and pan strainers.

6. *Beating, stirring, and mixing can be difficult for individuals with upper extremity involvement.* Some of these people may wish to use electric mixers, while others find it more

convenient to use a wire whisk, a Presto Whip, or a slanted-handle eggbeater.

7. *Handicapped people with hand limitations may need to use special techniques for breaking eggs:* dropping the egg into a bowl, using an egg separator, or cracking the egg as it sits in a carton with the pointed end facing upwards, and then removing it from the shell.

8. *Think about safety before lighting gas appliances.* It may be helpful to use long fireside matches.

9. *Some ways to make range-top cooking safer and easier for people with different disabilities are to use cookware with heat-resistant handles, cook in aluminum foil dishes, work with long-handled kitchen tools, or wear oven mitts.*

10. *Microwave ovens often have advantages for handicapped people.* Two of these are that they are much safer and one cannot burn the food.

11. *Table ranges can sometimes take the place of a standard or built-in type, since one can put them at a lower work level.*

12. *Electric skillets have appealing features for many handicapped people.* They are frequently able to cook an entire meal right where they intend to serve it, and cooking this way keeps them from having to reach over burners.

13. *Portable broilers can replace the need for cooking with a standard range.* Have a rest area in front of this appliance upon which to lay food before putting it in the unit.

14. *Electric hot pots eliminate having to use a teapot or kettle on a standard range.* One can boil water, make coffee, heat soups and sauces, or warm canned food.

15. *When washing, rinsing, and drying dishes, plan to make the work easy.* Find aids that make these tasks simpler to perform.

Chapter 7

KEEPING YOUR HOME
NEAT AND SPOTLESS

"Oh, I must polish the table and clean Tommy's room today," Molly, a polio victim, told her friend, Doris, while sitting in her wheelchair one morning as they drank coffee together. "I wish I could do my cleaning tasks easier."

"That's no problem," Doris replied. "Just be careful to select equipment with features that will simplify your work, and choose methods which make each job less of an effort."

This is good advice for any disabled homemaker. In this chapter some ways of putting these ideas into practice will be discussed.

SELECTING THE RIGHT EQUIPMENT

Choosing Your Vacuum Cleaner

Using a vacuum in many cases is much easier than operating a carpet sweeper, since a canister or bag confines household lint to one area. However, depending on your physical limitations, a vacuum cleaner might be awkward to move about. For example, this is often the case for a housewife with upper extremity limitations or one confined to a wheelchair. However, if you are thinking about purchasing one of these appliances, the following are some things to consider.

MANUFACTURER AND DEALER RELIABILITY. Be sure you buy a popular brand name vacuum manufactured by a reliable company. Check to see that the dealer is able to give you good service.

THINK ABOUT THE USE. Keep in mind the major cleaning purposes for which you intend to use your vacuum cleaner.

Upright Vacuums. Upright models with revolving brushes or an agitator make cleaning carpets easier than using a canister vacuum.

Attachments. Make certain you can use all the attachments easily. Those that lock together are better than the ones held together by friction. Check also to see that you are able to attach and use them conveniently.

Soil Container. Select a vacuum with a soil container that empties easily.

Canister Vacuums. Some disabled homemakers prefer to buy a canister or tank vacuum. If this is your desire, think about the following items.

Wheels or casters. Look for a vacuum that rolls on wheels or casters since this will reduce the stress when you are pulling it around from room to room. Additionally, that feature makes it easier to pass over rug edges or the vacuum's cord.

Bumpers. Bumpers on a model protect your furniture from being scratched.

Disposable dust bags. Vacuums with disposable dust bags rather than cloth ones eliminate the need to fasten them on the unit.

Bag release. Be sure the unit you select has an automatic bag release.

Cord. Make certain the cord is long enough for free movement.

Cord rewinder. To avoid bending, choose a vacuum with a cord rewinder.

Foot-operated switch. Especially for some individuals with hand involvement, a foot-operated switch might be preferable.

Attachment storage. Some vacuums have a place for storing attachments, which can be convenient.

Long-Handled Dustpans

A long-handled dustpan is handy for some handicapped people who find stooping and kneeling difficult or impossible. They are also especially useful for those confined to wheelchairs.

When choosing one, be sure that the handle will stay in an upright position while you clean. Furthermore, if you are chairbound, check also to see that the handle is long enough so it

Figure 7-1. Long-handled dustpan. Illustration furnished by Fulton Corporation.

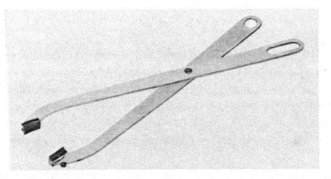

Figure 7-2. Better-Grip wooden reacher. Illustration furnished by Help Yourself Aids.

will not be necessary to lean forwards, since this might cause backache. Make certain, too, that the dustpan will be easy to carry without spilling dirt or lint.

Canes, Mopsticks, and Pickup Scissors

For wheelchair homemakers and others who are unable to reach hard-to-clean areas, wrapping a dust cloth around a mop handle or cane may be one solution.

You could also place your cloth in the Better-Grip® wooden reacher, which is 27 inches long. This scissor reacher with serrated rubber grippers provides good leverage and a strong grip. It is manufactured from sturdy, lightweight five-ply beach board and also has small magnets at the tip.

Mops and Mop Pails

MOPS. There are two varieties of mops: the dust mop and the wet mop. Just as with dustpans, brushes, and brooms, you should select one with a long handle if you have reaching difficulties.

One convenient dust mop is the Cotton Mitt-Mop®. It has a stainless steel handle that adjusts to any angle and glides easily under your furniture while you are either standing in an upright position or sitting in your wheelchair. The washable cotton head catches the dirt.

As for wet mops, you can select one with either a cloth or sponge head. Some of the sponge ones have a wringing device. One of these is the Squeez-a-matic®, which has a lever that you can pull to wring it dry.

MOP PAILS. Many handicapped homemakers find it easier to roll the mop pail along on the floor rather than to carry it. This is particularly true if you are confined to a wheelchair. One way of doing this is to put your pail on a platform with casters, which can be built from a square of plywood larger than your bucket. Use screws to attach a caster to each of the four

Figure 7-3. Cotton Mitt-Mop. Illustration furnished by Suburbanite.

Figure 7-4.   Squeez-a-matic. Illustration furnished by Suburbanite.

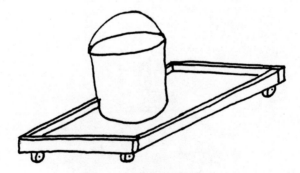

Figure 7-5.   Mop pail caddy.

underneath corners. Then tack strips of narrow molding around all the top sides to form a ledge so your pail will not slide off this platform. Depending on your handicap, you might want to push it with your feet, cane, or crutch or to pull the platform along with a rope, which you can fasten to a screw eye attached to one side.

Dusting and Polishing

DUSTING. Use a soft feather duster to dust around knickknacks, or fasten it to a long stick, which will enable you to reach high surfaces above your shoulder level. Also, a soft-bristled brush on a pole is equally good, providing you have enough strength and control in your arms. Be certain the pole is flexible, since a long, rigid one could break.

POLISHING. Aerosol silicone sprays, such as Pledge®, are the best for polishing furniture. Many handicapped people can use these with little effort. However, polishing floors should be avoided when at all possible. Often, carpets or vinyl tile with a built-in shine is easier to keep clean (*see* the section on floor coverings in Chap. 10).

Figure 7-6. Feather duster. Illustration furnished by Texas Feathers Incorporated.

MAKE YOUR CLEANING EASIER

Before presenting the methods some handicapped homemakers use to perform specific tasks, it may be helpful to examine four general principles that will help you make each job simpler.

Organize Your Work

Think about the best method and routine you can use to perform every chore. For example, Bonny, who walks with crutches, intended to clean her bedroom and bathroom on Monday, her living room and hall on Wednesday, and her kitchen and dining area on Friday. When you decide on a plan, keep in mind that you should allow yourself enough flexibility to cope with emergencies.

Another helpful tip is to list the cleaning tasks that you wish to accomplish daily, weekly, or less frequently. Avoid too many difficult seasonal cleaning chores by doing daily and weekly tasks more thoroughly. Remember also to avoid scheduling too many strenuous jobs in a short period of time, thus eliminating peaks of overwork.

Do Not Allow Dust to Accumulate

To make housecleaning jobs easier, try to prevent dust from collecting in your home. There are a number of ways to do this.

Make sure walks, steps, and porches are kept clean. Always remember to use doormats and foot scrapers so that you will not track dirt into the house. If possible, provide storage space inside near entrances to your home for sweaters, coats, rain jackets, umbrellas, rubbers, and boots. Sweep, vacuum, or mop surfaces before too much soil accumulates or becomes embedded in the floor. Select furnishings and fabrics that are easy to clean. For instance, you can wipe off the wooden arms of a chair much easier than you can vacuum upholstered ones. Remember, too, that plastic, vinyl coverings, and treated fabrics require less care. Reduce the number of knickknacks or other decorative items in your home because they must be dusted. Discard or store away the seldom used or nonessential articles and furnishings around the house.

Improve Your Cleaning Methods

Whenever you start working, pause and try to find ways of doing the task more efficiently. These tips might help you.

THINK ABOUT ONE CHORE AT A TIME. List all the steps involved in each of your cleaning jobs, and decide if you can improve the way you do any of them. If you have thought of a new approach, try it to see whether the method improves your work habits. Remember that this procedure may seem awkward at first until you have eliminated your old habit and established a new one. An important thing never to forget is to try isolating each of your cleaning tasks then organizing them into a series of small steps that you can try to refine and simplify each time you do them.

SELECT THE PROPER TOOLS. Choose the proper tools and equipment when you begin working.

Be sure you are using your vacuum cleaner to the best advantage. You may be able to use the floor brush to clean walls and bare floors instead of dust mops or brushes, which often scatter dirt rather than collect it.

As stated earlier, long-handled mops help to avoid bending or kneeling on the floor. Furthermore, you are able to use them for other household jobs, such as washing walls or cleaning the bottom of your bathtub. Cellulose sponges are also handy for wiping up spills.

PLAN THE ORDER OF YOUR WORK. Gather together all the equipment you need for a certain task; then when necessary, arrange the items in the order that you will use them. Do not forget that you can keep supplies and tools handy in cleaning baskets. You may also want to purchase an apron with small pockets for holding items you will need.

When considering the order of tasks, plan to do all your work in a given area before moving on. For example, with your vacuum cleaner attachments, clean all surfaces in one corner of the room before proceeding to another location.

BE FLEXIBLE IN YOUR CLEANING STANDARDS. This may particularly apply to someone who was once able-bodied but now is handicapped. As discussed in Chapter 4, ask two important questions about each task you plan to attempt: Is the job really important? Is it really necessary?

LOOK FOR NEW COMMERCIAL PRODUCTS. Often commercial products can make your work much easier. These include cleaning agents that require no rinsing, furniture polishes that clean and polish at the same time, and treated, disposable dusting paper. When you walk by the shelf where these products are located in your grocery store, stop periodically and examine the displays. You might find a product to make your work easier.

Develop the Right Attitude about Cleaning

Do not become frustrated about things you cannot change, but learn to accept them. For instance, Frances, paralyzed from the waist down, repeatedly asked her four-year-old son, Tommy, to stop tracking mud across the kitchen floor. However, he still continues. Frances then decided that instead of becoming too angry about cleaning up after him, she would still try to alter his behavior but not become disturbed by it.

As you go about your tasks, also remember not to expect the impossible. Even though you have a good cleaning plan and the best of equipment, it is still a chore. Above all, do not try doing too many heavy jobs in one day, since this could be quite strenuous and tiresome if you have a weakened physical condition.

SIMPLIFYING EACH CHORE

Previous sections of this book have already presented some features to look for that will help you when buying top quality cleaning equipment and four general principles to apply when doing your housekeeping chores. It may now help to examine some methods that could improve the way you do various cleaning jobs around your home.

Kitchen Cleaning

Spray and wipe off cleaners are ideal for washing away finger marks on walls and woodwork, on countertops, on the sink, or on the stove. These products are particularly convenient for handicapped people since when using them the person eliminates carrying a cleaning mixture, which possibly could be splashed on the floor. However, these cleaners have one disadvantage when doing such jobs as wiping off an entire side of a refrigerator or shining a coffee pot—often they leave a streaky appearance. For these jobs, it is better to use rubbing alcohol on a paper towel, since this method does a good job of cleaning metal and will not leave an antiseptic odor.

After you have wiped your kitchen center and shined your metal appliances, there might still be a corner on the countertop of the lower kitchen cupboards that you cannot reach. If this is one of your difficulties, you may want to try a large sponge in a reacher to make the task easier. If you are in a wheelchair and want to clean spots on the front of your counter, you can use a dish mop, which will extend your reaching distance about 10 inches.

For many handicapped homemakers, one of the hardest jobs is cleaning the oven. When doing this, you may want to use your vacuum first to take out the crumbs. Then decide if the racks need cleaning. If not, remove them so you can reach all areas of the oven. Select the type of appliance that works best, but depending on the cleaner used, it may be necessary to wipe out the dirt first. For that purpose, you could use either a small string or sponge dish-mop with an easy-to-grasp handle.

Dusting

One important thing for all handicapped homemakers to remember is that a long handle on a duster extends a person's reach. This is particularly true for someone confined to a wheelchair. Chairbound individuals may also want to wrap a dusting cloth around a cane so they are able to reach high dusting surfaces.

Picking Up Objects

Picking up objects from the floor may be somewhat difficult for someone confined to a wheelchair. Here is an approach that a person might try. He should slide back in his chair so that it will not tip over and lean down to grab the object alongside the pedal. If the object is behind something, he may want to roll the item toward him before picking it up. He can also use the Better-Grip® wooden reacher for grasping objects lying on the floor.

Wiping Up Spills

For those with poor balance, a small sponge dish mop could be the answer to wiping up spills, while others may prefer using dish cloths in the bathroom or kitchen. However, one should remember to be careful since wet floors can be dangerous.

If you are ambulatory and have good coordination but cannot bend, you might be able to drop a paper towel on the floor and move it around with your foot until you wipe the floor dry.

When someone is chairbound, just as with a person who cannot bend, he should drop a paper towel on the spill. Then he can use a broom to swish it around to soak up the spill.

Floor Care

Three major areas of floor care include: sweeping, mopping, and polishing.

SWEEPING. Previously it was stated that if you are confined to a wheelchair, long-handled dustpans are often handy. One method of sweeping some chairbound individuals have used successfully is the following: to begin by placing the broom on one side of their chair then the other and sweeping as they move forward. When collecting the dust, they lean the long-handled dustpan against the side of their chairs.

For an ambulatory homemaker who has difficulty bending, the problem is somewhat different. If you have such a disability, choose a dust mop with a strong but flexible handle that will enable you to sweep under furniture without stooping.

MOPPING. Those with hand limitations may have difficulty mopping. As mentioned before, you can purchase a self-wringing mop with either a cotton or sponge head.

After choosing the right mop, you need to decide how you will wet it. If you plan on using a mop bucket, you can fill it easily with a hose attached to the kitchen, bathtub, lavatory, or laundry sink faucet. To move the pail, put it on the dolly that was already discussed or place it on a lapboard if you are in a wheelchair.

The next problem is how to carry the mop. Here is one possible solution for a chairbound person: Cover your lap with several thicknesses of newspaper or plastic, which will protect your clothing from dampness, then set the mop on top of the paper with its handle resting on one of your shoulders.

POLISHING. If you have sufficient strength in your arms, you can use a mop to polish your floors. Remember, when choosing a wax, select one that cleans and polishes at the same time. However, if you have difficulty handling a mop, try using an electric polisher.

Making Your Bed

Depending on the handicap, a person may or may not have difficulties making a bed. In cases where someone has upper extremity weakness, incoordination, or other hand involvement, the task of tucking in the sheets could be difficult or even impossible. Furthermore, homemakers with poor balance might find it easier to sit in a chair with casters while doing this task.

Chairbound individuals should keep their bed about 36 inches from any wall so that they can approach it from two sides. Better yet, they should have casters put on all four corners of the bed so that they can move it with less effort. Also, beds with a higher frame are easier to clean under. Finally, while they work, they should think about putting a chair or table near the head of the bed on which to lay pillows, covers, and clean bedding.

Housekeeping tasks can be difficult and tiresome. Therefore, it is important to select the proper equipment and to find methods of simplifying your routine. For this reason, you should constantly be looking for ways to save time and energy when doing the cleaning chores around your home.

POINTS TO REMEMBER

1. *Some disabled homemakers rely on an upright vacuum to help them with cleaning rugs.* When selecting one, keep these guidelines in mind.
   a. Be sure the manufacturer and dealer are reliable.
   b. Think about the kind of vacuuming you will do most often.
   c. Choose an upright model with revolving brushes or an agitator.
   d. Make certain the sweeper attachments are easy to use.

e. Check to determine if you can empty the soil container easily.
2. *Canister vacuums can often simplify dusting for handicapped homemakers.* Look for the following features when you are thinking about purchasing one.
   a. A model on casters or wheels.
   b. Bumpers on the unit to protect your furniture from being scratched.
   c. Automatic bag release for easy removal of the dust bag.
   d. A long enough cord.
   e. If you have hand involvement, a vacuum with a foot-operated switch.
   f. A cord rewinder.
   g. An easy-to-use attachment storage area.
3. *Long-handled dustpans have advantages for people who are confined to wheelchairs or who are unable to bend.*
4. *Putting a cloth on the end of a mop handle, cane, or pickup scissors is one way of dusting hard-to-reach places.*
5. *Three types of mops are dust mop, wet mop, and short-handled mop.*
6. *An easy way to transport a mop pail from place to place is on a platform with casters attached to the underneath four corners.*
7. *Feather dusters or a soft-bristled brush on a pole works well for dusting.*
8. *Use aerosol silicone spray to make polishing furniture easier.*
9. *Remember four general cleaning principles.* Organize your work. Do not let dust accumulate. Try to improve your cleaning methods. Develop a positive attitude.

Chapter 8

DOING YOUR LAUNDRY

Besides meal preparation, doing the weekly laundry is one of a homemaker's largest tasks. Since providing clean clothes for your family can be a heavy chore, you could find it difficult. Therefore, planning a convenient work area and simplifying this process is important. To help you with this task some laundry room design features and ways of making this job easier for you will be presented.

DESIGNING YOUR LAUNDRY AREA

Over the last thirty years automatic washers and dryers have changed the way Americans plan their laundry area and wash days. Today with these modern appliances washing is much simpler. Consequently, housewives can do it easier, and a great deal of the drudgery has been eliminated. Once Monday was the laundry day but now homemakers wash and dry smaller quantities of clothes several times a week. Laundry tubs and wringer washing machines required a large amount of floor space; today modern equipment has made this unnecessary. Since laundry centers are now more compact, they can be more conveniently located.

PLANNING THE LOCATION OF YOUR LAUNDRY. All laundries should be in the best possible location in your home. This is especially important for someone with physical limitations. According to the University of Illinois Small Home Council, the laundry may be located in one of four places, all of which have advantages and disadvantages. Your individual needs, the house plan, and the home's construction will determine the laundry's location. Following are four possibilities:

Multipurpose room or hall. Since many disabled homemakers prefer to have their laundry area near the kitchen, you might want to plan it as part of a multipurpose room or hall. If you locate the washer and dryer in either place, make sure there is adequate lighting. Placing these appliances in a recessed space enclosed with an accordion door will hide them from view when they are not in use.

Kitchen laundry. You might choose to have your laundry in the kitchen. While this arrangement has many advantages, some disabled people raise one objection. They dislike the idea of having dirty clothes in any area where food is prepared. To solve this problem, you can use counter peninsulas, islands, or partitions to make an individual laundry area.

Bathroom laundry. Because bathroom floors are finished to withstand high humidities, a bathroom near the bedrooms is often suitable for doing your laundry. Two good features of this arrangement are that many clothes accumulate in this area and little additional plumbing is required. However, remember that just as with the other arrangements mentioned so far, this laundry design can accommodate only a washer and dryer. Therefore, you must find another place for ironing.

Laundry room near the bathroom or kitchen. You may prefer to have your laundry room near the bathroom or kitchen because then you will not need to clutter your kitchen or bathroom with dirty clothes. When planning a separate laundry area, if possible leave adequate space for shelving, a hamper, an ironing board, and a sink for soaking clothes or hand washing.

INSTALLING YOUR WASHER AND DRYER. Later in this chapter types of appliances that are best for people with certain disabilities will be discussed, but for now some of the general considerations when planning to include a washer and dryer in your home will be explored.

Plumbing. For both gas and electric washers you need to provide for a drain in the plumbing lines. You also can cut down on the installation costs by placing your appliances near existing plumbing lines. In fact, if you plan for a kitchen laundry, you may be able to put the washer on the same wall with the sink and dishwasher. Think, too, about installing it close to the hot water supply, since this helps insure you will have an adequate supply of hot water quickly for washing. It also conserves heat since the water flows only a short distance through the pipes.

Providing for LP or natural gas. While most disabled homemakers have electrical appliances, some may want a gas dryer. If this is your preference, be sure to provide for adequate connections for liquid petroleum or natural gas. Either install rigid pipe or flexible tubing to do this. Do not forget that the installation must meet local building codes, so check the regulations in your area for this information.

Electricity. An automatic washer requires 115 volt, 60 cycle electrical outlet. Furthermore, the dryer needs a 215 volt 60 cycle outlet to operate the motor and heating element. Both of these applicances should also have their own circuit. Make certain that they are grounded. If you want help in determining the best method for this, consult a local electric company or a washer and dryer repairman. Finally, when you are planning to sew or iron in your laundry area, be sure to provide for an ample amount of electrical sockets.

Venting. Vent all automatic dryers on an outside wall to prevent dust and lint particles from floating out into the household air. Moreover, a nonvented dryer creates a high level of moisture in the rooms. This interferes with the humidity control in your house and could cause blistering or peeling of wallpaper.

In addition, venting should be a prime consideration when locating your laundry. Long venting or the type with too many elbows reduces the efficiency of your dryer. To avoid this, follow the recommendations of the appliance manufacturer. However, a good rule to follow is to make sure that horizontal venting does not exceed 15 feet or exhaust into the garage or that piping is not installed in a vertical position through the roof.

When you are having a new home built, the contractor has more flexibility in deciding the best way of venting. However, this is more difficult if you are remodeling your home, so you may want to consult your appliance dealer for advice. In either of these situations, place an exhaust at least 1 foot from the ground. If possible, try to locate this vent in an inconspicuous place, since dust will accumulate around it.

SPACE REQUIREMENT. What are the dimensions of various laundry appliances? To answer this question, refer to Table 8-I.

Table 8-I
LAUNDRY SPACE REQUIREMENTS

	Maximum Width (Side to Side)	Maximum Depth[b] (Front to Back)
WASHING AND DRYING EQUIPMENT [a]		
Automatic Washer		
Top opening	30"	30"
Front opening	31"	30"
Automatic Dryer	32"	30"
Combination Washer-Dryer (front and top opening)	36"	30"
Combination Washer and Dryer (stacked)	31"	30"
Laundry Cart or Basket	16"	28"
Sink and Sorting Counter	48"	24"
IRONING EQUIPMENT		
Electric Ironer (opened)	65"	38"
Ironing Board	54"	15"
Chair (for electric ironer or ironing board)	18"	20"
Clothes Rack[c]		
Floor type	24"	22"
Hanging type	22'	20"
Pull-out type	18"	24"
Laundry Cart or Basket (same as that used for washing)		

[a] Water heaters and water softeners are considered as part of the plumbing equipment.
[b] Includes space for pipes and wiring in many, but not all, cases.
[c] Also used for fabrics which should be drip-dried.

While certain models are slightly larger in size, this diagram gives the average requirements for various types of laundry equipment.

Passageways. Not only should you take these space dimensions into consideration, but if you are chairbound and your laundry is small, you should remember to provide for an adequate passageway between your appliances and the wall. Allow at least 36 inches in front of your washer and dryer to maneuver your wheelchair and to open doors of the appliances.

Countertops. If space permits, any well-planned laundry

should have a countertop for sorting, mending, and folding clothes. However, if you are nonambulatory, make certain it is no higher than 31 inches. You might also wish to include some cabinets underneath for laundry supplies (*see* the section on planning your laundry storage in Chap. 9).

Since some disabled homemakers have upper extremity involvement, they might want to install two large snap clips on the wall above the countertop, placing one of these at either end. Clips can help a handicapped person fold hard-to-manage linens. Make sure they are the same distance apart as the length of one side of a sheet. Merely fasten both ends of one side of the sheet or bedspread to each of the two clips, then fold the other side of the item inward and secure the other two corners with the same clips. Loosen one side and fold it to the opposite side, and your sheet will be folded into quarters (see Fig. 8-1).

Sinks. If there is room in your laundry, install a sink for washing clothes by hand. If you are ambulatory, locate it about 36 inches from the floor; however, if you are chairbound, the sink should be no higher than 31 inches. Many of the same features discussed earlier regarding kitchen sinks also apply to the

Figure 8-1.   Clothes-folding clips.

laundry sink (*see* the section on using your sink in Chap. 5).

Laundry chutes. Some disabled Americans live in two-story homes. If the bedrooms and a bathroom are upstairs and the washroom is either on the first floor or in the basement, this situation poses the difficulty of getting soiled clothes to the laundry area. A way of solving this problem is to provide for a laundry chute. Installing one becomes difficult in an existing home, but you can easily plan for one if you are having a new home built. Remember to have the chute open into your bedroom, in the back of the closet, or in a hallway. It should be at least 3 feet above the floor, Then you can have it empty into a bin below. Furthermore, do not forget to plan the chute so it drops straight down. Be sure that you also line it with metal or other smooth material so that your clothes will travel along without snagging before falling into the laundry area below.

COLLECTING AND SORTING YOUR LAUNDRY

The first task in doing your laundry is gathering your family's clothes together and transporting them to the wash area. If you have mobility impairments, you can save time and effort by making this task as easy as possible. Aside from the laundry chute, which has already been discussed, there are other ways disabled homemakers can make collecting and sorting of clothes easier.

PUSHING A LAUNDRY CART. For those who have difficulty walking and carrying things, pushing a laundry cart allows a person to collect clothing from every room in the house and take it to the laundry area. While some carts only have one compartment, others have a bag divided into three sections. In the latter case, you could use one for white laundry, one for colored fabrics, and the other for delicate washables. Of course, you can use these differently. Some people prefer to have towels in one compartment and clothing in the others, because they may not be washed in the same way. By devising a system, you can eliminate work when sorting clothes (see Fig. 8-2).

PUT YOUR LAUNDRY IN A DISHPAN. You can keep a large dishpan on the floor of a linen closet and pile clothes into it. Remember not to fill the pan too full and hope to carry it, since

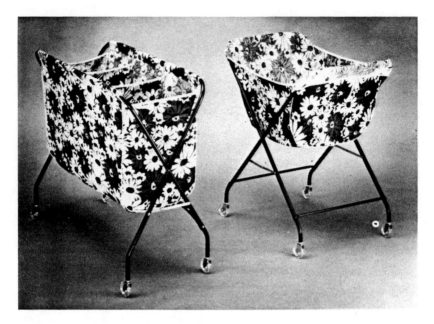

Figure 8-2.   Laundry carts. Illustration furnished by Lady Seymour House-wares.

underwear, shirts, and socks will probably fall on the floor behind you.

PLACE A PLASTIC BAG IN YOUR HAMPER. Use a plastic bag in your hamper for soiled clothing; when you are ready to wash, just lift it out. Do not forget that if you are confined to a wheelchair, you can put the bag on your lapboard and transport it to the laundry area.

STUFF SOILED CLOTHES INTO PILLOWCASES. When your family's clothes are soiled, stuff them into an old pillowcase. In fact, why not place one in every bathroom and bedroom for each person to deposit his clothing in when he or she takes it off.

USING A DIAPER PAIL. Using a diaper pail is an especially good idea if you have babies or toddlers, since it is an excellent place to store soiled diapers. Sometimes you might also want to keep a deodorant cake inside, while others may prefer to fill the pail with water then add disinfectant.

Those of you who are in a wheelchair or those of you who have other disabilities that make lifting and carrying difficult will find any container filled with wet diapers quite heavy. To solve this

Figure 8-3.   Diaper pail. Illustration furnished by Reliance Products.

problem, keep your pail on the dolly mentioned in Chapter 7, so that you can push it in front of you. Someone confined to a chair can use this method, but another person might need to lift the diapers off the dolly and into the washer. On the other hand, there is an easy way that a person can do this task himself. He can simply transfer half of the diapers from one pail to another and lift each onto a lapboard. Since this method can be strenuous, it would probably be easier to have another person's help.

SORTING BINS AND DIRTY CLOTHES. An excellent idea that will help you in the sorting process is to put different types of clothes in sorting bins. These could be labeled as follows:

1. Heavily soiled clothes
2. Light colored clothes
3. Dark colored clothes
4. Permanent press
5. Hand washables
6. Presoak
7. Mending

This system has a couple of advantages. First, since it is a waste of time and energy to wash only a small load of clothes in your machine, you may check easily on what type of clothes you must wash and when you must wash them by using this method. However, depending on the nature of your disability and your household routine, you might want to do your laundry several times a week. This often lightens your work because you will not have as many clothes to wash at one time. Storage bins also minimize the task of sorting on laundry days since part of the job has already been done.

WASHING THE DIRTY CLOTHES

To simplify washing, look for methods of laundering your garments in the most efficient manner. For instance, there are certain features that you should keep in mind when shopping for a washer. Another consideration is that, since most people do not wash all clothing in automatic machines, those who have some limitations should find ways of doing hand laundry with the least amount of effort.

WASHING HINTS. Following is a list of suggestions that may help you improve your washing process.

Sort your clothes. Before putting your garments into the machine, make certain you sort them carefully. You can do this according to the amount of soil, color, kind of fabric, or construction.

Prepare garments for washing. Be sure there is nothing in the pockets. Brush them out along with the trouser cuffs. Close the zippers and unbutton the buttons. Mend any tear since it may become larger when you launder the garment. Finally, remove any stain that might become set in the washer. Moisten heavily soiled areas and sprinkle on some of the detergent you will use for your washing. Wait a few minutes, then if needed, rub the garment will a small brush before putting it in your washer.

Do not soak clothes too long. Soak garments a maximum of fifteen minutes to remove any soil.

Choose the correct water temperature. Use a thermometer to measure the temperature of your wash water accurately. Keep it no hotter than 140° to 160° for washing white and light colorfast cottons, white Dacron® fabrics, acrylics and nylons. The reason for washing your clothes at this temperature is so that they will not be too hot to handle. Launder noncolorfast fabrics, silks, rayons, woolens, acetates, and other synthetic fabric fibers at 100°. After you wash the clothes, rinse them first in 115° to 130° water, followed by 100° for additional rinses.

Wash in soft water. Wash all your clothes in soft water. When it is too hard, you can install a mechanical system to help do the job, or you can rely on packaged softeners sometimes known as conditioners or normalizers. Using conditioners in your machine changes the mineral composition of the water to help in the cleaning process.

Make sure you measure the detergent correctly. Put the correct amount of detergent in your washer for the best results. Sometimes the trial and error method is the only way to determine this. Remember that too many suds only block the movement of clothes in the machine's tub and will hinder good washing action.

Carry your detergent in another container. If you use a powdered detergent for laundering and have difficulty managing the soap box, why not pour out what you need into a jar, plastic bottle, or cup, which may be easier to carry? You might want to pour through a funnel to prevent wasting any powder. Remember also that jugs do not spill as easily.

Be careful how you load your washer. Do not overload your washer. To avoid this, always watch to see that all garments are moving freely in the machine. Furthermore, when placing clothing in a washer, always keep a balance of small and large items in the machine.

Time your laundry. Use a clock when washing. If you keep clothes in the washer too long, unnecessary wear will result. Launder your garments according to the degree of soil. Wash those with only a slight amount from three to five minutes, those with more soil about ten minutes, and those with heavy soil twenty minutes.

Rinse adequately. Rinse clothes adequately to remove all suds, chemicals, and lint. Always use soft water when rinsing your garments. An easy way to do this is to let them stay in the machine while you drain out the sudsy water. Then, wash all the heavy suds off with a hose. After this, let clear water fill the machine and begin the rinse cycle.

Bleach garments seldom. Bleach clothes only when absolutely necessary. Remember that this is *not* a substitute for washing. Furthermore, when you bleach to remove stains, be sure that you follow the manufacturer's instructions.

Never blue clothes. You *never* need to blue clothes if they are washed properly. Bluing only makes garments whiter, and this is not a good reason for its use since most detergents have the same type of chemical in them.

Starch cottons and lightweight linens. For improved appearance, starch cottons and lightweight linens. How and when you do that is a matter of personal choice. To save time and effort, use prepared and permanent starches, although they are considerably more expensive than the type you can make at home.

Selecting an Automatic Washer

When you are planning to buy an automatic washer, remember some general guidelines. Depending on your disability, you might want to consider looking for some special features.

GENERAL GUIDELINES. Here are seven points to think about when shopping for an automatic washer, no matter the extent of your physical limitations.

Capacity. The washer tub's capacity is of prime importance. Do not be fooled if a salesman begins talking about how many pounds of laundry a certain machine will hold. Due to a wide variation in the kinds of fabrics, this information is meaningless. For example, 6 pounds of nylon curtains require more space than 6 pounds of bath towels. Therefore, regardless of any weight claims, be sure to find out if the volume of the machine will allow your clothes to circulate freely during agitation. Select a washer with a tub large enough to accommodate large and extra large loads of laundry to solve this problem.

Economical operation. Compare the gallons of water several different washers use during the laundry process. Find out also how much electricity each model requires so that you can make an intelligent choice.

Check the number of cycles. Check to see if the machine has a

variety of cycles, especially when you need to wash various types
of fabrics. Following are the principle ones:

1. *Permanent press cycle.* The permanent press cycle provides
   a cool rinse and keeps garments that require no ironing
   from wrinkling.
2. *Cycles for woolens and delicate fabrics.* Cycles for woolens
   and delicate fabrics make it possible for homemakers to
   wash such clothing in the machine rather than by hand.
3. *Bleach dispensers and fabric softeners.* You can use bleach
   dispensers and fabric softeners to control static cling so that
   permanent press and other no-iron garments will not
   wrinkle.
4. *Prewash and presoak cycles.* Prewash and presoak cycles
   are helpful if you plan to wash heavily soiled clothes.

Select a washer with meter fill. If there is low or fluctuating
water pressure in your home, choose a meter-filled washer. With
this feature, a pressure switch regulates the machine's intake of
electricity, thus making it impossible for the washer to begin
operation until the tub is completely filled with water.

Loading and unloading. Be sure you can load and unload the
washer easily.

Check the washtub. The best type of washtub is a perforated
one that spins as it drains, which helps to remove sand, grit, and
heavier-than-soil particles without straining the water back
through the clothes.

Water safety lid. A water safety lid is extremely important since
the machine's action stops a few seconds after you open it. This
feature eliminates the possibility of hand injury when you begin
to reach inside.

SPECIAL CONSIDERATIONS. Besides the general guidelines just
discussed, you may want to think about the following special
considerations as well.

Controls. Be certain you can reach the controls easily. Some
handicapped people with upper extremity involvement can push
buttons more efficiently, while others might operate dials easier.
The Maytag Corporation manufactures a special four-pronged
knob that fits over the standard one on most of their automatic
washers, which allows the disabled person to turn it with less
effort. Remember, too, if you are confined to a wheelchair, select a
washer with the controls at the front of the machine.

Figure 8-4. Four-pronged knob. Illustration furnished by Maytag Corporation.

Easy-to-reach filter. For all disabled people, especially those who are chairbound, the machine's filter should be located in the front so that it is convenient to reach.

Top-and front-loading washers. Depending on your physical limitations, select either a front- or top-loading machine. If you are in a wheelchair, you should choose one that opens from the front. On the other hand, a homemaker with poor balance should select a top-loading machine since he could lean against it for support while loading and unloading his clothes.

Doing Hand Laundry. Although you can wash most of your clothing in an automatic washer, there are certain garments you may prefer to wash by hand. This often poses some difficulties for disabled homemakers with upper extremity weakness. Furthermore, people with certain limitations may not be able to do hand washing, since the wringing process could place too much stress on their joints. Following are five hints that you may want to try.

Soak clothes overnight. To make washing less of an effort, soak

Figure 8-5.   Front-loading washer and dryer. Illustration furnished by White-Westinghouse.

heavily soiled clothes in detergent overnight.

Do not let clothes become too dirty. If you are planning to hand launder certain garments, be sure you do not allow them to become extremely dirty.

Do small amounts of laundry. Remember that it is sometimes easier to wash small loads of laundry daily.

Wrap garments in a towel. You can wrap small articles of clothing in a towel to absorb the moisture before placing them in the dryer.

Use a faucet to wring clothes. If you have a weak grasp or are limited to using one hand, use a faucet to help you wring clothes (see Fig.8-6). To accomplish this task, follow these five simple steps.

1. Wrap the garment around the faucet.
2. Twist lightly.
3. Drain the water out of the sink.

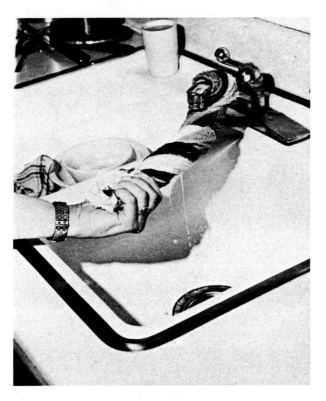

Figure 8-6.   One hand wringing method.

4. Press the garment against the sidewall of the sink.
5. Put the article of clothing in a bath towel to transport it to the dryer or clothesline.

DRYING YOUR CLOTHES

There are two ways of drying clothes: using an automatic machine, or hanging them on a line.

Your Automatic Dryer

CONSIDER THE ADVANTAGES. Automatic dryers have several advantages, since they eliminate much of the work of drying clothes which women had hung up to dry in years gone by. First, they do away with the need to carry heavy clothes baskets to an outside line. Second, this method is easier on garments, since it avoids the possibility of fading, which can occur outdoors and decreases the chance of weather damage. Third, dryers reduce the number of clothes you must store in your closets and drawers, since they can be dried quickly and put back in use. Fourth, these machines eliminate the necessity for an indoor drying area. Finally, clothes dry lint free and fluffier in a machine than on a line. Also, many garments taken from the dryer require no ironing.

SELECTING THE RIGHT MODEL. There are many different models on the market today, so choosing one to serve your needs is often difficult. The following guidelines can assist you, so think about them when you shop for a dryer.

Installation cost. Before you buy any model, check on the installation cost, because there is a wide variety of prices.

Gas or electric dryers. Both gas and electric dryers do their job well. However, a factor that will help determine the one you select is the price of gas fuel as opposed to electricity in your community.

Ten minute cooling cycle. Some dryers have a ten minute cooling cycle, so that after the clothes are finished drying, the machine will blow cool air on them for ten minutes. This is helpful to disabled homemakers who work slowly getting their clothes out of the machine.

An accessible filter. Just as with a washer, make sure you can reach the dryer's filter easily, as it needs frequent cleaning.

Front-loading dryer. Purchase a front-loading dryer. As with the washer, this is particularly important if you are in a wheelchair (*see* Fig. 8-5).

Large knobs. The Maytag Corporation, besides having large knobs for washers, also has knobs designed to fit dryers.

Using a Clothesline

Sometimes handicapped housewives may prefer to use a clothesline for drying to save money on the electric bill and to air blankets, linens, and other clothing.

Depending on what your physical limitations are, you may or may not be able to hang things on the line. In some cases, the disabled homemaker must depend on someone else for assistance or rely strictly on the dryer.

Others may want to put garments or miscellaneous items

outdoors. Disabled individuals who walk with difficulty or use crutches often find it easier to stand in one place while hanging clothes. This can sometimes be accomplished with the use of a pulley clothesline.

DOING YOUR IRONING

After you have dried your clothes, you may want to iron them. However, before we talk specifically about this task, there are some general considerations to keep in mind.

Understanding Some Basic Concepts

AVOID STRESS. When you iron, choose a method that helps you avoid stress. Disabled homemakers might try to reduce stress by sitting rather than standing; this is less strenuous on your lower extremities.

CHOOSE THE CORRECT ACCESSORIES. Select accessories that will make ironing easier. Some of the items include a sleeve board, a cellulose sponge to dampen dry areas, a spray bottle, and a basket nearby in which to keep unironed clothes.

REDUCE THE NUMBER OF TIMES YOU TURN A GARMENT. For efficient ironing, try not to turn a garment any more times than necessary.

HOLDING YOUR IRONING. You can use safety pins to straighten or secure items on the board.

SENSATION IMPAIRMENTS. If you have a sensory impairment in one of your hands, you might want to consider wearing an oven mitt while ironing (*see* the section on advice on ranges and ovens in Chap. 6).

Choosing an Ironing Board

When selecting an ironing board, purchase one that is the correct height so that you can maintain good posture when reaching in all directions. However, be sure it is low enough so that you do not have to raise your shoulders when working. If you find standing difficult or tiresome, a swivel chair permits you to sit but still have the range of motion you need to reach all places on your ironing board.

Wide ironing boards lessen the chance of a garment's slipping. For flat items the best surface is one 20 inches wide. If you know a handyman, have him make you an aid from ¾- or ⅜-inch plywood the same length as your ironing board (see Fig. 8-7). Fasten cleats along each side to hold it in place. Then lay this on top of your regular ironing board to have a wider surface.

Selecting a Pad

Select an ironing board pad that has a firm surface. One with silicone-aluminum, acetylated, Teflon, or some other burn resistant coating material is best. These types permit you to make free pressing strokes and speed ironing because they do not absorb heat. The cover should have drawstrings, elastic edges, two-way ties, or clamps to make it fit snugly over the board. You can also lace a cord through safety pins across from each other on the two underneath sides of the cover to hold it firmly.

Kitchen Table Ironing

Some disabled homemakers may wish to iron on their kitchen tables. If you want to use this method, simply find a thick pad of ½-inch foam rubber and cover it with muslin. Secure this mat

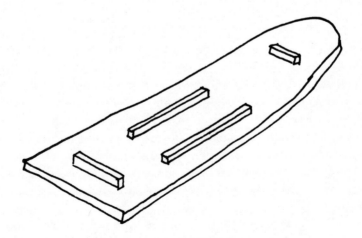

Figure 8-7.   Ironing board extension.

tightly with elastic sewn on all four corners. On a circular or oval table, sew elastic around the underneath edge. This provides a stable surface and allows for free range of motion without adjusting the ironing pad. Using foam rubber covered with muslin also has some advantages for a nonambulatory person, since most kitchen tables are a good height. Most of them also have ample clearance so someone in a wheelchair can roll the chair underneath. Finally, using a kitchen table enables you to fold the pad and put it away without lifting a heavy ironing board.

Purchasing an Iron and Equipment

Just as with all other household appliances, when buying an iron and other equipment, consider a few basic points.

CHECK THE WEIGHT. If your grasp is weak, you lack strength in your arms, or you are confined to a wheelchair, choose a lightweight iron. However, some disabled people, who cannot apply pressure while ironing, believe that a heavier iron weighing 3½ to 4 pounds will help counteract their unsteadiness and muscle weakness, particularly when ironing thick materials.

SELECT A STEAM IRON. Select a steam iron to eliminate the need for using sprinkling equipment.

CHOOSE A MODEL WITH EASY-TO-USE CONTROLS. Look for an iron with controls located on the top of the appliance, especially if you have hand impairments. This helps eliminate the possibility of burning yourself. Make sure also that you can read the fabric dial easily. If you iron slower than the average person does, be certain the unit has a wide range of fabric settings that will allow you to regulate the temperature.

CONSIDER THE GRIP. Before buying any iron, notice when grasping it where your knuckles lie. They should not touch any metal, since it becomes hot when you start to work.

BUY AN IRON HAVING AN INSULATED HANDLE. Select an iron with an insulated handle that remains cool during the time you are using it.

LOOK AT THE BASE. A properly shaped base point allows you to iron around corners and gathers. Going around buttons is easier if the iron has beveled edges.

EXAMINE THE SOLE PLATE. Examine the sole plate carefully.

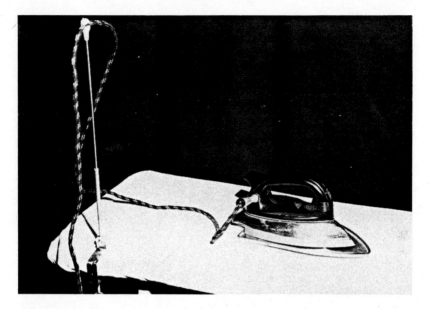

Figure 8-8.   Ironing cord holder. Illustration furnished by M. E. Heuck Company.

The type with a Teflon® coating is often recommended, since it helps you to slide the iron easier without sticking.

SELECT A DURABLE CORD. Make certain the iron's cord is well made and has an underwriter's label. If the cord attaches in the center of the appliance, you can use the iron with either hand.

USE AN IRONING CORD HOLDER. Ironing cord holders keep the cord from becoming tangled. There is also not as much danger of scorching your material.

One iron that many disabled people can use easily is Sunbeam's Today® iron (Model SW1), which weighs only 2½ pounds and has an insulated handle. You can use it with either hand since the cord attaches through the handle and will not interfere with its easy operation. In addition, the extra large push button on the top is simple to use. To prevent clogging, this appliance has a Shot of Steam® method for self-cleaning with an easy-to-see dial so you can pick one of several settings (see Fig. 8-9).

YOUR SEWING OR MENDING AREA

Depending on your individual preference and the space

Figure 8-9.   Today iron. Illustration furnished by Sunbeam Corporation.

available, you might want to consider including a sewing or mending center in your laundry. Some disabled homemakers like to have it near their ironing area because with various types of mending you merely need to press on the patch to repair the clothing. When you are doing this, remember always to wash the garment first so that you will not iron in the soil. If you use hem tape, too, be sure that you store it in a waterproof place since they stick together when damp. You may want to keep items like needles, spools of thread, thimbles, scissors and a button box near your laundry center, perhaps in the drawers beneath your countertop.

WORK ON A SOLID SURFACE. Mending is often easier for some disabled people if they lay the garment on a solid surface rather than hold the item or put it in their lap. This helps them maintain a better posture. If you also have trouble stabilizing the article, anchor it with a book or brick covered with fabric. People

Figure 8-10. Bernina 830H Handicap sewing machine. Illustration furnished by Bernina Sewing Machine Company, Inc.

who have a weak grasp can tie a strap around the center of the brick and lift it with their forearm. Smaller items can be anchored in a clipboard.

A SEWING MACHINE FOR THE HANDICAPPED. Some disabled homemakers may want to have a sewing machine located in their laundry area. If you are thinking about this, consider your physical limitations first. One sewing machine recommended for some disabled people is the Bernina 830H Handicap® sewing machine.

Winding the bobbin. A special holder permits easy removal of the bobbin case and returning of the filled bobbin to its original position. You can also lock the handwheel for the winding process by turning a lever with one hand. When the bobbin is filled, you may release and tighten the handwheel with a large key. To wind the bobbin, you only need to place the thread in position, and when the bobbin is full, the winder switches off automatically.

Inserting the needle. You can purchase a needle with a slot to the eye. Just insert the thread into the slot, and it falls into place.

Because of a special centering block, you may put the needle straight-forward into the right position. Use the large special screwdriver that comes with the machine to loosen and tighten the needle holder screw.

Threading. With one motion you can thread the machine from reel to needle. The machine also has an absolutely nonjamming bobbin hook. One more advantage is that you do not have to regulate the thread tension for thick or thin material.

Operating knobs. Nonslip, handy projections are on both the zigzag width and needle position knobs. You can also raise and lower the feeddog with a special built-up knob. The stitch-length knob has the same features and is simple to set, even for people with poor eyesight because it has a scale they can feel. An elongated lever also makes it possible for you to make fancy stitches without too much effort.

Electronic sewing speed regulator. Depending on your physical limitations, you may want to operate the sewing speed regulator with either your knee or elbow. A neck belt is also available for anyone who needs to manipulate this device using his chin.

Presser-foot lifter. With the presser-foot lifter you are able to raise and lower the presser foot with a specially designed lever. Although the lever is made for operation with your knee, an attachment using the elbow can be purchased for those who find this arrangement more convenient.

Finger guard. The finger guard keeps you from injuring yourself on the needle, since you can only open it when the presser foot is raised.

SEWING BY HAND. While some disabled homemakers can use the 830H Handicap sewing machine with ease, others may want to sew or mend garments using a needle and thread. One problem that those who have hand limitations might encounter when attempting these tasks is threading a needle. If you find that this is difficult or impossible, try doing it with a needle threader. Simply place your needle into the threader, position the thread, and push the lever.

STORING YOUR CLOTHES

Once you have collected, sorted, washed, dried, and ironed your

Figure 8-11. Needle threader. Illustration furnished by Help Yourself Aids.

clothes, it is time to store them. To do this with the least amount
of effort, you should have either a large table or, as stated earlier, a
laundry room near where you work. Some disabled homemakers
may also lay their folded clothes in a basket when taking them to
other rooms of the house for storage.

Other handicapped people might wish to use a bed for folding
purposes. For example, someone confined to a wheelchair can lay
garments on his lap and transport them from the laundry to a
bedroom before doing this task.

If you fold clothes in your laundry area but do not want to
spend time transporting them to each place where they are stored,
you may consider separating your clothes into piles; then each
time you go to a certain room you can take the laundry that
belongs in that place with you.

Many homemakers do not fold all their clothes but would
rather hang some on hangers. To help transport these garments

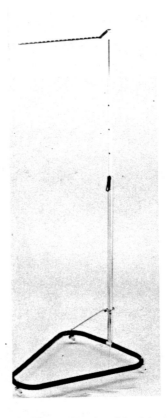

Figure 8-12.   Laundry rack. Illustration furnished by Lady Seymour Housewares.

to the clothes closet, you might want to purchase a laundry rack
on casters. You can put several garments on the rack, push it into
the closet, and then transfer your garments to the rod.

When you are disabled and are planning to have a new home
built, following the basic guidelines discussed previously will
help you make your laundry a convenient place to work.
Hopefully, you have discovered some ways of collecting, sorting,
washing, drying, ironing, mending, and putting your clothes
away that will make your work easier and less frustrating.

POINTS TO REMEMBER

1. *Design your laundry for convenience.* Good locations are
    a multipurpose room, hall, kitchen, or bathroom. However,

a separate laundry adjacent to the kitchen or bathroom is always the best.

2. *Provide for adequate plumbing, install the correct electric service, include proper venting, and make provisions for LP or natural gas in your laundry room when necessary.*

3. *Understand the various space requirements for washers, dryers, and ironing equipment.*

4. *Allow for an adequate passageway in front of your washer and dryer.* If you are chairbound, make certain to leave at least 36 inches between any appliance and a wall.

5. *Countertops are a convenient feature in laundry rooms.* If you are ambulatory, design the counter so you can either sit or stand while working.

6. *Space permitting, install a sink to launder hand washables.*

7. *Laundry chutes are often practical in two-story houses.* You can drop clothes from the upstairs area to a downstairs laundry.

8. *You may use a laundry cart, dishpan, plastic bag, pillowcases, or a diaper pail for collecting clothes.* Bins, too, are helpful in sorting garments.

9. *Consider the best method before beginning to wash your clothes.* Remember these helpful hints.
   a. Sort garments carefully.
   b. Empty all the pockets.
   c. Choose the correct water temperature.
   d. Do not soak clothes too long.
   e. Wash in soft water.
   f. Carrying detergent in another container rather than in its original box is often easier.
   g. Load your washer correctly.
   h. Time the laundry.
   i. Rinse clothing adequately.
   j. Bleach garments rarely.
   k. Bluing is unnecessary.
   l. Starch cottons and lightweight linens.

10. *Before purchasing a washer, check the capacity, electrical operation, number of cycles, existence of a meter fill on the model, instructions on loading and unloading the appliance, and existence of a spinning washtub and a safety lid.* Other guidelines some disabled people should consider

are location of controls, accessibility of the filter, and choice of a top or front loading machine.

11. *Simplify your hand washing.* Soak clothes overnight. Do not allow garments to get too soiled. Do small amounts of laundry at a time. Try using a faucet for wringing clothes.

12. *Automatic dryers have five advantages.* Eliminating the carrying of heavy laundry baskets to the clothesline, ending the concern about fading or weather damage, reducing the amount of space needed for storing clothes, banishing the necessity for an indoor drying area, and making your garments fluffier and more lint free than those which are line dried.

13. *Choose either an electric or gas dryer, depending on the cost and the availability of fuel in your area.*

14. *Some handicapped people should look for special features when selecting a dryer.* Ten minute cooling cycles often are helpful to the person who works slowly. Choose a unit with an easy-to-reach filter. Chairbound individuals should purchase a front-loading unit. Those with hand limitations often find large knobs easier to operate.

15. *A disabled homemaker may like to hang certain types of laundry on the clothesline.* The pulley line has advantages for those with mobility limitations since an individual can stand in one position while working.

16. *Keep a few general ironing concepts in mind.* Avoid stress. Choose accessories to make the task easier. Reduce the number of times you turn a garment. Secure items to your ironing board. If you have loss of sensation, it is a good idea to wear a mitt on the hand you use for this task so you will not get burned.

17. *Be certain you can operate the iron easily before making a purchase.* Check the weight. Buying a steam iron eliminates the need for sprinkling equipment. Buy a model with easy-to use controls. Consider the grip. Make certain the handle is insulated. Examine the base of the unit. Think about selecting one with a Teflon®-coated sole plate. A heel stand makes the iron less of an effort to lift.

18. *Iron cord holders help secure the ironing cord, thus reducing twisting and tangling.*

19. *With specially designed aids and techniques some handicapped people can learn to sew.* Among these are working on a solid surface, using a brick to hold down fabric or a garment, purchasing a sewing machine especially designed for the disabled, and threading a needle with a needle threader.

20. *When putting your clothes away, you can use a table, laundry counter, or bed for folding purposes.* Baskets and racks on casters are also helpful.

Chapter 9

STORAGE ORGANIZATION
THAT WORKS FOR YOU

" **A** place for everything and everything in its place." This common saying could apply to any homemaker but is especially important for someone disabled. For example, when Donna, a twenty-five-year-old college student, lived at home with her parents, her bedroom was always messy. In fact, Donna's mother often called it a disaster area. One afternoon on the way home from school, Donna was in an automobile accident and was paralyzed from the waist down. Now, seven years later, she lives independently with one big difference. No longer does she spend useless hours in prolonged searching for something. Instead, Donna applies certain principles to keep her apartment neat and orderly. This chapter discusses ways that can help you improve your storage methods.

ORGANIZATIONAL PRINCIPLES

Store Only What You Need

Did you ever realize we are a nation of pack rats? At least sometimes this is the case. Over the years many of us collect things that we store away and rarely, if ever, use. This was a problem Molly and her husband Dick had when they were planning to move.

One afternoon while cleaning their closets, Dick shouted, "Look at all these boxes! You haven't used some of this stuff in years!"

"I know," Molly replied. "But I might someday."

"Yes, but you haven't yet," he answered. "Anyway, because you

208

walk with crutches and have difficulty finding things, you should store all items in an orderly fashion and keep only what you expect to use in the near future, not clutter your shelves with items you may never work with!"

"I see what you mean. Let's take a little time to begin sorting."

Dick's advice is worthwhile for any disabled homemaker. Periodically take an inventory of the storage areas in your home and think about discarding things you seldom use. For instance, in the kitchen remove everything from your cupboard, then look at each item carefully. Decide if there are any utensils or other things you are unlikely to use. Another place to make a survey is your closet. Are there clothes you never wear still hanging on the closet rod? Make a similar assessment of every storage area in your house. Seldom used items take up space that you can utilize in a more productive way. Besides, clutter is also a potential fire hazard. So, frequently inspect each of your storage areas and throw away anything not worth keeping.

Analyze Your Storage Space

When you walk into a store to make a purchase, stop and ask yourself three important questions: where will I keep the item, how often will I use it, and is my selection worth the space required? Viola, a disabled shopper, considered these three questions before making a decision about buying a fur coat.

One afternoon Viola hobbled along on crutches, looking in department store windows. She stopped in front of one window and gazed at a mannequin wearing a black fur coat, then shuffled inside where a clerk greeted her.

"May I help you?"

"Yes," she replied, pointing her finger. "I want to see that coat you have on display in the window."

After a few minutes, the clerk returned.

"Here, I'll help you try it on."

"Yes, please do."

As Viola slid it over her shoulders, she said to herself, "Boy, I sure would like to have this." However, then Viola stopped a moment and thought about the three storage questions. She could keep the coat in her bedroom closet but decided if she were going to buy one, perhaps another style might take less space. Viola also wondered how often she would wear it and realized she would only use it a few times a year. Furthermore, on the matter of space, she decided that it could be used to a better advantage for something else, because she would wear the garment only rarely. Consequently, after considering the three questions, she left the store without making the purchase.

Just as Viola did, whenever you buy anything, remember to consider the three storage questions. Think about the amount of area you must have, and make certain there is enough. Decide how frequently you will use an item. Do not forget that something you seldom need may only take valuable storage space. These guidelines will help determine when you are making a wise purchase.

Select Multipurpose Items

Buying items that you are able to use for more than one purpose is another way of utilizing storage area. One disabled homemaker applies this guideline in her home management in the following ways.

Laura, a thirty-seven-year-old cerebral-palsied housewife, and her friend, Mary, went shopping together. As they were walking down an aisle in a local shoe store, Laura stopped at a rack and picked up a pair of low-heeled shoes to examine them.

"Laura, do you think you will buy those?" asked Mary,

"I don't know," she responded, "I'm looking for a certain color."

"Why are you so particular?" Mary asked.

"Well, I try to purchase ones that can be worn with many of my dresses. That way I don't have to buy so many pairs, which would only take up room in my closet."

Whenever possible, follow Laura's example and try to use an item for more than one purpose. Here are a few other ways of making this principle work for you: a table used for eating, writing, playing games, and sewing takes less space than a separate dining table, desk, card table, and free-standing sewing machine. Likewise, when cleaning, purchase supplies that you may use on several surfaces rather than choosing one for each specific job.

Keep Items Nearby

You will be able to find things easier if you store items near where you use them. Tom, who wears braces and lives alone, frequently applies this idea. He had a carpenter install hooks on the wall near his back door where he hangs coats and gloves. Tom also puts his boots in a closet nearby. Another way he uses this concept is that, since he plays chess with friends on the kitchen table twice a week, instead of keeping the board and chessmen somewhere else in the house, he keeps them in the kitchen cupboard.

As with the other storage guidelines already discussed, keeping an item close to where you use it will save time and energy. Whenever you begin searching for something, pause a moment and think about looking for another place where you can store the article near where you use it most often.

Group Things Together

When planning your storage, remember what items you generally use together. To make this even more convenient, put things you work with frequently at the front of shelves and drawers. Label whatever you will not be using for a long time. For example, Lois, a paraplegic, always makes sure her broom and dustpan are stored in the same cabinet. She also realizes that minor household repairs will take longer if she cannot find the hammer, so she keeps it alongside the nails. Similarly, Lois finishes mending jobs quicker if she does not have to spend time searching for her needle and thread. Therefore, she makes certain they are in the same box with her scissors.

Like Lois, when you are arranging your storage area, consider the items you use for each task. To help you do this, analyze every one of your household chores. Then think about what material or tools you need. That way you can be sure to store things together in the handiest location.

Make a List of Items

In order to easily store items together, make a list of everything you will use for a certain activity. By doing this, you can think about each area before you begin to put things in their places. David, an amputee, found that writing things down was a simple way to prepare for reorganizing his shop.

One Saturday afternoon as he sat at the kitchen table thinking about the task, he turned to his wife, June, and said, "Gee, I don't like to think about this job."

"Why?" she asked.

"I just don't know where to put things so they will be the most convenient."

"There is no reason to feel that way. Just list everything you have and the place you think will be the handiest to store each item before you tackle the job."

To save time and effort, how about taking June's advice and first make a list of items you wish to rearrange. Using this simple technique helps avoid needless frustration.

Plan Space Wisely

If you are planning to build a new house, be sure to analyze the storage space you will need. Mike and Beth, a married couple who both walked with crutches, did this when they were designing their home. Before construction was started, both of them examined the blueprints, making certain there was enough cupboard and cabinet space, while not having too much wasted area. When Mike and Beth moved into the house, they also stored things in convenient places and made sure adequate room was left above the items to allow them to lift those things without any overhead obstructions.

If you want to build a home, do not forget to study the plans and try answering this basic question: Have I included enough storage space? Remember to plan them carefully.

Provide Accessible Space for Frequently Used Items

What things do you use once a day, once a week, or once a year? Consider this whenever you start planning storage areas in your home so that you can allocate the space in the most efficient way. Marlene, a hemiplegic, keeps this principle in mind when storing dishes. She has two sets of china, one for everyday meals, and the other for special occasions such as Thanksgiving, Christmas, and New Year's. When storing them, Marlene keeps the dishes she uses daily on the lower shelf of her dining room hutch, where she can remove them easily, and keeps her holiday china on an upper shelf that is not so convenient.

When you are organizing your storage, think about placing frequently used items in easy-to-reach areas and things you seldom need in less handy locations.

Return Things to Their Proper Places

You can have the best storage plan in the world, but it does little good unless you remember to return things to their proper places after you use them. Melvin, a forty-year-old paraplegic who worked as a repairman at the Dial Clock Shop, learned the hard way.

One Thursday afternoon he went over to his tool box for a screwdriver but could not find it. Then he wheeled his chair over to Jack, one of his coworkers.

"Have you seen my screw driver?" he asked.

"No, Melvin. I though you had it yesterday."

For the next half hour, Melvin asked five other people a similar question. They all shrugged their shoulders, shook their heads, or did not respond. Finally, the foreman spotted Melvin going from workbench to workbench and called to him.

"Hey, what are you doing?"

"I'm trying to find my screwdriver. Have you seen it?"

"Yes, it's in my office."

"What's it doing in there?" Melvin asked.

"I picked it up where you were working yesterday. Haven't you learned yet how to put things away?"

Do not be like Melvin. Be sure you always know where everything is located. Never forget to store things away after you have finished using them since you might spend hours looking for the items in the future. Besides, such inefficiency only reduces the amount of work you are able to do in a day. Try to avoid this dilemma. Always return things to their proper places after you have finished using them.

HOME STORAGE AREAS

Avoid Corner Storage

Especially if you are confined to a wheelchair, do not plan cupboards or closets closer than 1 foot from the corner of any room, since they will be inaccessible. Be sure to allow enough space in front of the unit so that you can turn your chair around with the least amount of effort. Furthermore, if the cabinet or closet door swings out into a passageway, the distance between them and any wall should be a minimum of 2 feet 7 inches to allow your wheelchair to pass without any obstructions.

Use Closet and Linen Storage Areas to Good Advantage

To use your closet and linen storage space to a good advantage, you should devise special methods and consider certain design features. Remember, you always want to make the best possible use of all your areas in the most efficient way.

CLOSETS. Here are twenty-five ideas on how to improve your closet storage space. Why not try some of them?

Storing shoes. Without much cost you can store shoes in your closet conveniently. Cut off the top of a 16 by 18 inch cardboard box, and cover it with contact paper. Set this on the shelf to hold eight shoe boxes, which you can label to identify the shoes inside.

Smoothing pleats. When you plan to store a suit or skirt, be sure that the pleats are in proper position and secure them in place with a snap-on clothespin.

Use a shoe bag. Fasten several shoe bags to the back of your closet door to hold shoes or socks. You can keep dress socks in the top row of pockets and sport socks in a lower one. Particularly for men who often dress up, this will be a less confusing way to locate the pair he wants to wear. Besides, some people think it is a neater way of organizing socks than placing them in a drawer.

Keep your clothes separated. If your clothes have a tendency to bunch together in the closet, you can cut notches in a wooden rod at 2-inch intervals so that the hangers will stay in place.

Fasten your garments securely. Are your nightgowns, dresses, or slips falling off the metal hangers? To prevent this from happening, twist the hangers up slightly at both ends.

Putting away seasonal garments. If you have difficulty storing out-of-season clothing, stuff the sleeves of the garments with tissue paper. That way you will not need to press those clothes again before wearing them.

Hang purses in your closet. There is a simple method of hanging purses in the closet. Use a strong metal chain, and hook it over one hanger; then place metal curtain hooks on every few links of the chain to hang your purses. Be certain that you also cover the entire thing with a large plastic bag, which will keep dust from accumulating.

Storing belts. Fasten small hooks in your closet and hang your belts on them.

Put shoes in plastic bags. To keep your shoes from absorbing moisture, place them in plastic bags.

Ladies hat holder. Screw several small hooks below the closet shelf. Place your hats in plastic bags and, using spring clothespins, clip them to a wire or string hanging from each hook. You can then see them easily, decide which one you want to wear, and still leave your closet free to store other items. To prevent your hats from being crushed, make sure to blow air in the plastic bag before closing it.

Protect against mildew. Is your closet always damp? If so, take six pieces of chalk, bundle them, and hang this chalk in your closet to absorb moisture.

Brighten your dark closet. If your closet is dark or it has a dark shelf, place a mirror on the back wall to reflect the light that comes in when you open the door. Either set the mirror on the shelf or hang it on the wall for good results.

Avoid tangled jewelry. So that your necklaces will not tangle, install a curtain rod on the back of your closet door. Later, you merely need to slip your jewelry off the rod when you want to wear it. Small hooks attached to a wall are also handy for this purpose.

Preserve your gloves. Store away your summer and winter gloves in plastic bags until the appropriate season.

Prevent slacks from slipping. There is no need for a person's slacks to slip off a hanger. To keep this from happening, attach a couple of strips of tape around the hanger with the sticky side up where the trousers lie. This will hold them tightly even if the belt or other articles are not removed.

Coat hanger covers. Keep the neckties someone plans to discard. These make good coat hanger covers.

Wax your closet rods. So that your hangers slide easier on the rod in your closet, frequently apply a little paste wax on the rod.

Putting away comforters. An easy way to keep stored comforters from gathering dust is to roll them tightly and pull a pillowcase or plastic bag over the roll. By using this method, the comforter is held more securely than when placed on a shelf where it could slide off.

Dividing shelves into sections. If your son or daughter complains about your misplacing his/her gloves or caps, divide an upper shelf into compartments. Let each member of the family have one section, so s/he can store their garments in a separate place.

Shoe bags in closets. To avoid getting dirt in the closet from muddy shoes, hang a shoe bag inside so members of your family can put shoes there. During the winter months, you can also use the bag for mittens, earmuffs, caps and scarves.

Keep your guest closet dry. Does the wall-to-wall carpeting in your guest closet get wet on rainy days? If it does, purchase some desk blotters at a stationery store and cover your rug. Then when you have visitors they can place their damp boots in the closet without your needing to worry about your carpet. Blotters absorb the water and catch any loose dirt, and you can shake the dirt off easily when the blotter has dried.

Broomstick closet rod. If you want an extra clothing rod in your closet, select a broomstick and tie a piece of cord or rope to both ends. Secure the ends to the stationary rod, and let it hang (see Fig. 9-1). This is especially useful for youngsters, for homemakers who have limited reaching ability, and for people confined to wheelchairs.

Make dividers for closets. Use cardboard that usually comes in men's shirts, for dividers in your closet. For example, they could be used on an upper shelf to separate children's school clothing, their dress clothes, and their playthings.

Keeping sheets organized. If you have problems keeping sheets organized for twin beds and king-sized ones, purchase ink pens in several colors and mark each sheet with a different shade, so you can identify them easily.

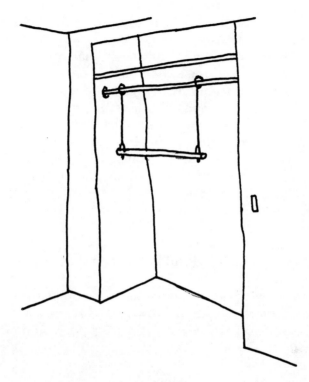

Figure 9-1. Broomstick closet rod.

Hanging blankets or comforters. If you have a blanket or comforter that you do not use or that is only needed at night, you might consider hanging it on a rod in your closet.

Make your garments smell fresh. To keep your clothes smelling fresh, put a bar of soap between your bed linens in your closet.

LINENS. If you are confined to a wheelchair, plan your linen cupboards so that you can store all items in single rows. Be sure the shelves are no wider than 1 foot 4 inches. However, if you must have wider shelves, they should not exceed 1 foot 10 inches. Because items sometimes hang over a particular shelf, make certain to keep the shelf a minimum of 1 inch behind the face of the door, so you can close it properly. Other good features to include are slide-out shelves that enable you to reach for things more conveniently and magnetic catches that help insure your cupboard doors will remain closed after you shut them.

Planning Your Kitchen Storage

Using space wisely is especially important in your kitchen because many handicapped homemakers spend a majority of the day there. Others with hand involvement may find it difficult to pick things off the shelf, and those who have only one hand might become frustrated when trying to lift items out of the way so that they can remove another one. Furthermore, people with a weak grasp or lack of coordination often have the tendency to tip something else over while reaching for a jar, bottle, or can. If you have these difficulties, be sure to arrange all items so that you can reach them easily. Some disabled individuals also arrange storage areas according to the types of meals they wish to prepare. For example, a person might place convenience foods in readily accessible places.

MAKING THE BEST USE OF YOUR KITCHEN CABINETS. Why not try using some of these helpful hints when storing items in your kitchen cabinet?

Make raised shelves. Use small, narrow cardboard boxes and place them bottom side up in a row to the back of a shelf. Two-pound cheese boxes are ideal for this purpose. You now have a raised shelf on which you can place items that are not too tall and can be readily seen.

Store foods in a pantry. Since the average American family usually buys many nonrefrigerated foods, a pantry can be convenient. Locate it near your cooking area. If you do much canning, be sure to have a cool dark place. For many foods, such as those in number 303 cans or smaller, shallow shelves 4 inches wide and 12 to 48 inches long are preferable.

Storing paper bags. Store paper sacks in your cabinet according to size. Then you can see them easily without searching through a pile.

Hang a shoe bag. Hang a small shoe bag on the back of your kitchen door to hold gravy ladles, big spoons, spatulas, bottles and other utensils so that they do not clutter a drawer.

Keeping your cabinet door shut. If you have problems keeping your cabinet doors closed, place a piece of tape on their top edges. You can see the tape, but it will hold the door securely. If one piece does not work, try using two of them.

Lighten your shelves. When shelves are dark under the sink, put aluminum foil on the side and back of the area. It will then reflect the light to brighten the space.

Use cardboard dividers. Use cardboard dividers to divide your canned goods and to separate each variety.

Store knives using wooden spools. Attach wooden spools with glue or screws to the inside of your cupboard door. Place two of them side by side so that the slots between the spools will just be large enough to hold a knife. These are convenient for small paring knives.

Aluminum foil storage. Use aluminum foil underneath pots and pans as shelf paper. To make the foil last longer, lay several thicknesses of newspaper under it.

STORAGE AIDS AND DEVICES. Today there are many storage aids and devices that help make work in the kitchen easier for disabled homemakers. Listed below are eleven which can be particularly helpful.

Wrap and bag organizer. Do you have difficulty finding a place to store your plastic wrap and paper bags? If you do, purchase a Wrap and Bag Organizer®, which you can fasten with screws and attach to walls or the inside of cabinet doors.

Figure 9-2. Wrap and Bag Organizer. Illustration furnished by Rubbermaid Incorporated.

Plate rack. Vinyl-coated plate racks hold dishes separately on cushioned dividers so that you can grasp them easily.

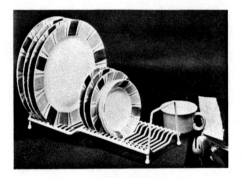
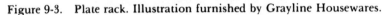

Figure 9-3.   Plate rack. Illustration furnished by Grayline Housewares.

Spice rack. A spice rack will keep spices neat and orderly. You can secure it to your cupboard door or to the wall with the fasteners provided. Since it is vinyl coated, the rack will never rust.

Sliding Pot 'n Pan® rack. You are able to store eight utensils with a slide out Pot 'n Pan rack, which makes them quite accessible. The 18 inch long black steel sliding channels with plated wire hooks may be secured to either a wood or steel wall.

Figure 9-5. Sliding Pot 'n Pan Rack. Illustration furnished by Grayline Housewares.

Adjustable Helper Shelf®. The Adjustable Helper Shelf will hold a variety of assorted sizes and shapes of jars, tins, and packages. You may also store small appliances on them. This shelf is designed to extend from 11 inches to 20½ inches.

Figure 9-6. Adjustable Helper shelf. Illustration furnished by Grayline Housewares.

Bottle rack and can dispenser. The bottle rack and can dispenser can hang below a shelf in your refrigerator to make use of that often wasted space. The bottle rack is 12½ inches long by 5 inches wide and 4¼ inches high. The can dispenser holds six 12-ounce cans.

Figure 9-7.　Bottle and Can Dispenser. Illustration furnished by Rubbermaid Incorporated.

Spacemaker Drawers®. Utilize space under your kitchen cupboards by installing Spacemaker Drawers, which measure 15 inches wide by 12 inches deep. These attach to the base of wall cabinets with two fasteners.

Figure 9-8.　Spacemaker drawers. Illustration furnished by Rubbermaid Incorporated.

Turntables. Turntables rotate, bringing spices, small jars, and bottles within convenient reach. They are easy to clean and measure 10½ inches in diameter by 5¾ inches tall. You may purchase a turntable with either one or two shelves.

Figure 9-9. Turntables. Illustration furnished by Rubbermaid Incorporated.

Vegetable storage bins. Disabled people can often reach produce with less effort using storage bins. Some types can be installed in a cabinet and are readily accessible; others may be concealed inside a cupboard when not in use.

Figure 9-10. Vegetable storage bins. Illustration furnished by International Paper Company and Rubbermaid Incorporated.

Drawer dividers. Storing silverware or kitchen utensils is easier with drawer dividers, which make finding items simple.

Figure 9-11.   Drawer dividers. Illustration furnished by Rubbermaid Incorporated.

Grab-All® extension arm. Reaching for things is often less of an effort with the Grab-All extension arm, which you may purchase in two sizes. One extends your reach 29 inches, while the other helps you grab items 42 inches away. The all-metal arms work with a lever action. and the rubberized tips hold articles securely once you have a grasp on them.

Figure 9-12.   Grab-All extension arm by Miles Kimball and Help Yourself Aids.

Storing Items in Bathrooms

A major shortcoming of most bathrooms is that they simply do not have enough storage space. When planning in this household area, think about some of the articles you frequently will use there. These might include toothpaste and brush, deodorant, razors, towels, washcloths, comb, and hairbrush. If you intend to store medicines there, be sure to include a locked cabinet so that children cannot reach them.

An additional problem with bathroom storage is that often there is inadequate closet space. To remedy this difficulty, you might want to consider installing hooks to hang such items as bathrobes, pajamas, towels and washcloths, or clothing you take off at night and will wear the next day.

Besides using hooks, other methods also help keep your bathroom orderly; here are two of them.

Prevent peeling labels. So that medicine labels will not peel off or become illegible because of frequent handling or spilling, apply a coat of clear nail polish over the label when you make a new purchase.

Use blotters in medicine cabinets. Line the shelves with blotters cut to size, which will absorb any spills and eliminate containers from slipping.

Planning Your Laundry Storage

Depending upon your physical limitations, you may want to plan either more shelf space or more cabinet space or a combination of both. If you are ambulatory, consider adjustable shelves. But, if you cannot reach the upper ones easily, store items seldom used there, such as seasonal bedding. This is also a good place to keep laundry supplies out of the reach of children. However, people confined to wheelchairs may have difficulty using shelves. In these cases they should have at least one locked cabinet to store toxic bleaches and detergents.

Another convenient laundry feature for disabled homemakers is a hamper where you can store soiled clothing. To save space, locate it under your countertop in the laundry area. If you are confined to a wheelchair, it may be necessary to use a reacher or utility stick to remove the clothes from the bottom.

Finally, do not forget to provide some space for keeping clothes that have been washed and dried. If you have enough room, a full-length closet is best. Otherwise, the portable laundry racks discussed in Chapter 8 or hooks will suffice.

Keep Cleaning Supplies Handy

As with other home storage areas, plan to keep cleaning supplies in a handy place. To do this, ask yourself two important questions: How much space do I need for my cleaning equipment and supplies, and where do I use them?

LOCATION. Answering these questions will help you determine the best location for your cleaning supplies. You should also take into account the space you need. Determining this is easy. Just think about how many items you must store, the size of each one, and the total amount of area required. Above all, remember that too much room is better than not enough.

PROVIDE FOR EASY ACCESS. Be sure that all parts of your cleaning storage area are as accessible as possible. One of the best ways is to have a full-sized opening in front.

DISABILITIES AND CLEANING STORAGE. When it comes to planning your cleaning storage, as with other facets of independent living, consider your physical limitations. For those who walk, use crutches, or find it difficult to bend or reach high places, store items at a height of between 2½ and 5 feet. If you are chairbound, make certain to place items at a height of between 1½ and 4 feet.

DUPLICATE ITEMS. To avoid carrying cleaning equipment and supplies from one area of your house to another, you may want to consider purchasing a duplicate set of some items. These might include dust cloths, sponges, and scouring powder.

AIDS. Here are two aids that might help improve your cleaning storage problems.

Clean-up Caddy®. The Clean-up Caddy may be mounted inside a standard-sized cabinet door and conveniently holds cleaning supplies out of sight. This unit attaches with screws and measures 11 inches wide, 5½ inches deep and 14¾ inches high.

Broom and mop holder. The broom and mop holder in Figure 9-14 keeps cleaning items handy. Brooms and mops hang on

Figure 9-13. Clean-Up Caddy. Illustration furnished by Rubbermaid Incorporated.

Figure 9-14. Broom and mop holder. Illustration furnished by Rubbermaid Incorporated.

special vinyl-coated hooks, and the dust pan fits into specially designed holes. The dimensions of the unit are 13½ inches wide, 2¾ inches deep, and 10 inches high.

Planning storage areas is extremely important for homemakers with physical impairments. To arrange well-designed storage areas is difficult in any household, but employing some of the principles, thinking about the design considerations, and using some of the other hints discussed in this chapter will make it easier for you.

POINTS TO REMEMBER

1. *Store only what you need.* Periodically make an inventory of your household areas. Discard seldom used items.
2. *Analyze your storage spaces.* When doing your planning, ask yourself three important questions: where will you store the items, how often will you use them, and is your selection worth the space required?
3. *Select multipurpose items.* Purchase things that you can use for more than one purpose.
4. *Locate items nearby.* Store articles close to where you use them.
5. *Make a list.* When you are thinking about each storage area and what you will place there, write down things that you intend to store.
6. *Plan space wisely.* If you are having a new home built, look over the blueprints beforehand and decide if there is enough storage space.
7. *Avoid corner storage.* Disabled people who are designing their home should not plan cupboards less than 1 foot from the corner of a room, since these cabinets are inconvenient for someone who is using crutches or who is confined to a wheelchair.
8. *In the kitchen, when planning storage areas leave enough room to lift items over one another, and also be sure you can arrange your space in a convenient way.*
9. *Many bathrooms do not have enough room for storing items.* One way to remedy this problem is to install hooks for clothing, towels, and washcloths.

10. *Plan your laundry storage carefully.* Handicapped people who can walk should consider installing adjustable shelves, while those confined to wheelchairs need more cabinet space. When possible, include a hamper in your laundry for soiled clothing. Provide a locked cabinet for bleaches and other toxic substances. A closet, a laundry rack, hooks, or a portable valet are ideal for hanging laundered clothes.

11. *Keep cleaning supplies handy.* Consider the location, the accessibility, and your physical limitations when planning your cleaning storage area. Think, too, about purchasing duplicate inexpensive items to avoid carrying them from place to place in your home.

Chapter 10.

STRUCTURAL MODIFICATION
AND HOME ADAPTIONS

Today many disabled Americans are building their own houses. Some of them, especially those in wheelchairs, must think about special considerations when planning a home. Previous chapters have discussed laundry and storage arrangements as well as designing an efficient kitchen. However, there are several other features you may want to take into account.

EXTERIOR CONSIDERATIONS

Sidewalks

If you are chairbound, remember four important points when designing sidewalks. First, so you can use them easily, they should measure at least 4 feet 6 inches in width. Better yet, to allow two wheelchairs to pass each other with adequate clearance, a 6-foot width is preferred. Second, be sure that the slope of the sidewalk is no more than 1-inch rise per 40 inches of length, or 1½°. However, if this is not possible, a 1-inch rise in 20 inches is acceptable. Third, always provide at least a 5-foot by 5 foot landing in front of an exterior door. Finally, to provide for a non-slip covering, be sure the ramp is slightly corrugated.

Steps

Going up and down steps is an effort for some handicapped individuals. In this case the person may wish to install a ramp. But, if you are planning a home with steps, make certain each one is no more than 5 inches high and at least 12 inches wide. Be sure, too, that you install a sturdy handrail. It should be easy to grip, with a diameter of 1½ to 2 inches. Remember, large railings are sometimes difficult to grasp for people with arthritis in the finger joints. The entry to your house should also be well lighted and easy to see.

Ramps

Design ramps for convenience and safety. All people confined to wheelchairs must use ramps to enter buildings, but those with limited ankle or hip movement may also prefer to use them. With these thoughts in mind, here are a few guidelines for ramp construction. Be sure they are between 48 and 54 inches wide with a slope of 1-inch rise for every 12 inches of length. It is best to have them constructed of concrete or metal and have them covered with corrugated rubber to increase traction.

Build a ramp with platforms for resting in the following three conditions: when the ramp changes directions, when it approaches a door, or when the incline is excessively long and the person pushing his wheelchair needs to stop periodically due to limited arm strength. *(Note:* No ramp should be over 30 feet long, preferably not more than 20 feet without a platform.) Build platforms at least 5 feet square with 18 inches minimum on the side where the doorknob is located.

Be certain, too, that curbs are attached securely to the ramp so that a chairbound person does not accidentally run over the edge.

Depending on the individual's reach, place handrails between 26 and 32 inches high, extending 12 inches beyond the end of the ramp at the top and bottom.

HOME AREAS

Bathrooms

When building a house for someone using a wheelchair, a prime consideration is designing an accessible bathroom. You should ask yourself five important questions: How many bathrooms will you have in your house? What size should they be? Can you place them back to back to avoid additional plumbing expense? What utilities should you include? What special features do you need because of your physical limitations?

On the matter of size, plan your bathrooms to be at least 6 by twelve feet. This allows a disabled person to maneuver his wheelchair easily in the bathroom. Extra space may also be needed for the person with hip and knee involvement.

CHOOSE AN EASY-TO-USE TOILET. You can install one of five basic types of toilets. The *one-piece* and *close-coupled* types are mounted on the floor. The *two-piece* toilet has the tank hung on the wall, and the bowl is secured to the floor. A *wall-hung* model is completely fastened to the wall with no floor connection and is frequently recommended for disabled people, since these units can be placed at any height. Finally, a *corner* toilet is a real space saver. Some of the newer bowls have a built-in ventilation system that helps eliminate odors from a room. You can also purchase toilets with elongated bowls, which have more space at the front and rear of the seat. Depending on the physical handicaps, this kind might make toilet functioning and personal hygiene easier for a disabled person.

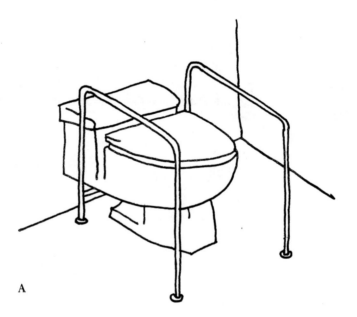

A

Figure 10-1. Bathroom toilets and handrail mountings. A. Floor mounted toilet with floor-mounted handrails.

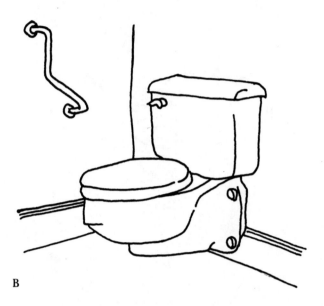

B

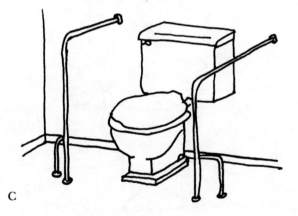

C

Figure 10-1.   B. Wall-hung toilet with wall-mounted handrail. C. Two-piece toilet with floor-mounted handrails.

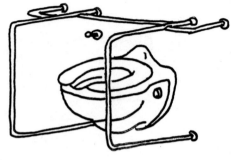

D

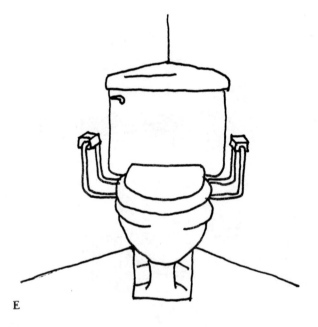

E

Figure 10-1.　D. Flush valve wall-hung toilet and wall-mounted safety bars. E. Corner toilet with integrally mounted safety frame. Courtesy of Paralyzed Veterans of America, Inc.

Furthermore, toilets are also classified according to their water action. Plumbers usually install the siphon jet, reverse trap, or washdown types. Although the siphon jet has the quickest action, it is expensive. To maintain cleanliness, have the trap located at the rear of the bowl and use a deep water seal to give protection from sewer gases. Reverse traps work the same way as siphon jets but have a trapway, smaller water surface, and a water seal that is not so deep. Washdown water traps cost the least, and the trapway is at the front of the bowl. However, when you flush the toilet, it makes a noise.

After you decide on the toilet you wish to purchase, be sure to make a careful choice about its placement. The correct height and width can mean the difference between your needing assistance or being self-reliant in the bathroom. For instance, some disabled people may only be able to slide onto a stool from either the right or left side, while others may want to do this from the front. Therefore, make certain you are aware of such considerations before installing your toilet.

Other handicapped individuals need a higher stool so they can transfer from their chair to the toilet easier. Chapter 3 already discussed how to use a raised toilet seat and a bathroom commode chair. However, here are two other ideas to make the toilet seat more comfortable. You might wish to put a block of wood under the bowl and tank, raising them to the desired level (see Fig. 10-2). If you often have pressure sores, you might want to cushion the toilet seat by laying pieces of foam rubber on it.

Another important consideration is installing safety bars near the stool. There are a number of different types; five of these are shown in Figure 10-1. The type a disabled person needs will depend on his limitations and the support he requires for stabilizing himself. One aid that may help a severely handi-capped person to stand from a seated position is a trapeze, which he can grab as he rises (see Fig. 10-3). Use an eyebolt to mount it to the ceiling. However, be sure when the trapeze is not in use to have it tied back so another person will not hit his head on it while using the stool.

Lastly, when you are thinking about installing a toilet, do not forget to plan for an overhead exhaust fan connected to a timer, which will eliminate objectionable odors.

SELECT A CONVENIENT LAVATORY. Most lavatories are manufactured from steel or iron covered with porcelain enamel or vitreous china. Basically, there are two types: the countertop lavatory units or the wall-hung units, which are fully mounted on the wall and supported by two legs.

If you are building a new home, there is no reason why you cannot place the lavatory in the best location to suit your needs. Be sure to locate it and the adjacent countertop at the best height for accessibility (if you are in a wheelchair this means 31 inches). You can cover the top with ceramic tile or install Formica®.

Figure 10-2. Raised toilet bowl. Courtesy of Paralyzed Veterans of America, Inc.

For a person confined to a wheelchair the basin is important. One advantage to having an oval porcelain bowl is that you can mount it flush with the countertop, and because of its size, the wheelchair's arms will slide easily under it. While steel sinks are most often thought of for kitchen use, there are also some for bathrooms that are less bulky than the vitreous china type. Often there are exposed drain pipes; if this is the case, cover them with asbestos or some other insulating material so that you will not burn your legs on them as you sit in your chair. One of the most convenient basins for chairbound people to use is a *wheelchair*

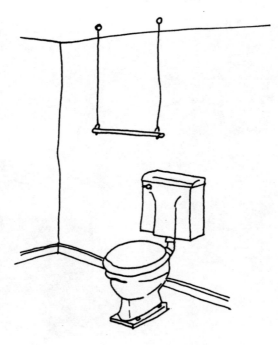

Figure 10-3. Bathroom trapeze. Courtesy of Paralyzed Veterans of America, Inc.

lavatory. You can also install faucets with goose neck spouts that have wrist control handles which are easy for some individuals with upper extremity weakness to operate.

INSTALLING A BATHTUB. When installing a bathtub, space is a prime consideration. The standard tub length is 5 feet, but some may be longer. The width is approximately 32 inches. Some tubs also have wider rims, which help make transferring from your wheelchair into the tub easier.

Always remember that a bathtub can be a dangerous place because it is smooth, slippery, and hard. Therefore, be sure to install grab bars behind the tub. Horizontal rails are best for pushing oneself into a wheelchair, while vertical rails enable one to pull easier. However, placing one rail in a diagonal position serves both purposes. For your bathroom make certain that you choose a type with a nonslip finish for greater safety. Remember also that you should mount your grab bar 1½ inches from the wall.

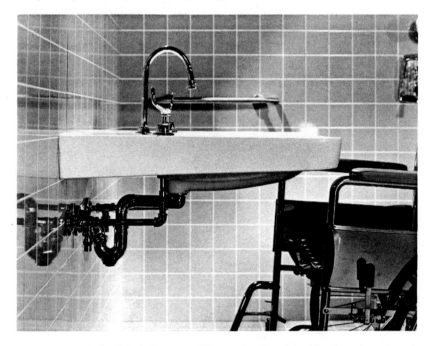

Figure 10-4.   Wheelchair lavatory. Illustration furnished by American Standard U. S. Plumbing Products.

WHEEL-IN STALL SHOWER. Some disabled people confined to wheelchairs prefer to take a shower rather than a tub bath. To do this easily, they must be able to roll their chairs inside, maneuver them into position, close the curtain, and operate the controls.

Unfortunately, no company makes a premanufactured shower that is practical for nonambulatory individuals, since most of them are too small for a wheelchair. Furthermore, they also have a water ledge, which makes it impossible to push a wheelchair over the barrier and into the shower.

However, you can solve these problems with a wheel-in stall shower. Locate it at one end of the bathroom and provide space for a 3-foot by 5-foot stall shower. Tile the wall or use laminated plastic, being sure the floor slopes inward to a center drain. Remember also that the floor should be sunken at least ½ inch

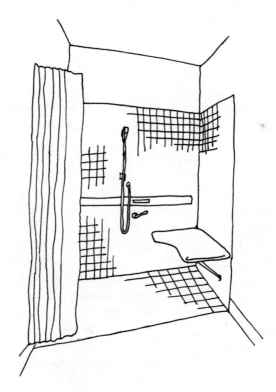

Figure 10-5.   Wheel-in shower.

with a nonskid surface. Do not install a shower door, because the tracks only gather water and dirt, making another cleaning job. Instead, place a shower curtain 2 inches in from the edge of the shower's opening to avoid splashing into the bathroom. Have a 15-inch seat mounted 18 inches from the floor, which will fold up when not in use. Make certain your contractor places plumbing on an inside wall of your house in cold climates. You might want him to provide for a hand-held shower head you can use while sitting (*see* the section on bathing hints in Chap. 3). Sometimes a special faucet adapter is necessary. Furthermore, install a window to allow good ventilation, and plan for an electric light in the ceiling.

Unlike bathing in a tub, showering does not pose as many hazards. However, be certain to install a wall railing for safety. These are the same as those placed behind tubs. In a properly designed shower, the person can roll his chair in and then come out wet, since the bathroom floor should not be slippery. Another option is to install indoor-outdoor carpeting, which is water-proof and mildew-proof.

CHECK THE FAUCETS. Pay special attention to the type of faucets you select for bathtubs, sinks, or showers. Some older ones have rubber or plastic washers that wear out quickly and need to be replaced.

While many faucets have two handles, certain models have a single handle that handicapped people can operate with the elbow or heel of one of their hands. The lever can be moved from left to right to regulate the temperature. Another kind is the Scald-Guard® with a single knob control. It has three important safety features: valves are equipped with limited stops, which can be adjusted to prevent the valve from being opened fully, a Hot-Stop® button on the handle to prevent the hot water being unintentionally turned on, and a convenient lever on the valve, which will control the flow of water.

Depending on the faucet, the water spout could be either long or short. Some are fixed in one position and may be straight or have a goose neck, while others swivel. Even though the swivel kind is most often used in kitchens, there is no reason why one could not use them in the bathroom, since the faucet can swing away from the center of the basin.

Figure 10-6.   Lever-handle faucet.

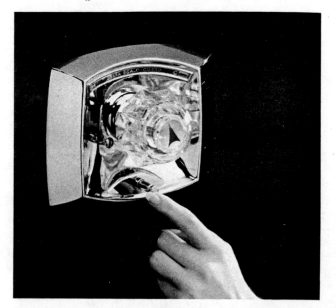

Figure 10-7.   Scald-Guard. Illustration furnished by Delta Faucet Company.

SHOP CAREFULLY FOR ACCESSORIES. Accessories in this chapter refer to such items as toilet paper holder, towel racks, medicine cabinets, and recessed shelves.

A medicine cabinet can have several uses. This is a handy place to store items used for cleaning and grooming as well as medicines. These are usually recessed, have a built-in mirror, and are also attractive and functional. They come in various sizes and styles to fit a person's needs. When selecting a cabinet with sliding doors, make sure they slide easily, preferably on nylon wheels or by another minimum-friction method.

For disabled people to use tissue holders and towel rods easily, these must be wall hung. So that a chairbound person can reach tissue holders without too much effort, mount them above the toilet's grab bars, which should be installed 30 to 36 inches from the floor. When it comes to towel rods, metal ones are preferred; mount them 40 to 42 inches from the floor. Make sure they are fastened securely to the wall.

A linen closet is convenient in the bathroom. Wall-hung cabinets protruding into the room can be hazardous if they are not properly placed. Consider also the placement of toothbrush holders, soap dishes, glass holders, and ashtrays.

BE SURE GOOD LIGHTING EXISTS. In the bathroom, overhead lighting is never good enough; additional light is always necessary near the lavatory for such tasks as shaving and grooming. However, if properly selected these fixtures can light the entire bathroom. You should choose fixtures with care to reduce glare, reflection, and strong shadows. Two linear flourescent lights on either side of the mirror are a good source of lighting.

When considering the kind of lighting you want, you ought to think about the selection of switches. Silent mercury switches are the best. Install them approximately 36 inches from the floor. Depending on your individual preference, they can be located inside or outside the bathroom door. To make sure no one will get an electric shock from the switches, place them so you cannot reach them from the tub or shower. Some disabled people shave with an electric razor. In this case, be sure to install electric outlets near the lavatory so that you can plug it in.

Bedrooms

When planning a bedroom, consider three important things: design, furnishings, and linens.

DESIGN CONSIDERATIONS. One of the first rules you should remember is to make your bedrooms as accessible as possible. Unless you are chairbound, this will require no structural modifications. If you use a wheelchair, however, you must plan the bedroom accordingly. The preferred minimum space required for a king-sized bed is 72 inches by 80 inches, a queen-sized bed, 60 inches by 80 inches, a double bed, 54 inches by 75 inches, and a twin bed, 38 inches by 75 inches. When your bed is against one wall and another piece of furniture is on the opposite one, you should have at least 2 feet 6 inches between them. These are only minimum space requirements, and if you can leave more room, so much the better.

Closets. One handy bedroom feature is a walk-in closet, since this eliminates the need for a dresser. As discussed in Chapter 9, you can have portable bins on the closet shelf for shirts, handkerchiefs, socks, and underwear. Also, if you are in a wheelchair the rod should never by higher than 48 inches from the floor. When planning shelving, install it no higher than 45 inches.

Windows. In placing windows to reduce glare, be sure that you locate your bed on the opposite side of the room. Plan the windows as low to the ground as possible. The average distance from the floor to a person lying in bed is 2 feet 2 inches. When he is seated, it is approximately 2 feet 11 inches. Place windows with these measurements in mind. This subject will be discussed in more detail later in this chapter.

FURNITURE. Besides making the structural modifications in your home that have already been discussed, purchase furniture that makes living more cheerful and restful. Following are some ways of doing this.

Beds. Take considerable time when selecting a bed. Make certain the frame is strong and large enough so you will feel comfortable. Since some disabled people are prone to develop pressure sores and must turn over frequently, a twin bed would probably be best, because the individual can easily grip the mattress edge for added leverage in changing positions or turning. Additionally, do not forget that if the footboard has spindle posts you can tie ropes to them to aid yourself in moving about (*see* the section on you and your bed in Chap. 3).

If you are confined to a wheelchair, be sure that your bed is high enough so the foot pedals of your chair can roll under it. Lower beds are easier to transfer to and from. Make certain there is at least 10 to 12 inches between the bottom rail and the floor. If your bed does not meet this standard, you can put blocks under each of the four legs or install casters. Also, be sure that the seat of your wheelchair and the bed are the same height since you will be able to transfer easier. For those with arthritis and heart conditions, this is especially important. The best height for these people is 17½ to 19½ inches. However, regardless of your handicaps, you can make a bed much easier if you keep in mind the previous dimensions.

Mattresses. Basically, there are three types of mattresses: foam rubber, available in different firmnesses and thicknesses, solid upholstered, and upholstered innerspring. Although the upholstered innerspring is the most popular, the best type's weight is at least 45 pounds. For people who cannot turn themselves, there are various antipressure materials available, such as ripple mattresses or sheepskins.

Before purchasing any mattress, however, remember three general principles. First, consult your doctor, physical therapist, or occupational therapist to see what type would be recommended considering your disabilities. Then be sure the mattress has reinforced padding and is covered with ticking around the borders. Finally, lie down on it and test it for comfort.

Mattress pad. Purchase a mattress pad with flaps that you can tuck in, and make sure it will protect the mattress against soil.

Gatch spring. If you decide to buy a hospital bed, look for one with a Gatch spring, which enables you to raise and lower its foot. Some of these have manual controls, while others operate electronically.

Night tables. Select night tables with generous drawer space and bottom shelves with doors. Make certain they are roomy so that everything will be at hand with no need for you to get out of bed.

Lamps. Choose lamps that can be raised or lowered and hung on a wall above a bed. Make sure that the chain is within easy reach and long enough so you can turn the lamp on or off with little effort. A variation of this type is a reading lamp that attaches to the headboard and gives ample light without disturbing others who sleep nearby.

Signal bell. Place an electrical or hand operated signal bell near your bed so you are able to call someone if you need assistance.

Mirrors. Center large mirrors over a dresser. When using wall-hung ones, be sure they are no smaller than 24 inches high and they are located 30 inches from the floor. You can also mount full-length ones on the back of a bedroom door.

Chairs. Select chairs that are 18 inches high. Those without front rungs make transferring from a wheelchair easier.

LINENS. For general use, to be found are blankets, spreads, pillowcases, and towels along with sheets in a number of sizes. Depending on your hand limitations, you can choose either fitted or unfitted ones. You might want to choose those made of muslin or percale. Percale is finely woven and more luxurious but will cost more than muslin.

Think twice before purchasing nylon or any other slippery material because, even though you tuck them under the mattress, they will invariably slip out. Wrinkling is also a problem, and it can disturb your sleep.

Living Rooms

There is little need for much structural modification when designing a living room for disabled individuals. However, you might want to keep a few things in mind. First, if you are chairbound, perhaps you should make the room a little larger than you had originally planned to allow for easier movement from place to place without any obstructions. Remember also that you need at least 60 inches to turn your wheelchair completely around. Second, make certain the windows are at a good height so you can get a good view of the outdoors. If possible, plan for a bay window that permits a maximum amount of light to enter the room and enables you to have a clear view of the landscape. This is especially important because many handicapped people are either confined to a wheelchair, are bedridden, or may be unable to be outside for any part of the day; a good view of the out-of-doors can be psychologically beneficial.

FURNISHING YOUR LIVING ROOM. While a living room does not require much architectural modification, you should select furnishings that are both functional and comfortable. Below is a list of furniture that you might want to consider for your living room and some reasons why certain features are recommended for people with various physical limitations.

Sofa. When you are chairbound, having your sofa's seat 16½ inches high with firm cushions is handy. Nonambulatory people should choose one at this height because they can transfer from their wheelchair to it easier.

Armchairs. Preferably select armchairs that are 18½ inches high with firm cushions. In choosing them, be certain the backrest and head support are adequate. If you are chairbound, avoid buying chairs with crossbars that will interfere with your wheelchair.

Coffee table. A square coffee table with ball-bearing casters is conveniently moveable from place to place. Some have one or two shelves that will hold everything a person might need in the living room for entertaining.

End tables. End tables with shelves can be used for books and other storage.

Desk. If you have a desk in the living room, select one with generous drawer area, sturdy design, and large enough working surface. Be sure it has ample knee space to allow you to approach it closely in your wheelchair.

Large table lamps. Place large table lamps where you will get the greatest benefit of the light.

Writing lamps. You can adjust and attach writing lamps to the wall so that your desk's surface is free for working.

Standing or wall lamps. Be sure that standing or wall lamps have a switch you are able to reach from a standing or sitting position. You can put a chain on some to aid in turning them on and off.

Dining Area

Locate your dining area as close to the kitchen as possible so that you need not carry food long distances. This is particularly important for someone who is confined to a wheelchair, who is using crutches, or who is having some upper extremity involvement since people with these disabilities can often have difficulty transporting pots, pans, and dishes to and from the serving area. Depending on the floor plan of your house and on whether there is a partition between the dining room and kitchen, you may want to have on opening cut in the wall so that you can pass food from one room to the other.

Just as with all rooms in your house, the dining area should not be cluttered with expensive furnishings. Remember that the essentials are a table with chairs. When more eating space is required, you can always bring in extra seating. If you sometimes need additional eating area, a card table can seat four people comfortably. Should you need a larger dining space, extension tables may accommodate as many as sixteen guests.

The height of the table is important. For those who are ambulatory, the preferred measurement is between 2 feet 3½ inches and 2 feet 4 inches. However, you must consider other factors if you are chairbound. A major thing to keep in mind is that the table should clear your wheelchair's arms, allowing the chair to roll underneath easily. Therefore, a minimum of 2 feet 7½ inches is needed. This means that the overall table height must be approximately 2 feet 7½ inches.

Carport or Garage

If you drive an automobile, you will probably want to include a carport or garage as part of the plan for the house. However, before you start construction, there are some things about which to think.

CARPORTS. Depending on your physical limitations, a carport may be preferable to a garage because with a garage you must get out of your car, open a heavy door, return to the auto, drive inside, and then close the door. On the other hand, a carport eliminates these steps.

In the design of your carport, the platform for your car should be almost level, with a little slope to allow good drainage. Make certain also that you make the concrete pad wide enough. A good width is about 11 feet; this gives 7 feet for your automobile and an extra 4 feet on the driver's side so a nonambulatory person can transfer from the car seat to a wheelchair.

Finally, design your home so you can walk directly from your carport into the house. However, if you cannot accomplish this, provide for a weatherproof covered walkway between them.

GARAGES. While some disabled people find a carport more convenient, others prefer a garage. As stated earlier, an open area has certain advantages, because it eliminates the necessity of lifting a heavy door. On the other hand, a locked building offers better security against vandalism and weather. Just as with a carport, the garage should have direct entry into the house.

When considering the plans for your garage, you should take your disability into account since that will help determine its size. Be sure there is at least 3 feet 2 inches between the car door and the wall. Furthermore, if you are ambulatory, the overall garage width should be a minimum of 10 feet. If you use crutches, canes, or a walker, allow no less than 10 feet 3 inches. This gives a clear access of 3 feet 3 inches to maneuver your walking aid. Finally, if you are chairbound, you should have a minimum of 10 feet 9 inches of access space. However, so that you will have enough room, it is better to build the garage 11 feet 3 inches wide. One advantage of this larger measurement is that an attendant can help the disabled individual in and out of the car.

Once you have left the automobile and the garage, you must close the garage door. Most people do this manually, but it is often difficult or impossible for a handicapped person, particularly someone in a wheelchair. Consequently, one solution is an automatic garage door opener.

Stanley Vemco® manufactures several garage door openers, including the Standard Model 200, Stanley Delux Model 202, Model 5030 Deluxe Dental Screw Drive, Deluxe Digital Gear Drive Model 5010, and the Heavy Duty Model 307R. These openers are designed for convenience, and they can be operated by pressing a wall button or using a radio control to close or open the garage door. The light can be turned on and off automatically. If you are planning to work in your garage, you can also open the door halfway for ventilation. Other manufacturers also make electric garage door openers.

OTHER STRUCTURAL MODIFICATIONS

Windows

In our earlier discussion of bathrooms and bedrooms the placement of windows was mentioned, but now this subject will be presented in more detail. The first thing to remember is that you should install windows at the right height so you can comfortably look outside. Consequently, keep in mind that the average eye height, measured from the floor, of someone sitting in a wheelchair is 3 feet 9½ inches, for an elderly woman standing, 4 feet 8¾ inches, and for a young man standing, 5 feet ¼ inch.

Taking these measurements into consideration, place window-sills between 2 feet and 2 feet 6 inches from the floor. Remember that a sill over 2 feet 9 inches high will obstruct the view of a seated person. Another thing to consider is that someone on a second floor or above must look down; therefore, in these cases locate the sill at a height of no more than 2 feet.

FOUR BASIC DESIGNS. Basically, there are four types of windows used in homes. The *casement window* can be opened with a hand crank on the sill. When you open it, a hinge moves the glass outward. The *awning window* has several panes of glass that also open with a crank. Since panes are on a slant, they will protect the interior of a house from the elements, even though the windows are not shut. *Double hung windows*, which were used in many

Figure 10-8.   Window designs. Courtesy of Paralyzed Veterans of America, Inc.

older homes in America, have two halves that slide up and down but are usually difficult for a handicapped person to operate. Unless you have strong arms, pushing either section back and forth may be impossible. Therefore, someone with upper extremity weakness or incoordination might not be able to fasten the latch. The last type of window is the *sliding window*, which is easy to manipulate from a wheelchair, since it moves smoothly and easily. Moreover, the buttons on these aluminum windows lock them, and they can be placed at any level. In fact, if you are living in a home with casement windows, it probably would be a good idea to replace them with the sliding type.

In placing windows, one of the prime considerations you should think about is how you will clean them. Here are three good rules to remember. First, they should be in an accessible position. Second, avoid installing small panes. Last, be sure that all window hardware is easy to clean.

LATCHES. At what height should you place the latch? This depends on your disability. If you can walk unassisted, a good measurement is 5 feet 4 inches. If you use a cane, crutches or a walker, 5 feet 1 inch is a suitable height. If you are confined to a wheelchair, 3 feet 11 inches to 4 feet 5 inches is proper.

Doorways

Imagine yourself confined to a wheelchair approaching a narrow doorway that you cannot pass through. This is one reason why a chairbound person, when designing a home, must plan it carefully. Not only should you consider the dimensions of the entrance way and the openings to all rooms of the house but also you should think about the width of the door itself since it too can reduce the space. For example, a side-hung door, one of the most common types, has a thickness of 1⅜ inches. Therefore, a 36-inch doorway actually only leaves approximately 34 inches of passing space when it is standing open.

Besides the side-hinge door, there are other types, such as the accordion door, that also causes a space reduction. Only a sliding door that disappears back into the wall will not cause this problem.

ENTRY DOORS. Install a 36-inch entry door, which will leave a 34-inch opening. Most builders consider this standard, and in some areas this is part of the building code regulations. Since front doors usually open inward, the screen or storm door should swing outward. Consequently, always position your wheelchair properly so that you can pass through the door. Remember also that you should allow enough room so you can swing the outside door towards your wheelchair without pushing the chair out of the way.

Be sure that the approach inside and outside your door is level and that the threshold is no higher than ½ inch. In addition, make certain the front, screen, and storm doors open at least a full 90°. Since screen doors are difficult to operate from a wheelchair, you can also equip them with a spring-loaded closing device to prevent them from banging shut. Finally, if you are in a wheelchair and accustomed to using your footrests to open the door, install a stainless steel or brass kick plate along the base of the door.

INTERIOR DOORS. Place all interior doors so they will not interfere with each other. Under no circumstances should you install thresholds in any interior area of the house. For tight spaces such as in a closet or bedroom opening, consider using sliding doors that operate from an overhead track or those which are recessed in a wall. In some areas where you have less room, you may choose to install an accordian door. However, it will require considerable space.

DOOR FASTENINGS. Place door fastenings between 36 and 38 inches from the floor. If you install doorknobs, be sure they have rough finishes and are easy to grip. Some people with a weak or limited grasp may find a horizontal lever door latch or a vertical handle together with thumb squeeze latch much simpler to operate than a knob. A rubber doorknob lever that fits over the doorknob is also handy for some disabled individuals. It provides added leverage for a person who has difficulty turning the knob.

For someone in a wheelchair, passing through a side-hung door is somewhat difficult, because the person must turn around, reenter the door opening, grip the knob, then back up into the entrance while holding the knob, and finally pull the door shut. To eliminate this process, install a pull handle a few inches away from the hinge side of the door, which enables you to shut it as you pass through in your wheelchair. Make certain to align this handle evenly with the doorknob.

Figure 10-9.   Rubber doorknob lever. Illustration furnished by Help Yourself
Aids.

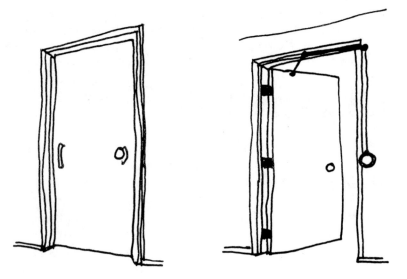

Figure 10-10. Two doorknobs
on sidehung door. Courtesy of
Paralyzed Veterans of America,
Inc.

Figure 10-11.   Sash door closing.
Courtesy of Paralyzed Veterans of
America, Inc.

Another closing device for a nonambulatory person who wants to close a door after passing through is a sash cord that runs through two pulleys, one located on the right-hand corner of the door casing, and the other in the middle of the molding. One end of a rope is attached to a screw eye fastened to the door, while the opposite end is tied to a curtain ring or small loop that a disabled person can grasp (see Fig. 10-11).

Electrical Service

Plan to have adequate lighting in your home both for efficiency and for safety. The National Electric Code recommends a minimum of 3 watts of lighting for every square foot of building area. Therefore, be sure that each individual light serves the purpose for which it was intended, either direct lighting or overall illumination. Of course, daylight is the best source, but sometimes this is not enough in dark rooms, cupboards, or places you plan to do close work. Also, general lighting is sometimes not as satisfactory as selectively placed fixtures for specific purposes. Following are three other aspects of an electrical system that are important.

SWITCHES. Make sure that switches are conveniently located and are horizontally aligned with the knob just inside the door to every room in the house. With a master switch at the front entrance you can light an entire house. However, no switch should be higher than 40 inches from the floor and for wheelchair users no more than 36 inches.

In addition to taking height into consideration, remember not to place more than two switches in one group, since a multi-switch panel is somewhat confusing. If a person has upper extremity involvement, he may be able to use rocker switches the easiest, since a severely disabled individual merely needs to tap the switch with either his arm, elbow, or wrist to turn the light on and off. Furthermore, switches with delayed action have some advantages because the light remains on for a few minutes after you leave the room so that you will not be groping in the dark. Last, do not forget to think about two-way switches. These make it possible for you to turn a light off or on at two different points, such as at either end of a hallway.

Figure 10-12.   Final Touch switch. Illustration furnished by General Electric Company.

OUTLETS. If you are confined in a wheelchair, install outlets between 2 feet 4 inches and 3 feet from the floor so that you can plug in appliances easily. Appliances should be grounded for safety to guard against shock. To avoid the need for extension cords, plan the arrangements of outlets carefully. For instance, most appliance cords are 6 feet long. Therefore, you ought to make sure to place one outlet at least every 12 feet, and at least one on every wall. In the dining area, be certain that outlets are available at table height for such things as electric skillets and hot pots.

METER PANELS. Meter panels are located on the outside of the house. Their location and height is normally regulated by the city or county building codes. Consequently, they are not accessible to most disabled people. If you are building a new home, you can ask your electrical contractor to install another panel with circuit breakers inside your house. Locate this panel in a convenient place such as a hall, closet, or utility room, but if there are children in the home, the meter panel should be locked at all times. Install a panel with circuit breakers rather than fuses. These have a time-delay mechanism. If a problem arises after the fault has been remedied, the current can be restored when you replace the circuit breaker. This system is the most convenient for someone who is disabled.

Floor Coverings

The type of floor covering you choose for your home can depend on your disability, the cost, the location in your home, and your ability to maintain it. Following are some specific considerations to think about if you walk with difficulty or use a wheelchair.

SELECTING FLOORING FOR THE CHAIRBOUND. For chairbound individuals linoleum or wooden flooring is better than carpet, since a chair will roll on it easier. A person usually has difficulty propelling himself on thick carpet pile. Terrazzo, cork, or vinyl tile are nonskid materials you might want to use. Whatever kind of floor you buy, be sure it is easy to maintain with an occasional coat of nonskid polish.

However, if you choose to carpet some rooms of your home, make certain the rug is very low density pile with a tough fiber. Nylon rugs are some of the best. Do not select deep piles or shag rugs since they are more difficult to wheel your chair over. Something else to consider is that dirt and marks are not as obvious on patterned surfaces. Be certain that you test the carpet before making an investment. Simply roll your wheelchair over it; if the wheels drag or the carpeting mats down and shows tracks, do not make the purchase.

Indoor-outdoor carpeting produced from a man-made fiber, polypropylene, is another option, and it provides a flat surface. This carpeting can be installed on porches, patios, swimming pool decks, bathrooms, and other places where a great deal of moisture and heavy soil accumulates.

No matter what type of carpeting you buy, be sure that it is installed correctly and stretched tightly from wall to wall. Sometimes these rugs bunch up and slide out of place due to the swinging action of the front wheels of your chair.

CHOOSING FLOORING FOR THE AMBULATORY. Some of the same types of flooring found in homes of those confined to wheelchairs are also suitable for the ambulatory who walk with extreme difficulty or who use crutches. It is important for every person to have a nonslip floor. Slipperiness is due to the type of flooring, and slippery surfaces are particularly hazardous for those who walk with crutches. Take care to choose a type for comfort, for instance, one with a sponge backing. Look, too, for the kind that will not show crutch marks, and do not wax it heavily—perhaps not at all. Finally, never forget that floor mats on a polished floor can be dangerous, since a person without good balance may fall.

Heating and Cooling Your Home

Depending on what a person's handicaps are, he may require more heat than able-bodied individuals. Therefore, disabled people should have some control over the temperature in their homes. One of the best ways of doing this is with forced air heating. Some units also cool the house and, consequently, are called dual systems. When having the registers installed, be sure they are located near the floor rather than in the ceiling for the most efficiency. In placing the thermostat for best cooling and heating results, place it 54 inches from the floor.

Provide for Good Communications

For some people with mobility handicaps, going from one room to another to communicate with someone can be tiring and ineffective, if not impossible. You might be able to use a tapping, ringing, or other noise device. For example, you could have a prearranged signal, such as two rings for "I need help" and three for "please come quickly." However, often these systems are not adequate.

In recent years a host of electronic devices have become available. Although they are usually meant for interoffice communications in the business world, you can use them in residences to a good advantage.

Probably the best known of these is the intercom. The bedroom and bathroom are two important locations for call boxes. Depending on what your household routine is, you should plan the other places where they will be the most convenient. Be sure that you place receivers in locations where people will be present most of the time. You can also run a wire and put a receiver in a neighbor's house 200 or 300 feet away. Some intercom models sold on the market today are transistorized and operate from a battery or household current. Most of them are compact, and you may place them on a table or mount them on a wall. When installing these devices, make sure they have their own wiring for better clarity and power for carrying the voice signal. Those which require no special wiring are sometimes called "wireless" (not radio) and have an advantage because they need no special wiring but use a regular alternating current. You can move this type of intercom from room to room, but it may have poorer sound quality since often electric interference causes an annoying crackling sound. Avoid this problem by purchasing an intercom with frequency modulation, which is a little more expensive but suppresses the interferences. Above all, whatever kind of equipment you buy, make sure you can return it if you are not satisfied.

Installing a Telephone

For some disabled people the telephone is a valuable link with the outside world, because it may allow them to work from their homes and communicate with others without leaving home. The phone should be as convenient as possible so that someone with physical limitations can do these things. If you are confined to a wheelchair, one of the first considerations is the height of your phone. It should be no higher than 3 feet 3 inches from the floor.

Today many telephone companies are providing special equipment to assist disabled persons with communication. The Bell System is one of the leaders in this field. Following are three of the devices they are able to provide.

If an individual cannot hold the receiver, a single-button set with a small on/off switch may be installed. An adjustable arm can then hold a headset in a convenient position.

When a person is confined to bed the Speakerphone® allows the individual to use telephone equipment and free the hands. To make or answer a call simply push a button without removing the receiver from the phone. You then talk into a speaker. This device is also excellent for quadriplegic or others with impaired hand use.

Some disabled people who find it difficult to dial a phone might find using a Card Dialer® easier. Those with partial paralysis or lack of hand coordination may want to insert a prepushed telephone number into the unit, which presses a start bar and automatically dials the number.

Select the Proper Chair Lift

When people usually· think about designing homes for the chairbound, they assume the house must be on one level. This is not necessarily true. Think for a moment about the problem Jean, a fifty-four-year-old paraplegic, faced when she was injured. At that time she lived in a home with a basement that she wanted to make accessible. To accomplish this, Jean decided to install a lift. Many handicapped people who live in a home with a second story face a similar problem. Three of the most popular wheelchair lifts are the stairway chair lift, the wheelchair stair lift, and the wheelchair platform lift.

STAIRWAY CHAIR LIFT. Although the stairway chair lift has many limitations, some handicapped people operate it successfully. To use this lift independently, you must have good arm mobility, upper extremity strength, and the ability to transfer to a wheelchair at both the bottom and top of the stairs. Incidentally, this requires having two wheelchairs. You can control the upward and downward movement of the lift with a push button. Install a button at the top and bottom of the staircase that will also control the movement of the chair.

One such model is the Stair-Glide Delux®, which meets both Canadian Standard Association and American Standard Institute safety codes. With a fingertip control switch, you can stop and start the unit anywhere along the track. Furthermore, a person can call or send the unit to any position on the track by using the call-send controls located at both the bottom and top landings. This stairway lift has a capacity of 250 pounds. The motor is completely enclosed under the seat for clean, quiet, and safe operation. The seat rotates 180° for easy access at the top and bottom of the stairs. You can get on and off this unit in a normal sitting position, facing away from the stairs.

A Stair-Glide Delux is easy to install on either the right or left side of your stairway. The track is designed for straight stairways; however, it is adaptable to fit most situations. The track rests on the steps, securely fastened at the top and bottom landings. Because the track is only 12 inches wide, the stairway is left open for normal use. There are no attachments to the wall or individual steps to mar the stairs. No special wiring is required

Figure 10-13. Stair-Glide Delux. Illustration furnished by American Stair-Glide Corporation.

because this lift runs on standard 110-volt current. Simply plug it in and your unit is fully operational.

WHEELCHAIR STAIR LIFT. A wheelchair stair lift consists of a platform that carries the person and his wheelchair safely up and down flights of stairs. If you purchase one, be sure the controls are easy to reach, and make certain you choose the type with limit switches, which are used to stop the platform when it reaches the top or bottom of the stairs. Remember, too, that a wheelchair stair lift should have safety devices to keep the wheelchair from rolling off the lift during operation, that lower it gently in the event of a power blackout, or when the drive mechanism fails, that will stop the elevator if there is an obstruction in its path.

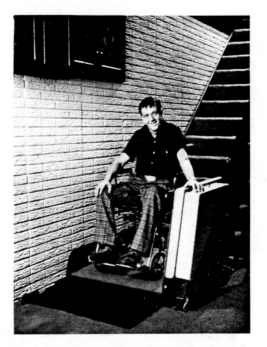

Figure 10-14.   Cheney Wheelchair Lift II. Illustration furnished by the Cheney Company.

One type is the Cheney Wheelchair Lift II®, which is powered by a plant. Designed to be stairway mounted, it carries a person in a wheelchair safely from one floor to the other. To mount this lift, the stairway should be at least 40 inches wide and accommodate a platform of at least 27 inches in width. Ideally, a 42 inch stairway would give a width of at least 29 inches. The wheelchair lift stops level with the upper landing for entrance at the top of the staircase; at the lower landing, a person may wheel his chair on the lift from either side of the platform or straight ahead.

WHEELCHAIR PLATFORM LIFTS. Wheelchair platform lifts are short vertical lifts that can be installed at ground level to raise your wheelchair from the outdoors to the interior of your home and vice versa. Provisions can be made for such a lift with little need for additional construction expense. However, the purchase and installation of the lift may be quite costly. These units serve when it is not practical to ramp an entrance. In operating this type of lift, you will not be using much household current, so it will not increase your electric bill substantially.

Figure 10-15. Porch lift. Illustration furnished by American Stair-Glide Corporation.

If you decide to install a wheelchair platform lift, one unit to consider is the Porch Lift®. These units permit the rider to simply roll his wheelchair onto a 12 square foot platform having a nonskid surface, which can be raised or lowered to the proper level. You can operate the Porch Lift with a push bar control that is easy for anyone who has limited finger use to manipulate. This unit is powered by the standard 110-volt current. The motor and lifting mechanism are completely enclosed to prevent contact with moving parts. The units are shipped assembled and ready for installation.

ACCESSIBILITY CHECKLIST

To this point only designs for new homes for disabled people have been discussed. However, many handicapped individuals rent instead of owning their own home. What are various things they should take into account when evaluating rental property? Table 10-I is a checklist that you can use for determining whether a rental unit is accessible to those in wheelchairs.

This chapter has focused on various things disabled people should think about when designing or renting a home. However, if you are planning to build your own home, you should consult an architect or contractor and read other material on the subject

Table 10-I
ACCESSIBILITY CHECKLIST

	YES	NO
1. Is the building accessible with no steps or curbs?	_____	_____
2. Can you enter the apartment from street level?	_____	_____
3. If the rental unit is on an upper floor, is there an elevator with a wide enough doorway to let you enter in your wheelchair? Does it have a device to hold the door open while you push your chair in and out? Can you reach the elevator buttons?	_____	_____
4. Will the width of the exterior door allow you to enter the apartment without any obstructions?	_____	_____
5. In the bathroom can you transfer to and from the tub and stool easily? Are there grab bars mounted near them?	_____	_____
6. Is the kitchen countertop a convenient height? Are the kitchen cabinets accessible?	_____	_____
7. Can you maneuver your wheelchair in all rooms, in all halls, and through interior doors of the apartment?	_____	_____
8. Will your wheelchair roll smoothly on the floor covering?	_____	_____
9. Does the landlord permit you to make simple modifications?	_____	_____
10. Can you use other facilities, e.g. laundry room, garbage chute, recreation room, office, etc?	_____	_____
11. Is there parking for yourself or visitors?	_____	_____

before you begin. When renting a house or apartment, be sure you inspect it for accessibility before you move in.

POINTS TO REMEMBER

1. *Sidewalks should meet three important criteria.* To accommodate a wheelchair, plan them 4 feet 6 inches wide, or so that two wheelchairs can pass one another, allow 6 feet clearance. Be sure also that sidewalks have a 1-inch rise for every forty inches of length. Make certain you provide a nonslip surface.

2. *Design steps no more than 5 inches high and no less than 12 inches wide.* Provide for a sturdy handrail.

3. *Build ramps with a slope not exceeding 1 inch rise for every*

12 inches of length. Construct the surface of concrete, metal, or corrugated rubber. Be sure you install platforms periodically when ramps are excessively long, when they change directions, or when one approaches a door.

4. *For someone in a wheelchair, bathrooms must be large enough.* Other considerations include choosing an easy-to-use toilet, selecting a convenient lavatory, installing an accessible bathtub and shower, purchasing faucets you can use without too much effort, giving special attention to your choice of paper and towel racks, buying medicine cabinets and recessed shelves with care, and making certain the lighting is adequate.

5. *If you are chairbound, take certain features into account when planning a bedroom.* These include leaving enough space to maneuver your wheelchair, being sure you purchase comfortable furniture, and making certain the closets and linens are adequate.

6. *Plan a living room that is large enough and has good lighting.*

7. *When possible, locate the dining area near the kitchen.* The table height is important for people in wheelchairs.

8. *Plan carports and garages carefully: Carports eliminate opening heavy doors.* On the other hand, a garage offers more security against vandalism and weather. Electric garage door openers are often necessary for people confined to wheelchairs.

9. *Consider the placement of windows: Locate them at a convenient height.* The four types are casement, awning, double-hung, and sliding windows.

10. *Think about doorway openings.* For nonambulatory people, exterior doorways should be 36 inches wide. The preferred interior door width for crutch users is 2 feet 8 inches. If you are confined to a wheelchair, allow at least 36 inches width for passage. Be sure door fastenings are easy for you to operate.

11. *When planning the electrical system in your house, make a wise choice of switches, outlets, and meter panels.*

12. *Choose the right floor covering for safety in your home.* Select the nonskid type, particularly if you use crutches or

have poor balance. Maneuvering wheelchairs on thick pile carpeting is difficult.

13. *A forced air heating system is both economical and efficient.* Consider how far you can reach when locating the thermostat. If possible, operate the system with natural gas rather than electricity to save money.

14. *Intercoms reduce walking or making nonambulatory persons move their wheelchairs from one room of the house to another.*

15. *Some handicapped people need to use special telephone devices.* Three of these include single-button sets, Speakerphones, and Card Dialers.

16. *Three types of wheelchair lifts include a stairway, wheelchair, and platform chairlift.*

Chapter 11

COMFORTABLE CLOTHING

For some disabled people it is difficult to move around. An individual's gait, use of braces, or use of crutches can make this even more of an effort. Anyone confined to a wheelchair may become uncomfortable sitting in the same position all day. Therefore, selecting a garment that feels good as well as one that looks attractive is important. This chapter discusses some guidelines to consider before buying clothes.

GENERAL CONSIDERATIONS

Because many disabled individuals have special clothing needs, following are a few basic things to keep in mind.

MOBILITY AND COMFORT. Analyze how you walk or sit. Chris, a college freshman who has cerebral palsy, spends much time traveling from class to class. Since he cannot bend his knees when making each step, he puts both crutches out in front of him. Chris must be able to move freely without his clothes restricting him in any way. Therefore, something an able-bodied person might wear may be uncomfortable for one who is handicapped.

SERVICEABILITY. Chris's clothes should be serviceable to withstand the stress from walking. Some features to look for in well-made garments are flat-fell or neatly finished seams, adequate seams with small and even stitches, underarm seams and crotches that are double stitched or reinforced, inconspicuous, even hems, matching material, and well-made buttonholes.

TYPE OF CLOTH. Select sturdy, lighter weight fabrics that help prevent fatigue and withstand stretch and pull. Always remember to buy absorbent clothing whenever possible. Cheri, a sixteen-year-old cerebral palsied high school student, drools. Since she wants to look neat at all times, she wears blouses that absorb damp spots to make herself more socially presentable. Printed material rather than plain also helps disguise dampness. Cotton, rayon, or blends of these fabrics are often recommended for disabled people to wear.

CONVENIENCE. Choose garments that are easy to take on and off and are easy to unfasten. Remember to select large roomy ones with front openings that slip over your head, or buy those with features especially made for handicapped people. For example, Chris has found slacks that he can pull on over his braces. He cannot fasten buttons, so he buys garments with other types of closings. Because of his lack of arm mobility, Chris has difficulty using hip pockets, so he must find pants with big ones on the side.

SAFETY. Look for clothes that you can move around in easily without worrying about tripping or falling. For instance, a girl with a clumsy gait should not wear a long dress that she might step on while walking which could cause her to lose balance. Some other points to remember are the following: select pants having legs that are not too wide, and buy dresses that are not too long, too full, too awkward, or too tight. Also buy clothing made of flame retardant fabric such as acrylics. Do not purchase those with brushed textures because they will ignite more quickly. Choose garments that are close fitting so that you will not be in danger when wearing them near open flames or heat.

ATTRACTIVNESS. Clothing affects the way you look, so select it wisely. This is especially important for a handicapped person, because he should purchase garments that minimize his disabilities. Color, fabric patterns, lines, and styles are four important considerations.

Bright colors attract attention; but small amounts, such as on a collar, add interest, However, wearing darker shades usually make handicaps less obvious.

Fabric patterns capture a person's eye, so be sure they enhance rather than detract from your appearance. Kate, who sits in a wheelchair, does not want people to notice the lower part of her body, and she selects printed cloth blouses and plain material for skirts.

Lines in garments draw emphasis to your body. For instance, a loosely fitted dress will disguise defects by creating an imaginary figure image. Clothing with lines that run vertically in the front of a dress may call attention to your neckline or legs, depending on the trimmings.

Finally, styles accentuate personal features, so always try to cover your irregularities. As an example, a man's boxy jacket can hide a back brace, and long shirts worn over slacks camouflage protruding hips. For women, full skirts or fullness at a raised or lowered waistline and in a yoke will conceal impairments; graceful ankle length dresses also detract from a woman's legs.

DISABILITIES AND CLOTHING

Some people with handicaps have specific dressing problems. The following are a few possible solutions for the most common of these difficulties.

CLOTHING AND CRUTCHES. There are two major concerns for those who use mobility aids: tearing clothes and keeping your shirt or blouse tucked in. Particularly for people using the underarm type of crutches, this is a real problem because constant rubbing often weakens the fabric. You can solve this in several ways: by adding a cloth patch to the underside of the garment, lining the inside with material to add strength and warmth as well as longer wear, or stitching the underarm seam with tape.

Choose materials that also wear well. Knit and stretch garments are long lasting and will not restrict body movements. Avoid tightly fitted clothes that cling to the underarm area and that do not allow you to move freely.

Keeping garments tucked in is sometimes another difficulty if you use crutches. To remedy this, buy shirts having long tails. Overblouses, bodyshirts, and sweaters hide the clothing that often becomes untucked from your waistline. Special binding with rubber strips fastened to the inside of the waistband may help keep your clothes in place.

LIMITED HAND, ELBOW, AND SHOULDER MOTION. There are four ways to simplify taking clothing on and off. Front openings reduce shoulder motion needed for dressing and undressing, use wraparound fashions when possible. Action pleats provide more fullness and flexibility, and raglan and kimono sleeves, which are larger, allow for easier movement.

Pulling on a garment is often difficult, so make this less of an effort. Buy slip-on clothes that attach buttons with elastic thread or decorative elastic on cuffs so that your hand slides through the sleeve easily. If you have limited hand use, find clothing that works the best for you, and sew easy-to-use fastenings on everything you wear. Later in this chapter five different types that some people with various kinds of hand limitations can use with less effort will be discussed.

LEG BRACES OR CASTS. Sliding trousers on over braces and casts is always difficult, so buy loose clothing that will slip over these appliances. Sewing a zipper along the inseam of your pants provides convenience. Another idea that helps is to attach a loop on the inside of your pants' waistband so that you may use large hooks to pull the slacks on.

Braces also often rub the clothes, but you can remedy this problem by stitching an extra layer of fabric on the underside of the garment. Better yet, select clothing that is lined to provide greater protection against this rubbing action.

WHEELCHAIRS. Since people confined to wheelchairs may develop pressure sores from sitting for an extended period of time, finding the right clothing can help alleviate this problem. Short length jackets and capes are practical because they do not bunch up beneath a person who is sitting in a wheelchair. Both garments are less bulky than longer styles. Full skirts and slacks also provide greater comfort for those who must be lifted out of their chairs.

EASY-ON AND EASY-OFF FASTENINGS

Fastenings on clothes present frustrating problems for some disabled people who are visually impaired, who have poor hand coordination, or who are one handed. Dressing and undressing can be a real problem. If this is your problem, do not give up. There are many solutions. Five easy to use closings are zippers, buttons, hooks and eyes, grippers, and Velcro fastenings.

ZIPPERS. When you are buying clothing with zippers, be sure the zipper is strong enough to withstand daily wear and tear. A nylon one is the best type to prevent snag. If it becomes difficult

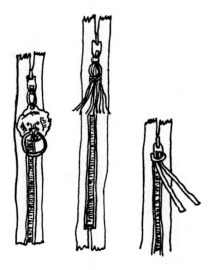

Figure 11-1.   Zippers with pulls.

Figure 11-2.   Long shank button.

Figure 11-3.   Hook and eye.

Figure 11-4.   Grippers.

for you to grasp, you can attach a pull, which may be either a fabric loop or a metal ring. As stated before, often a zipper opening is necessary for people who wear braces or casts, and if you must insert one, make certain it is long enough for the purpose and will blend with the fabric.

BUTTONS. For people with poor hand coordination, medium-sized or large buttons make it easier to take clothing on and off. Those with long shanks and smooth heads fit through the buttonhole with the least amount of effort.

HOOKS AND EYES. Small hooks are more difficult to fasten, but large ones work well. However, clothing with hooks is frequently difficult to locate and buy in large sizes.

GRIPPERS. These are usually easier to unfasten than to fasten because closing them requires considerable pressure. In order for this fastening to work the best, it should be easy to see, reach, and grasp. Grippers in the front of clothing are more convenient for the handicapped than those on the back or side of a garment, but for the severely disabled, this type of closing could present considerable difficulties.

VELCRO FASTENERS. One of the most innovative fastening discoveries in the last twenty years is Velcro, which is made of polyester hooks and nylon loops which press tightly together and peel apart with little effort. You can replace clothing fastenings with this material, which is available in ½-, ¾-, ⅞-inch widths, and 10-inch strips. Use half-inch strips in places of light stress, such as cuffs, lapels, pockets, and belt ends. Select the medium stress, ¾-inch type for dresses, jackets, and robe closings. Choose ⅞-inch, heavy stress Velcro for sportswear, coats, and belts. Ten-inch, all purpose strips are often used to prevent gaping of blouses or to provide an opening in trouser seams that can accommodate short casts or leg braces. Velcro may also be cut to size and used at the neckline for a hook and eye closing above the zipper in the back or front of a garment.

MEN'S FASHIONS

Physically disabled men often find it difficult to purchase comfortable clothing. Those who wear braces or sit in wheelchairs frequently have special problems.

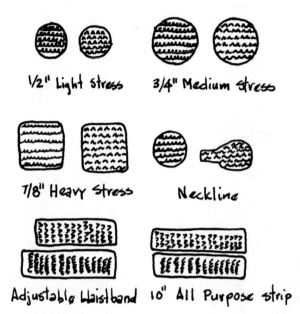

1/2" Light Stress   3/4" Medium Stress

7/8" Heavy Stress   Neckline

Adjustable Waistband   10" All Purpose strip

Figure 11-5.   Velcro fastenings. Courtesy of Talon/Velcro Consumer Education.

BRACES AND CLOTHING. One of the major difficulties, for people who wear appliances, as discussed earlier in this chapter, is finding pants that can be pulled on over them. Today some manufacturers are designing garments for the disabled with this is mind.

In the near future The Clothing Research Design Foundation plans to manufacture easy-on and easy-off denim blue jeans that are preshrunk, machine washable, and long wearing. A heavy pair of nylon zippers in the side seams of both legs allow them to be opened from either the bottom up or top down. Another good feature is an inside half-belt, which buttons just in front of each side seam so that when the side seams are unzipped the front of the pants will remain in place while the seat drops. This belt can also be reversed and the back of the pants held in place while the front part is dropped.

The Vocational Guidance and Rehabilitation Service (V.G.R.S.) is another agency that offers specially designed clothes for disabled men, such as slacks in various colors and fabrics with

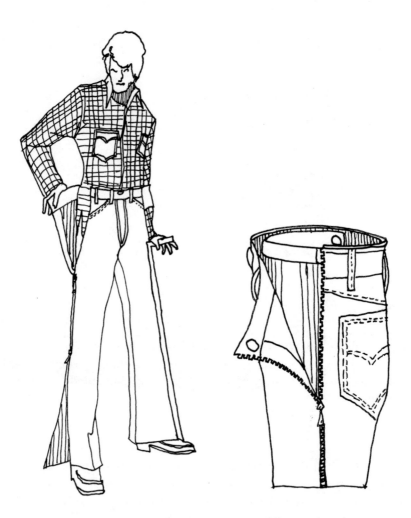

Figure 11-6.   Jeans with half-belt and zippers. Illustration furnished by Vocational Guidance and Rehabilitation Service.

right, left, or no inseam openings and with either Velcro or gripping fastenings. A man's robe is available with front openings in small, medium, or large sizes. Other types of clothing that V.G.R.S. offers are hospital gowns and night shirts with back or front openings.

WHEELCHAIRS AND CLOTHING. Often trousers designed for the able-bodied person are uncomfortable for someone who must sit in a wheelchair. As a man sits and moves, his pants frequently slide down, and his shirttail works itself out from the waist. Pockets also are often in the wrong place and unhandy to use. A topcoat may become caught in the wheel spokes. Of course, disabled men can have their clothing custom tailored, but it is quite expensive. Many cannot afford this and must buy their clothes at regular retail outlets, so here are three points to remember:

1. Look for short-length coats.
2. Select clothes with buttons in front.
3. Be sure there is no excess material to add weight or to become caught in the spokes of the wheelchair.

WOMEN'S FASHIONS

There are some special considerations to think about when buying women's clothing; following are just a few.

THE CUT IS IMPORTANT. Make sure the garment fits easily everywhere on your body, especially around the waist, abdomen, hips, and shoulders.

CHECK SLEEVE LENGTH. Choose sleeves that are short enough to remain out of the way while you work and that allow for easy movement. Three-quarter length sleeves interfere less with your work than full-length ones and are not as likely to become soiled.

CHOOSE WELL-DESIGNED NECKLINES AND COLLARS. Open necklines with low rolling collars are more comfortable. These also have fastenings that will aid in dressing, while the collars do not ride up to hinder a woman's shoulder movements as she operates her wheelchair or uses crutches. Select front-opening clothes to make dressing and undressing easier. Three-quarter length openings are the best because they prevent damage due to strain on the fasteners, which may occur if you use full-length ones.

BUY EASY-TO-CARE-FOR FABRICS. You should consider three major points when deciding what type of material to choose. First, disabled women often perspire excessively from doing household tasks. Soft, smooth cotton clothing has absorptive qualities and will not cling to their skin. Second, select fabric that is soil resistant and does not wrinkle. Such cloth helps you keep a neat appearance, even after lying down. Try to select fabric that will have minimum shrinkage to avoid a tight fit, be uncomfortable or have the possibility of tearing. Woven fabrics often have some of these same advantages.

Now that some of the general things women should consider when selecting clothes have been discussed, some of the special features to look for in buying four different types of garments will be presented.

DRESSES. Women usually buy three major types of dresses: the year-around, the shirtwaist, and the hot weather variety.

Purchase a year-round style without a belt for convenience and one that has an elasticized back, which allows for ease of movement. When trying on a garment, make sure it has hidden pleats that open when you raise your arm. Then check to see if the dress is full enough around your waist and hips. Before taking it off, stop a minute and examine the sleeves. Raglan sleeves provide room under the arm. Also ask yourself whether the front opening is large enough. Most women prefer a three-quarter-length style with a rolling collar because this is more comfortable. Remember, too, that if you have good hand coordination, snaps are more secure, easier to manage, and quicker to unfasten than buttons.

If you are thinking about purchasing a shirtwaist dress, look for an open cardigan neckline for comfort, a gored skirt with a moderate flare to allow for smooth fitting, and an underarm extension of the blouse into the sleeves to avoid tear in the seams.

In the spring and summer of the year, some women think about buying a hot weather dress. If you decide to purchase one of them, here are a few suggestions you might want to consider. Choose a sleeveless and collarless garment that can be worn with a bolero. For maximum comfort, select a moderately full skirt that has a waistline with elasticized insets at the sides. So that you will know the sleeves provide for easy arm movement, look for pleats in the back and near the arm holes. Make sure the center front opening is roomy enough; a 20-inch one can simplify dressing and undressing. For the chairbound, styles with a split-skirt back enables one to snap the skirt in front and move the split section to the back. Also, the skirt is less bulky than a wraparound.

BLOUSES. Some clothing experts suggest that raglan sleeve, hot weather, and tailored blouses are the most functional for disabled women because of their convenience features.

The raglan sleeve blouse is sometimes designed as an over-blouse to be worn out or to be tucked in. One advantage of this garment for people with a shoulder impairment is that it has no seam over the shoulders, which may be uncomfortable or unbecoming. Roomy sleeves lessen the chance for wear and tear. Pleats at the side and back provide for greater comfort, while many of these have pockets on the lower front side, which are handy.

A sleeveless hot weather blouse that is cool has no sleeve restraints and makes an ideal garment for use with shorts or pedal pushers, giving an image of a one-piece dress. However, make sure the back pleats in this garment allow for ample spread and ease of movement. The pockets located beneath the bust are stitched flat for maximum serviceability.

When shopping for a tailored blouse, purchase one that can be either tucked in or worn over your pants. To enjoy the most comfort, select those which will allow for easy reaching in all directions. This is even more important for a woman in a wheelchair, since she must do all her work from a sitting position. Also, buy blouses with side vents that adjust to your hips without creating bulk and choose ones with slippery linings below the waistline so the blouse can move up and down freely when you want to reach.

SKIRTS. Some of the most practical skirts for disabled women are the wraparound, those which are gored with side openings, or those which open in the center front.

The principle consideration with a wraparound skirt is that it be in one piece. You should choose those which have released hip darts that will enhance your figure. This garment may fasten in the back or the front, depending on your preference and disability. Someone in a wheelchair usually manages a back closing best and can drape the wraparound skirt over her body while sitting, then she can fasten it when she stands up. As previously mentioned, another good feature to look for is elasticized insets in the waistband that keep the blouse tucked in and secured by Velcro fasteners or two snaps. Finally, make sure pockets are located in a convenient place so that you can use them easily.

Simply styled gored skirts are extremely comfortable for women who must sit for a long period of time. Side front openings are less likely to buckle than ones in the center front and probably are best if you are confined to a wheelchair. Choose waistbands that fasten with strong snaps or buttons. To make a slip unnecessary, select firmly woven, soil resistant cotton fabric.

A third type of skirt is one with a center opening. If you buy this kind, remember that darts at the waistline give more comfort and easy-to-alter hip room. Check the fullness to see that the skirt will stay down, especially if you sit in a wheelchair where it could interfere with the wheels. As with other types of skirts, select the center opening that has elasticized waistbands which respond comfortably for easy, even breathing and help keep your blouse tucked in.

TROUSER GARMENTS. Slacks and pedal pushers are the two kinds of clothing that will be discussed here. Think about these few basic guidelines if you want to buy high quality and comfortable fashions.

When purchasing slacks, select those with long backs and short front rises that help relieve strain in the knee and crotch area. This also lessens lap puff, which might occur with other styles. Check to see whether there is enough adjustment in the hip, in the waist, and around the abdomen; such a fit may be accomplished with elasticized webbing, stretch fabrics, or released darts. Tapered legs with simple hems rather than cuffs are best for those who often lose their balance. If you wear braces, choose slacks with wider legs and flat inside seams so that strings from fabric will not become caught in these devices.

Some of the same general rules apply to pedal pushers. As with slacks, choose ones with long backs and short rises, but a 9-inch placket can also make dressing simpler. In addition, select fabrics that have strong, flat workmanship for quick, smooth drying and that require little or no pressing. If you do not wear braces, buy styles with shirred knees and replaceable elastic at the side seams for more length to provide for greater comfort and safety. A bias-covered waistband would allow for ease of movement.

CLOTHING CARE

When you think about the care of your clothing, there are many things to take into account. Following are some of the more important ones.

GENERAL CONSIDERATIONS. Here are a few points to keep in mind. Select garments that are washable and need little or no ironing. Permanent finishes and knit fabrics require minimal care and do not show soil or wrinkle easily. Light-colored plain materials show stains more than the printed ones do. Of course, you will not want to wear dark clothing all the time, but even light prints conceal spots better. Choose nonclinging under-garments or use antistatic agents to prevent clothes from riding up. Two of the most important rules to remember are to read the laundering instructions and make sure the garment has a guarantee. The law requires that all clothing have a tag which explains how to wash it. Some items are only guaranteed under normal washing conditions and for a certain period of time. However, when fabric does wear out in one particular spot, sew a piece of material to the underneath side for reinforcement. Sometimes large patches that you can sew onto the garment or appliqués can also add strength.

VELCRO CARE. Always close fastenings when you are not wearing the garment or when you are cleaning it because the closing may snag other fabrics if it touches them. Velcro is machine washable, and it can also be dry-cleaned. When ironing this fastening, remember to use a permanent press setting on your iron. Sometimes the fabric becomes gummy when you wear Velcro fasteners. If this happens, wipe it clean with alcohol or cleaning fluid. Lint may collect, too, on the hook portion of this fabric, so simply use the hook portion of another fastener to comb the lint free.

ZIPPER CARE. Four basic rules apply to zipper care. First, you can use an iron to press cotton fabrics. If possible, select a smaller iron so that you can get close to the zipper. Set the iron on the low setting to avoid scorching the nylon or melting the zipper. Second, shut this fastening before washing or dry cleaning your clothes so that the garment will not get caught on the center agitator in your washer. Third, you can apply wax to zippers to make them work easier. Do this everytime you wash your clothes to avoid zippers' snagging and to keep them in good working order. Finally, remember that longer openings put less strain on the fabric, so use longer ones whenever possible.

In this chapter many things people with disabilities should consider when selecting clothing have been discussed. Weekly, department stores have sales and try to lure people into buying merchandise. Do not be swayed by the fancy advertising and low prices. Remember, quality is important too. Take your time and consider each purchase carefully, following the guidelines set forth previously. (*See* also the list of clothing resources in the appendix.) Then apply these rules to your own individual needs so that you will always look your best in comfortable and durable clothing.

POINTS TO REMEMBER

1. *Think about these four principles when buying clothes: mobility, serviceability, safety, and attractiveness.*
2. *Consider the limitations of your particular disabilities as they apply to the garments you buy.*
3. *The five types of fasteners that work the easiest for disabled people are zippers, large buttons, hooks and eyes, grippers, and Velcro fasteners.*
4. *Make sure the pant legs are wide enough for men or women who wear braces.*
5. *The tails and buttons on suits often present difficulties for people confined to wheelchairs.*
6. *Check the sleeves, necklines, collars, and fabrics of all clothing.*
7. *Look for special features in ladies' dresses, blouses, shirts, and trouser styles.*
8. *Follow simple rules for clothing, Velcro fasteners, and zipper care.*

Chapter 12

CARING FOR YOUR CHILD

During her sixteenth year, Joan contracted polio and was confined to a wheelchair. However, this did not dampen her strong desire to rear children. At twenty-five, she married Jerry who had been injured in an automobile accident and now walked with crutches. Two years later, Joan became pregnant with their first child. Neither friends nor relatives supported the decision, insisting they should never have children. Even her doctor advised Joan to have an abortion during the third month.

Despite this opposition, Joan carried the pregnancy to termination and gave birth to a son. Today, he is a healthy, happy, and well-adjusted child. After this experience Joan always advises other disabled couples who are thinking about having children to explore the possibility with an open mind.

Little by little the myth that handicapped individuals are asexual is disappearing. Today more people with physical limitations are getting married and choosing to become parents. Admittedly, deciding to have a family is a big decision. What are some of the things you should think about when planning to have children? How will you cope with the many problems that can arise? This chapter will discuss some of the considerations and ways handicapped parents can make child rearing easier, rewarding, and more enjoyable.

DECIDING ON A FAMILY

Think about Genetics

If you are not sure that genetic defects caused your disability, consult a doctor or a family planning counseling service. If this is the case, without proper knowledge you could pass your handicapping condition on to your youngsters. Two examples of inherited disabilities are osteogenesis imperfecta and neurofibromatosis.

Osteogenesis imperfecta is a condition passed on through a dominant gene to the child and results in a youngster having brittle bones that break easily. For instance, Ken was born with a broken arm and leg, has had thirty-three fractures in the last twenty-three years, and is now confined to a wheelchair.

Neurofibromatosis causes tumors on a person's nerve endings. People with this health impairment have a 50-percent chance that their child will be born with a similar medical problem.

Timing

For some disabled women choosing the right time to have children is important. Judy, who had polio and spinal meningitis, knew as she grew older her physical condition would deteriorate. Therefore, when she married, instead of engaging in a career and then having children as some women do, Judy decided that if she wanted youngsters, she should have them during her younger years. Consequently, during the next four years, three daughters were born and when Judy was in her early forties, the girls were married. Now, even though she is confined to a wheelchair and has a lower energy level, Judy still operates a gift shop in a seaside town. However, if Judy had not planned this way, she might never have been able to enjoy her two greatest pleasures: rearing three beautiful daughters and operating a successful business.

Consider Your Limitations

Before you become serious about having children, consider your physical limitations and how they could affect your ability to care for them. Try to decide what you will need help with and the things you can manage alone. To assist you in making this assessment, use Table 12-I. For each child care task, simply check the appropriate column: *I Can* or *I Need Help*. This will give you a fairly good idea of your abilities.

Table 12-I
CHILD CARE ASSESSMENT SHEET

CHILD CARE	I CAN	I NEED HELP
1. Lifting child	⎯⎯	⎯⎯
2. Carrying youngster.......................	⎯⎯	⎯⎯
3. Holding infant	⎯⎯	⎯⎯
4. Preparing formula	⎯⎯	⎯⎯
5. Feeding baby	⎯⎯	⎯⎯
6. Burping infant	⎯⎯	⎯⎯
7. Bathing child............................	⎯⎯	⎯⎯
8. Putting oil on baby	⎯⎯	⎯⎯
9. Powdering the youngster	⎯⎯	
10. Positioning for changing diapers	⎯⎯	⎯⎯
11. Fastening diapers	⎯⎯	⎯⎯
12. Unfastening diapers	⎯⎯	⎯⎯
13. Dressing an older child	⎯⎯	⎯⎯
14. Supervising play activities	⎯⎯	⎯⎯
15. Disciplining youngster	⎯⎯	⎯⎯

What if you are not sure whether you want children? You might want to talk with some mothers with disabilities similar to your own. Find out what some of their difficulties were and how they coped with them. You may also wish to consult a doctor or an occupational therapist.

After you make a careful analysis of your abilities and if you decide to have children, vow to handle the problems as they arise and not worry. For example, if you are chairbound do not be overly concerned about how you will discipline your child if he is unruly. After all, he may be shy and not adventuresome. Remember also that child development is a gradual process. First, your youngster learns to sit up without assistance. Then he may or may not start to crawl before beginning to walk. Since children grow slowly, you can stay alert for these signs and have plenty of time to prepare before the child reaches a certain age. Do not forget that planning at the right time is intelligent, but often planning prematurely invites needless worry.

WATCH THE MINUTES

Your children are only young once, so spend as much time with them as possible. However, there are always those routine tasks to perform, so here are two ideas on how you can get more time with your baby during the first few months of his life. To begin with, have your spouse and the other children assume an increasing amount of the household duties. If they grumble, simply tell them you need time to spend with the new arrival. Second, when there are younger children in the home, think about enrolling them in a preschool program. This will give you more free time during the day so that you can have those extra minutes to be with your baby.

SELECTING CHILD CARE EQUIPMENT AND PROCEDURES

Some General Guidelines

A study of 100 disabled mothers conducted by the School of Home Economics of the University of Connecticut revealed that there were six major problem areas for handicapped mothers. These included lifting, bending, stooping, grasping, carrying, coordination,and lack of strength. If you have one or more of these problems, be sure to select child equipment carefully. According to Neva R. Waggoner and Garland W. Reedy, two home economists specializing in home management for the physically disabled, homemakers should ask the following questions before purchasing child care equipment.

1. Can you manage the equipment?
   a. Is it adjustable in height?
   b. Will you be able to move it easily?
   c. Do the controls, if any, manipulate without too much effort?
2. Are you able to use the equipment for different purposes over an extended period of time?
   a. Is it sturdy and durable?
   b. Is it adaptable to the rapid growth of your child?
   c. Is it easy to care for?
3. Does the equipment help promote the early independence of your child?

4. Is it safe for both you and your youngster?*

Your Baby's Bed

One of the first pieces of furniture most parents think about buying is a baby's bed. Therefore, it is important to discuss some of the features to look for when purchasing two common types.

BASSINETS. Bassinets provide a place where your baby can sleep and be fed and changed. Although the infant will outgrow it in about six months, most mothers want to use a bassinet since it keeps their children warmer than a standard bed. For chairbound mothers, locate the bassinet approximately 1 foot off the floor. Be careful also that you do not put this bed too close to the floor since you never want your baby to become chilled with cold drafts of air.

CRIBS. When purchasing a crib, choose one with care. Most full-sized cribs are manufactured from wood or steel. Unfortunately, you cannot allow for knee height to accommodate a wheelchair mother. On some kinds the mattress adjusts to facilitate easier lifting. Following are some things to consider when selecting a crib.

Size. The small three-quarter size is versatile and fits well in most apartments and small houses. Handicapped mothers frequently leave their babies in these cribs and use them for playpens. Furthermore, they can easily be pushed from room to room and adjusted for height without too much effort. If you set the mattress at the lowest level, a child can climb in and out of the crib independently.

Construction. Be sure the crib is well made to withstand the abuse your child will give it. This is also important if you have impaired balance, since you may need to grasp the railings for support. An additional feature to look for is solid head and foot panels, which add to the stability.

Casters. If a crib has oversized swivel casters, this will make it easier for the disabled mother to move it about.

---

*Adapted from N.R. Waggoner and G.W. Reedy, *Child Care Equipment for Physically Handicapped Mothers,* Storrs, Connecticut, University of Connecticut, School of Home Economics, no date, p. 55.

Height adjustments. Many smaller cribs have adjustable legs. Remember, too, that you should select one where you are able to raise and lower the mattress to prevent stooping or bending.

Adjustable springs. Larger cribs often have notches so you can raise and lower the level of the springs. This valuable feature enables you to set the springs at the top level of approximately 29 inches. With a 3-inch mattress, an ambulatory mother usually can work at a height of 32 inches comfortably. If you are confined to a wheelchair, 31 inches is desired. Consequently, adjust the springs to a 28-inch level, then use a 3-inch mattress.

Drop-down sides. Purchase a crib with drop-down sides. With this feature, you can place the crib anywhere in the room and also put your baby inside with minimal effort. This is important, since some handicapped mothers cannot use cribs without drop-down sides.

Latches. For disabled mothers, one of the principle concerns should be whether or not the latches on your baby's crib will lock securely and are easy to manage. Depending on your limitations, you may want to choose one of these four basic types:

1. *Hand buttons* work best for people with good use of both hands, since they can fasten the latch on either of the two ends at the same time. However, hand buttons are very difficult for a mother with the use of one hand to operate, but they are ideal for someone with no upper extremity limitations.
2. *Toe releases* lower the sides of some cribs. Many one-handed mothers can work this type well, while obviously someone in a wheelchair could not.
3. *Knob into slot locks* are excellent for keeping the infant in the crib. However, you must have considerable finger strength and dexterity to use the latch.
4. *Recessed safety locks* are located on the crib and are quite safe for the child. However, you need fairly good hand control to fasten them.

One convenient type of crib for handicapped mothers is the Port-a-crib®. You can raise or lower the mattress level, and the crib's legs retract so that you are able to use it as a play area. The hinged sides swing down for easy access. In addition, there is still enough room underneath for the foot pedals of a wheelchair.

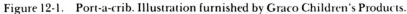

Figure 12-1.   Port-a-crib. Illustration furnished by Graco Children's Products.

Your Youngster's Playpen

When purchasing a playpen, always consider where you will locate it in your house, since it may be difficult to unfold, fold, and put away. Some handicapped mothers cannot manage the folding kind without assistance.

Most playpens are built of wood, steel, or aluminum. Remember to select one that is sturdy and that will withstand your child's shaking it. As with the crib, some disabled mothers need to grab the railings for support when lifting the child. If this is your case, check the catches; make sure they lock securely. Be certain that you have the coordination and dexterity to operate them yourself. Do not forget that you can move the playpen more easily if it has swivel casters.

Some handicapped mothers cannot stoop to pick up their child from inside a commercially built playpen. A wheelchair mother could also have this difficulty. Raising it 27 inches off the floor and installing a gate solves the problem. The following are the directions for modifying a crib:

1. Cut a 24-inch gate into rail on the rigid side of the pen.
2. Add a bottom rail to form gate.
3. Fasten 1-inch butt hinges in center.
4. Fasten latch on the post side.
5. Cut the legs the maximum height desired.
6. Drill holes 6 inches apart in old and new legs.

7. Position a ¼-inch bolt with a wing nut at the desired height.
8. Replace the center leg.
9. Install casters.

Gates for Safety

Many disabled mothers are unable to move swiftly to rescue their children from accidents. In these cases it is a good idea to install safety gates to close off stairways that might present a hazard and to keep your youngsters from entering any potentially dangerous areas around the house. There are many popular types of safety gates. One of them is the Nu-Line® mesh pressure gate (Model 202), which can be purchased with either smooth plastic or vinyl-coated mesh. Different sizes fit door openings between 27 and 48 inches wide. You can choose one 26 or 33 inches high. A pressure bar mechanism holds these gates in place, while rubber bumpers eliminate the possibility of marring or slipping.

Figure 12-2.   Nu-Line Mesh Pressure Gate. Illustration furnished by Nu-Line Industries.

Toileting Your Child

When it is time for toilet training a child, some disabled mothers start thinking about the equipment they will purchase and the techniques they will use. For instance, one method handicapped parents who cannot bend may use is to ask the child to jump while they assist with lifting.

SPECIAL SEATS. Some mothers with physical impairments might wish to buy a specially designed child's toilet seat. You can lay one type, the Protect-o® seat ring trainer, on the stool each time your youngster goes to the bathroom. When choosing any toilet seat, be sure it is made of durable, heavy-grade, acid-resistant material.

NURSERY CHAIRS. Handicapped parents might prefer to use a toilet or nursery chair because they are at the youngster's own height. Using these enables children to slide off and toilet themselves without their parents' having to lift them. You can also place the chair anywhere that is convenient. If you are unable to reach this lower level, you can put the chair on a platform and

Figure 12-3.   Protecto Seat Ring Trainer. Illustration furnished by Reliance Products.

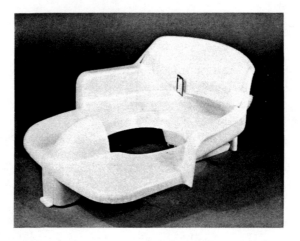

Figure 12-4.   Nursery chair. Illustration furnished by Reliance Products.

raise it up to your height. Purchase one that is sturdy enough so
your youngster will feel secure when sitting in the chair. Some
have a tray or a safety strap to hold your child in place and prevent
him from falling.

PORTABLE URINALS. If you have a boy, one excellent way to
teach him independence is showing him how to handle a
portable urinal. Since these are lightweight and do not spill
easily, your son can learn to use this and empty it himself.

Your Baby's Bath

When bathing their infants handicapped mothers might want
to use specially designed equipment. As with other types,
carefully analyze your needs and the extent of your limitations.
To simplify bathing your child, you should set aside a particular
area in your home and find a place where you can store the
equipment at a comfortable height for you.

SMALL TUBS. Easy-to-lift lightweight plastic tubs are probably
one of the simplest pieces of equipment to use when bathing your
baby, since they do not require much space to store away. Some
oval models have a slanted bottom that enables your infant to sit
safely in the water without support from his parent. One feature
to look for is a tub with a plastic pad inside to prevent your child
from slipping. If the type you have does not, put a towel under the
youngster to serve the same purpose.

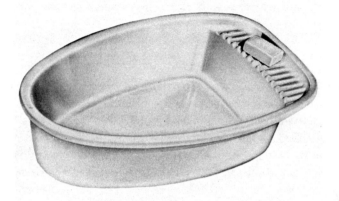

Figure 12-5.   Plastic infant bathing tub. Illustration furnished by Lustroware, Borden, Inc.

THE KITCHEN SINK. Some handicapped parents may like to bathe their infants in the sink, since it is easy to fill and drain. When using this method, remember to put a rubber mat on the bottom of the sink to keep your child from slipping. It is also wise to cover the ends of the faucets with rubber tips to protect your baby's head if he bumps them. If possible, you should also store bathing supplies nearby for convenience. Finally, mothers who can stand or sit on a high stool usually can use a sink easier than someone in a wheelchair who might find this tiring unless the sink is lower than the standard 36 inches.

TUB BATHING. Other handicapped parents might wish to bathe their children in the family tub. When needed, they can often use special techniques to make this task easier. For example, they could sit on a stool or put it inside for their children to use to raise the youngsters to a desired height. This latter point is a particularly good suggestion for mothers confined to wheelchairs. Some chairbound parents can also move alongside the tub to bathe their child. One final advantage is that a bathtub is easy to fill and drain.

Safety is important, so make sure to instruct your youngsters always to hold onto the grab bars when getting in and out of the tub. You can also put a wet cloth or a small towel on the rim to provide a degree of stability. Additionally, as with the kitchen sink, using a nonskid mat is another safety measure.

Feeding Your Baby

Many handicapped mothers prefer to breast-feed their infants not only because it is more healthy for the child but because this eliminates having to prepare a formula and having to wash dirty bottles. However, when feeding your baby fruit juices or water, you will need to use special equipment.

BOTTLES. Most bottles are made of heat-resistant plastic or glass. Be sure to select ones that have wide mouths, since you can fill and clean them with less effort. For someone with hand limitations, lids that screw rather than pull off may be easier to use. If you want to eliminate washing bottles, you might consider purchasing the Playtex Nurser Kit®, which has disposable bottles, holder, and accessories. However, even though they are lighter in weight than glass bottles and no sterilization is necessary, they can be difficult to assemble for someone with hand impairments.

PLASTIC INFANT SEATS. Many handicapped mothers find plastic infant seats quite handy. Most of these are padded and will support a baby's back while elevating his head. Parents often hold these seats in their lap or prop them on a chair or sofa. One kind is the contoured Maxi-Mite® Baby carrier, which is extra wide and deep and also has a luxurious wraparound cushion. The multiposition stand swings up to serve as a sturdy carrying handle that locks into place for safety.

HIGH CHAIRS. High chairs will put your infant at a convenient height for feeding. Most models are made of fiberglass or wood and have seats that are padded. When selecting a high chair, there are four things to consider. First, check the legs. Choose chairs with legs adequately supported with crossbars. Second, a high chair should have footrests to provide your child with the most comfort. Third, look for a well-constructed tray. One manufactured of strong plastic that you are able to adjust is ideal. Some feeding tables have swing-away trays, which are often easier for disabled mothers to manage; you need only to release one side,

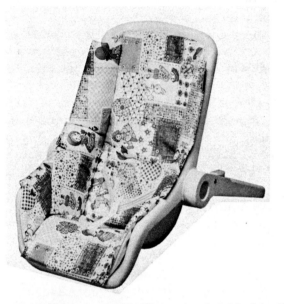

Figure 12-6.   Maxi-Mite baby carrier. Illustration furnished by Questor Juvenile Furniture Company.

Figure 12-7.   Sidewinder high chair. Illustration furnished by Questor Juvenile Furniture Company.

and it drops down over the arm of the chair. Finally, for safety be sure the high chair has a strap that when fastened, will prevent your child from sliding out of the seat but still does not hold him too securely so he cannot move. A soft-cushioned webbing or plastic strap that fastens back of the seat is easiest for a handicapped mother to manage.

The Sidewinder™ high chair has some of these features, including a Squeeze-Ease latch mechanism that you can release with one hand. The extra wide and deep tray lifts up and then swings downward. However, when it is in place, you can wipe the tray clean with little effort. The armrests, too, provide for maximum comfort. A safety strap will hold your child securely in place to prevent him from falling.

FEEDING TABLES. Disabled mothers may want to use feeding tables because they are more convenient. These may also serve as play surfaces. Select one that you can move on casters. Choose a table manufactured of wood, metal, or fiberglass, which has a stain-resistant top; some also fold for storage. One good feature to look for is a model with adjustable legs. Sometimes these will telescope into several different positions. For instance, they may slide from 21½ inches to 28½ inches. You can then adjust the table to suit your needs. Finally, do not forget to give the same considerations to safety straps and footrests as you would when purchasing a high chair.

One type is the Baby-Tenda® safety feeding table, which has a seat that reclines where you can place the child in a comfortable position when he is three or four weeks old. Your youngster is then completely surrounded in a tip-proof unit. You can also use it for a high chair, and in this position you can adjust the model to fit about any size child. Furthermore, the legs of the feeding table are adjustable in three positions. This device is made by the Baby-Tenda Corporation.

Dressing Your Infant or Toddler

Since some handicapped parents find it difficult to dress their infant or toddler, begin teaching the child as young as possible to dress himself. According to a University of Connecticut Home

Economics study, children can put on and take off specially designed garments at an early age. Many of the same considerations discussed in the last chapter on clothing also apply to buying garments that youngsters can put on themselves.

Another way to make dressing easier for your sons or daughters is to select furniture they can use conveniently. Its proper placement in the dressing area is important to allow for easy movement.

Some handicapped mothers choose to dress the baby on a portable dressing table, in a crib or carriage, or on their laps. Even an older child can often jump or hop on a wheelchair mother's lap so that she will not have to lift him. If you choose to use this procedure, it is helpful to arrange the child's clothing on a chair nearby beforehand.

Carrying Your Little One

Did you ever stop to think that when you give birth to a baby its life is in your hands? Particularly if you have upper extremity weakness, incoordination, or mobility problems, you should think about this whenever you lift or carry your baby. Mary, an arthritic, still remembers the day she almost had an accident.

One morning, she walked over to Debbie's crib, stooped, and put the baby in her arms, then started carrying the child into the kitchen. Half-way across the room, she felt pain in her right knee and the joint locked. She stood there forty-five minutes until her husband came home and took Debbie from her. During that time Mary worried, concerned she might tire and drop the child. After this, whenever Mary moves her daughter, she puts her in a carriage and wheels her from place to place, so that such a mishap will not happen again.

There are many ways to carry a youngster. If you have good arm use, hold the child on your hip on the same side as your good functioning arm. Use the pelvis to distribute weight and to reduce strain on your arm. Remember, too, when handling the child, do it slowly, making sure you have a firm grasp on your youngster.

SELECTING A CARRIAGE. When you are considering purchasing a carriage, be sure it is well constructed and has good springs and large wheels that will roll over small items without upsetting. Some carriages even have removable beds, a factor worth considering. In choosing those with beds, make certain you can grasp the handles to lift the bed from the carriage. If your balance is good but you have poor grasping ability, you may be able to tow the carriage. Simply tie a belt to the handle bars then around your waist. This will enable you to pull the carriage along as you walk. However, do not forget that you should remain at the center of the handle bars for maximum control.

One type of carriage is the Strolee® travel trio (Model No. 543), which is extra large and has an exclusive Glide-O-Flex™ suspension system for a smooth ride.

GERRY® KIDDIE PACK. The Gerry kiddie pack distributes children's weight evenly, and a strap suspension holds your youngster in place. You can adjust the waist strap to keep your youngster in a secure upright position. This pack has a hinged, wide angle stand for stability, and it also converts to a baby chair.

Figure 12-8. Strolee Travel Trio. Illustration furnished by Strolee of California.

Figure 12-9. The Gerry Kiddie Pack. Illustration furnished by LL. Bean, Inc.

Manufactured of strong, lightweight tubing, this carrier has nylon shoulder straps and a sturdy canvas carrier. Storage for diapers or other items is provided underneath the seat.

DIAPERING YOUR CHILD

Caring for an infant's diapering is one of the most repetitive jobs for every mother, so since it may be difficult for you if you have physical limitations, you should always purchase convenient equipment and find the best method for doing this chore.

Changing Your Baby

A TABLE ON WHEELS. If you are chairbound, you could find

changing diapers on your lap awkward. To solve this problem you might want to use a table on wheels (*see* the section on carrying without spilling in Chap. 6). These tables make transferring the child fairly easy. If you cannot lift your baby onto the table, you can place a board between the crib and table to slide the infant across. Of course, be sure it is smooth and has no splinters.

FASTENINGS. For some mothers with hand limitations, fastening diapers can be difficult. Parents with weak fingers may find it impossible to push the pins through cloth, so they can use soap to lubricate the ends, which makes the pins glide through the material easier. In other cases, a person might wish to sew Velcro fasteners on the youngster's garments.

Diaper Pails Are Sometimes Handy

In Chapter 8 diaper pails were discussed, but now they will be dealt with in greater detail. Enamel ones with a foot lever that lifts up the lid often work well for mothers with impaired hand and arm use. Although you need not have a strong grasp to open them, you must be able to lift out the inner pail. Another alternative is the less expensive lightweight plastic kind, which can also be easy for you to carry. Remember when selecting one to make certain the lid does not fit too tightly so that you can lift it off with ease.

Cloth Diapers or Disposable Diapers?

Washing diapers is a laborious and time-consuming task for anyone, but this may be more of an effort for a handicapped parent. To eliminate the chore from your daily routine, use either of these two ways. First, you might try disposable diapers, such as Pampers®. In the past, mothers often claimed that the diapers leaked, but some manufacturers now say this is not a problem. However, some people warn that if you use disposable diapers over a long period of time your infant may develop a rash on his buttocks. Second, if you can afford the expense, hire a diaper service to pick up, wash, fold, and return the items to your home.

PLAY EXPERIENCES AND THE DISABLED MOTHER

As your child grows older, you probably will want to participate in and monitor his play activities. Certain ones can be
shared, while others are only supervised. You can fulfill your role
as a parent to oversee, plan, and engage in various play
experiences with your child.

Supervising Outdoor Play

For handicapped mothers with severe mobility limitations,
supervising outdoor play can be difficult and requires a little
ingenuity. Karen, confined to a wheelchair, had a clever plan for
monitoring the activities of her twins when they were outdoors.
Their play area was in the back yard, enclosed with a sturdy high
fence and a gate that she kept locked for safety. The only entrance
to this area was through the house. This gave her complete
control over her girls.

DOORS AND YOUR YOUNGSTERS. You can give your children
freedom at certain times, but not at others, by placing a low
handle on the door along with a hook high above that you can
unfasten on proper occasions.

MONITORING CHILDREN'S PLAY. Some mothers with severe
physical impairments must oversee their youngster's outdoor
play activities from inside the house. If this is your problem, try
one of these solutions.
1. Use a whistle to summon your children at various times.
2. If your child can tell time, mount a clock outdoors for his
   use.

Active Indoor Play

When supervising your children's play activities is difficult,
you may wish them to play indoors most of the time. If you decide
on this plan, be prepared to allow your children to make noise in
the house. Do not take this normal pleasure away from them.
Learn to tolerate the noise. One way to accomplish this is to set a
specific time each day when your child can engage in active play.
Many mothers find they can withstand the noise better if they

join in their child's fun and games. Most children are also happier when they are playing near their mothers. Consequently, you might want to arrange your child's play area close to where you are working to make supervising the youngster easier.

TEACH YOUR CHILD TO CLEAN UP. From an early age start teaching your child that all toys have a place, and he should store them away when he finishes playing with them. There is no point for you to exert effort when your youngster could put playthings away himself. However, do not forget that young children do not have the same attitude about order and neatness as you might, so encourage and teach them.

Some youngsters may not know how to begin when it is time to pick up their toys. To help your son or daughter and to guide the child through the process, you could say, "Pick up the doll clothes, now the doll furniture, next the blocks," and so on. Stand or sit near your youngster to give encouragement. Show that you care about what your boy or girl is doing. Usually, guiding your child through the cleaning up process is better than the general statement "Clean up your room."

SELECTING TOYS. All parents should think about safety when buying toys for children, but this is especially important for disabled parents, since they are often less able to react speedily in emergency situations. A good rule to remember is to never purchase anything on impulse, but always read the label carefully, especially when buying things made of plastic, which can break and leave sharp edges or points that might hurt the child. Do not buy any glass items. While plastic toys are hazardous, some toys have wires in them which could puncture children. Wires holding the toy together are also potentially dangerous if metal pieces are exposed. Another thing to avoid is a toy with small parts because a child could swallow them. Some cheaply made toys also have small pellets inside, which infants or toddlers might put in their mouths.

Enjoying the Outdoors

Some disabled parents may feel it is impossible to explore the outdoors with their children, but this is not necessarily so. Today many of our nation's state parks have accessible trails for people confined to wheelchairs. However, even if you cannot go into the woods or wade in streams, you can still open a child's eyes and ears to the mystery, wonder, and beauty of growing things. Remember to use your children's formative years to expose him to his natural surroundings. In this way, youngsters can develop a better appreciation of nature.

ANIMAL OR INSECT VISITOR'S HOUSE. Many children love animals and like to bring them indoors. The problem with this habit is that you must teach the child that some animals cannot survive inside over a long period of time. On the other hand, you may want to provide a safe place where a child can keep animals for a few days. To do this, build a *visitor's house* or terrarium with netting, glass, and masking tape. The reason for calling it a visitor's house instead of a terrarium is to impress on your son or daughter that the visitor can only stay in your house a little while.

HOUSEHOLD PETS. Encourage your children to have household pets. They may enjoy guinea pigs, hamsters, birds, white mice, and fish in preference to the common dog and cat. Giving your child a pet and teaching him to care for it helps teach him responsibility.

Sharing Musical Experiences

No matter what the extent of their physical limitations is, most handicapped mothers can share some musical experiences with their children. From infancy youngsters love soothing music. One early musical game you can play with your child is patty-cake. Remember, if you develop a sense of appreciation for good music, much of your son's or daughter's desire for loud noise, banging, whooping, or yelling, may be satisfied.

INSTRUMENTS. An important thing to keep in mind when purchasing instruments for your child is that having no instrument is better than having a poor one. For instance, the toy varieties are usually disappointing to children, since they often cannot be tuned accurately and may have an unpleasant sound. On the other hand, resonator bells frequently satisfy a youngster, since they have a good sound quality.

You need not always purchase expensive instruments, since you can make some yourself. Children may pound out a beat on pie tins. A small barrel will serve as a good drum, particularly if part of an inner tube from an old tire is stretched tightly across one end. Finally, clothes pins in a cardboard carton make a good rattle.

When your child grows older, he may become curious about the piano. If you have one and your son or daughter starts exploring the different parts, do not worry because the child probably will not damage it. If possible, you should learn to play and demonstrate the instrument to your youngster. This could help eliminate your child's haphazard banging on the keys and may spark a desire for him to study music seriously in the future.

SINGING TOGETHER. One pasttime that many disabled parents can participate in with their chldren is a sing-along. To begin with, teach your child songs that are easy to remember, such as "Polly Wolly Doodle."

At an older age, why not teach your youngster folk songs? Some like "I've Been Working on the Railroad" and "Twinkle, Twinkle Little Star" can be sung in rounds. Singing games associated with body movement in songs may also be fun for both young and old, for example, "Here We Go 'Round the Mulberry Bush (This Is the Way We Wash Our Clothes)."

LISTENING. Develop an appreciation for good music by listening to it with your child. Buy a phonograph and remember that you can teach children to handle records carefully. Let them learn to choose and to play the ones they enjoy.

Creative Art Activities

Art experiences are relatively easy to provide. This is a creative way of giving children an opportunity for self-expression. You do not need elaborate equipment for a son or daughter to enjoy art: simple materials, such as a blackboard, chalk, crayons, water colors, finger paints, paste, scissors, and clay, can give hours of enjoyment. On the other hand, you should set limits on when and where to use these items. Show your child how to use them; however, do not be too rigid by dictating what your child should create. Let him feel free to express himself.

BLACKBOARDS AND CHALK. A youngster can spend much time with a few pieces of chalk at a blackboard. Teach him how to use a sponge as an eraser so that he can clean the slate without assistance. For easy supervision you might want to place the blackboard in the kitchen or wherever you do most of your housework.

CRAYONS. Crayons help your son or daughter develop imagination and creativeness. This is even more true if your child does not use a coloring book. To keep the youngster from breaking crayons, buy the heavy, unbreakable kind. When only short pieces remain, scrape them together and mash them between two pieces of waxed or freezer paper. Your child then can rub a warm iron back-and-forth over the paper to make a beautiful design.

WATER COLORS. You can purchase water colors in powder form and mix them yourself. Use a jar with a lid for this purpose. Fill it half full with an equal amount of paint and water. Some disabled people who have difficulty stirring can pick up the jar and shake it. Depending on what your limitations are, this might be impossible, so you may want to put the powder in a mixing bowl and use an egg beater.

When painting, some youngsters like to work on a tabletop, while others prefer standing at an easel. Whatever your child's preference, do not allow him to dip his brush into all the paint at once since he might spill it. Instead, put a smaller amount in a container.

If you intend to supply your child with an easel, you do not need to purchase an expensive one. Simply make one from a cardboard box, and cut it from corner to corner in triangular shape. Then, using an apron to protect his clothing, a flat brush about ½ inch wide, a jar of water to clean the brush, and an old sponge or paint cloth, your child is ready to start painting.

FINGER PAINTING. Finger painting is fun for any age group, and it requires little equipment or skill. Of course, you can buy commercial finger paints but to save money use this recipe.

¼ cup laundry starch
1 cup cold water
1 envelope of unflavored gelatin
2 cups hot water
½ cup mild soap flakes or synthetic detergent

Stir the starch along with 1 cup of cold water in a bowl. Add hot water to the mixture, and cook it over medium heat until the substance comes to a boil. Keep mixing constantly. Then remove the mixture from the heat and stir in the gelatin that has been soaking for five minutes in ¼ cup of water. Add the soap or detergent and stir until it is thoroughly dissolved and the mixture has thickened. If desired, you can add coloring.

PASTE. Many children like to stick things together. Of course, you can buy commerical brands of paste, but you can make it at home yourself using 1 cup of laundry starch and 1 cup of water. After mixing these ingredients together, add 2 gallons of boiling water and stir until the substance has become transparent. When cooled, the paste is ready to use. Show your youngster how to hold the sheet of paper at the corners and pull it through the paste until both sides are covered. Having done this, the child can then put the sheet on a large piece of dry paper and press carefully until the sticky sheet has adhered to the dry one. Your youngster can then stick things such as flowers, seeds, leaves, sticks, feathers, grains of sand, cereals, yarn, ribbon, or cotton on the sheet or make any kind of design. If you wish to have a tinted background, mix a small amount of food coloring into the paste after it has been cooled.

FREE-HAND CUTTING. You can let your child use scissors with blunt points at an early age. This type will not scratch furniture or harm the youngster. However, teach your son or daughter how to use them. Remember, even many two-year-olds have the ability to use scissors successfully. Children begin cutting around edges of paper; then after awhile, the youngster will begin to make more complicated designs.

PLAY WITH CLAY. Often you can satisfy a child's desire for getting down in the dirt by giving your youngster a ball of clay with which to play. In addition to developing your child's creative ability, this increases coordination and builds strength in his hands and arms.

PLAY MATERIALS AROUND THE HOUSE. As stated earlier, you do not need to spend much money on art supplies. In fact, you can find many around the house that will provide your child hours of enjoyment (see Table 12-II).

Youngsters Enjoy Stories

Providing you do not have much speech difficulty, you will be

Table 12-II
HOUSEHOLD PLAYTHINGS

Sewing And Clothing

Wooden packing crates	Spools	Aluminum foil
Orange crates	Buttons	Seed catalogs
Apple boxes	Scraps of material	Sears-Roebuck catalog
Cardboard mailing tubes	Old coats	Wallpaper
Milk cartons	Trousers	Magazines
Egg boxes	Nylon stockings	Shirt cardboards
Qt. or pt. containers	Ribbon	Paper plates
Suit boxes	Sequins	Old road maps
Candy boxes	Crinoline	Paper napkins
Cigar boxes	Yarn	Tinsel rope
Hat boxes	Darning needles	Paper cups
Shoe boxes	Embroidery thread	Paper doilies
Match boxes	Cotton thread	Crepe paper
Plastic cheese boxes	Leather straps	Cellophane tape
Bias tape	Old calendars	Colored felt
Tissue paper	Dress-up clothes	Stencil papers
Old felt hats	Paper straws	Socks for soft dolls
Construction paper	Old pieces of fur	Tracing paper
Gold stars		

Miscellaneous

Kitchen Items

Pipe cleaners	Food coloring	Glass tumblers
Old toothbrushes	Drinking straws	Dye for coloring eggs
Feathers	Clothesline	Linoleum blocks
Marbles	Nut cups	Bar of soap
Wire coat hangers	Old wooden bowls	Steel wool
Lollipop sticks	Cake mix	Cake tins
Orange sticks	Macaroni	Muffin tins
Wire	Salt	Lids
Wire screening	Beans	Cookie sheet
Chicken wire	Sponge	Mixing bowl
Shells & pebbles	Birthday candles	Pots & pans
Artificial flowers	Candle pieces	Egg beater
Aquarium	Sugar	Beans to plant
Pocket mirror	Coffee cans	Corks
Lollipops	Gallon cans	Envelopes of seeds
Balloons	Vegetable cans	Bottle caps
Pine cones	Vegetables	Bottles
Christmas tree balls	Cookie cutters	Alphabet soup macaroni
Pencils	Washboards	Alphabet cereal
Nail file	Soap powder	Marshmallows
Sachet powder	Rolling pin	Gumdrops
Absorbent cotton	Clothes pins	Plastic bags
Cup hooks	Fruit jars	Measuring cups
Paper clips	Whisk broom	Measuring spoons
Plywood	China plates	Rice

Table 12-II continued

Miscellaneous	*Kitchen Items*	
Ink Pad	Toothpicks	Wooden or paper spoons
Comb		

From Jessie Wall, *Play Experiences Handicapped Mothers Can Share with Young Children.* Published in conjunction with the University of Connecticut, Storrs, Connecticut.

able to tell your child stories. Over the last several years fewer parents do this, but it can be quite stimulating for the youngster. You may create a tale that helps share experiences with your child or could stress important moral values. Furthermore, encourage your son or daughter to also tell stories himself, and when the child does, make certain you plan time to listen. To help your youngster develop story-telling ability, you might start one, then ask the child to complete it. This helps children learn to plan, think, and create.

Some parents enjoy reading to their youngsters. As your child grows older, he may enjoy various types of material: classic stories, folklore, animal tales, cowboy and Indian yarns, as well as others. Remember, reading to your boy or girl when s/he is young may cultivate an enjoyment of literature later in life.

But how do you judge what is good reading material for children? Here are six questions to ask yourself when making an evaluation.

Is the content wholesome and worthwhile?

Are the ideas well expressed?

Does the book fit your child's interests or develop new ones?

Will your child want it himself?

How likely is your youngster to treasure, read, and reread the story?

Does the book have good printing and illustrations?

EXPLAINING YOUR DISABILITY

One day your child might ask you about your disability. If he does, do not avoid the questions, but answer them forthrightly. After all, the youngster should be aware of the special considerations regarding your health. For example, some handicapped mothers may become overly tired and need rest in the afternoon. In such cases, these parents should make their youngster aware of why the child ought to be quiet during those times. Furthermore, as your son or daughter grows older, continue to counsel him/her concerning your limitations.

Explaining about your physical limitations should begin when your child is young. Remember, do not make your explanation too technical. Always adapt it to the age level of your child. Here are two suggestions and illustrations for accomplishing this goal.

USE LANGUAGE YOUR YOUNGSTER CAN UNDERSTAND. Be straightforward and use words that convey your message to the son or daughter simply. Dotty did this when Bobby asked about her limitations. One Sunday afternoon at a church picnic, he and some of his friends were preparing to run a race. Suddenly, before Bobby began he ran over to Dotty who was sitting in a wheelchair.

"Mommy, why can't you get up and run this race against our team like my friends' mothers?"

Dotty was prepared for Bobby's question and knew she probably would have to answer this query someday.

"You know, Bobby," she began, "I have sat in this wheelchair ever since you were born. I cannot walk like other mothers. I probably will never be able to. A car hit me when I was a little girl. I have no feeling in my legs and cannot move them."

"I'm sorry Mom," Bobby replied, putting his arms around her. "I still love you."

Dotty's explanation seemed to satisfy her son, because he asked no further questions.

TALK ABOUT THE MEDICAL ASPECTS OF YOUR DISABILITY. Depending on the age of your youngster, you might want to explain the medical aspects of your disability to him. Bill responded this way to his son Jim, while they were building a go-cart in the shop one day.

"Dad," Jim asked, "Would you wheel your chair around to the end of that sawhorse and hold this board?"

"Sorry, son; my hands are too weak to hold anything today."

"Why Dad? You never told me the reason."

"When I was twenty-three I contracted multiple sclerosis. At times this disease affects me worse than at other times. For instance, this morning my hands are weak. If I were to hold the board now, I might drop it."

THE TASK OF DISCIPLINE

When disciplining a child, parents with physical disabilities might encounter special problems. For example, your youngster might try to run from you, thinking that you cannot catch him. Three-year-old Mike did this when he and his father, Joe, were passing by the courthouse.

"I'm going to climb those steps," Mike declared as he left Joe's side.

"Come here, Mike. Come here!"

"You can't catch me. You can't catch me," he said looking back at his father.

"Oh, yes I can, Mike. That's what you think." Then Joe got out of his chair and on his hands crawled up the steps. Finally, he caught Billy by the leg and on the courthouse steps gave him a spanking.

Other chairbound parents use different methods. One mother who reared four children had a standing rule: If her children tried to get away from her when she started to reprimand them, she would give them one spanking for running and an additional one for the offense. Another father who walked with crutches always told his child when the youngster threatened to disobey, "If I can't catch you now, I will catch you later, and when I do you will be punished."

BUILD YOUR CHILD'S RESPECT. Since it may be difficult for some disabled parents to physically discipline a child, from an early age teach your youngster to respect your wishes so he will obey you. Remember, children know by the time they are three or four months old when you express displeasure with their actions. Then gradually most youngsters learn to respect your wishes. On the other hand, if you fail to reprimand children when they are small, you may have a much bigger problem when they are older.

USE A SENSE OF HUMOR. You can sometimes use a sense of humor to help discipline. Judging by one of the experiences of Barbara, a mother of two and confined to a wheelchair, it worked well in one situation. Often, when her children became obnoxious and Barbara and the youngsters began yelling at each other, it reached the point where it was really funny. On some occasions, all three of them would sit down and laugh about it.

One other example of where humor worked well for Barbara was the morning she yelled at her daughter from the bottom of the staircase, "Linda! Clean the upstairs bathroom."

"But, Mom, I'm late for school. I'll clean it when I get home."

"No, you'll do it now. You're just trying to get out of your work."

"Oh, Mom, I'll do it later."

"No Linda, you must . . ." Before Barbara finished her sentence, Darlene, her other daughter, came up and tugged on her skirt to ask a question. Barbara, who should have lowered her voice to answer the question, instead turned around and without thinking screamed "OK!" Darlene, who thought this was quite an unusual response, started to laugh. Then Linda, also giggling, said, "Mom, I guess if you're going to raise your voice when talking to Darlene because of something I didn't do, I'd better get busy right now."

TEACH SELF-RELIANCE

For all children, learning to become self-reliant is important, but for youngsters of handicapped mothers, it may be vital. There are two good reasons for this. First, a disabled person may be limited or unable to perform all the tasks around the house himself, and second, the youngster should learn to accept responsibility. A good illustration of the first point was Carol's arthritic condition. Depending on how she feels on a certain day, she may or may not be able to do any housework since her joints could be painful. In fact, on certain occasions she was confined to bed for two weeks at a time. Luckily, she had taught her teenage daughters to cook and clean house. As early as age five, they had learned to make a bed, and when her children reached seven, they could operate a vacuum.

At what age should you give your children responsibility? The best guideline to remember is to watch to see when your child is physically able to perform the tasks and has shown a desire for wanting to help. Usually, a youngster's willingness to assist and to be independent is at its height when the child is three or four, so take advantage of this time and teach him to do things for himself.

Do not confuse self-reliance with dependence. In other words, no child likes to feel he is a servant to a disabled parent. To avoid this, do all you can for yourself and only ask for help when it is absolutely necessary.

Today more and more disabled couples are choosing to become parents. A person's having physical impairments does not necessarily rule out this possibility. Being a mother or father can be one of the most wonderful experiences of a lifetime, so if you have this strong desire even though you are physically limited, it may be possible for you to enjoy the rich rewards of being a parent.

POINTS TO REMEMBER

1. *Before deciding to have children, consider the genetic background of your family.* Consult your doctor for advice.
2. *Choosing the right time to give birth to a child may be a consideration for some handicapped mothers.* Some physical conditions are progressive, and the woman may become more disabled as she grows older. In such cases, she may wish to have her youngsters early in her marriage.
3. *Think about whether or not you will physically be able to care for children.* Talking to other disabled mothers may help you decide. After you have thought about this matter carefully and made a decision, do not worry about the problems you might encounter before they arise.
4. *Plan to use your time to the best advantage.*
5. *Two popular types of infant beds are bassinets and cribs.* Select these carefully.
6. *Shop carefully for your youngster's playpen.* Consider where you might place it in your home.
7. *Safety gates prevent children from going into hazardous places.*
8. *There is special equipment for toileting your child.* You can use a special toilet seat, nursery chair, or portable urinals for boys.
9. *Set aside a particular area in your house for bathing your child.* Choose a place that is of a comfortable height. This

might include either a small plastic lightweight tub or a family bathtub.

10. *Feeding an infant requires forethought.* Decide what type of bottles you wish to use. You may also want to use a plastic seat for feeding.

11. *Look for certain features when purchasing a highchair.* Check to see that it has sturdy legs. Make sure to buy one with adequate footrests. Be certain the chair has a well-constructed tray.

12. *Many mothers like to feed their child on an easy-to-move feeding table.*

13. *Think about how you will diaper your child.* You can change your baby on a table on wheels. Some disabled mothers must find special ways to fasten diapers. Using a diaper pail can be handy. Consider a laundry service or disposable pants.

14. *Teach your child to dress himself at an early age and purchase clothes he can put on independently.*

15. *You might want to carry your child one of several ways.* These can include using infant chairs, a kiddy carrier, or baby buggy.

16. *Blowing a whistle to summon your children or mounting a clock outdoors so your youngster will know to report to you are two ways of making supervising their play easier.*

17. *If you cannot oversee your youngster's active play, have him play indoors.* Teach the child to pick up his playthings and store them away in the proper places. Remember, also, to select safe toys for your son or daughter.

18. *Help your youngster enjoy the outdoors.* Build a visitor's house. Encourage your child to have pets.

19. *Share musical experiences with your child.* Select quality instruments, sing together, and listen to quality music.

20. *Provide creative art activities for your youngster.* These can include using blackboards and chalk, drawing with crayons, painting with water colors, finger painting, pasting, free-hand cutting, and playing with clay.

21. *Inspire your child to enjoy good literature.* Read to your youngster, and tell him original stories.

22. *When children ask questions about your disability, answer them.* Use simple language. You might want to explain the medical aspects of your disability.

23. *Discipline youngsters from the time they are small.* Teach them to respect your wishes.

24. *Help you child to become self-reliant.* Begin when sons or daughters are young. However, do not unnecessarily rely on youngsters to do things for you.

APPENDICES

APPENDIX A

CLOTHING SUPPLIERS

BAKA MANUFACTURING COMPANY, INC.
7-11 Cross Street
Plainville, Massachusetts   02762

Catheter leg strap—"Dale Combo C. L. S." Eliminates tape and pins. Catalog available.

CHICK ORTHOPEDIC COMPANY
821 75th Avenue
Oakland, California   94621

Boot fits over lower extremity cast. Available in small, medium, or large sizes. Write for information.

FASHION-ABLE
Rocky Hill, New Jersey   08553

Supplier of clothing for physically disabled men and women. Catalog available.

HANDEE
7674 Park Avenue
Lowville, New York   13367

Supplier of clothing with special features for the disabled. Brochure available.

LEINWEBER, INC.
Brunswick Building
69 West Washington Street
Chicago, Illinois   60602

Custom tailor of suits designed for men in wheelchairs. Information folder available.

SOLVE GARMENTS INC.
Box 123-B
Bayport, Minnesota   55003

Ready-to-wear clothing for the disabled. Catalog available.

TEXTILE RESEARCH CENTER
Box 4150
Lubbock, Texas   79409

Clothing design patterns for people confined to wheelchairs. Brochure available.

VELCRO CORPORATION
41 East 51st Street
New York, New York   10022

Suppliers of Velcro. Write for information.

VOCATIONAL GUIDANCE
AND REHABILITATION SERVICES
2239 East 55th Street
Cleveland, Ohio   44103

Supplier of garments for those with physical impairments. Catalog available.

APPENDIX B

MANUFACTURERS, DISTRIBUTORS, AND RESOURCES

Below is an alphabetical listing of manufacturers, distributors, and other resources useful to disabled people. Many of these companies supplied photographs included in this book, which is greatly appreciated.

American Stair-Glide Corporation
4001 East 138th Street
Grandview, Missouri   64030

American Standard U. S. Plumbing Products
River Road and Centennial Avenue
Piscataway, New Jersey   88854

Baby-Tenda Corporation
911 State Line Avenue
Kansas City, Missouri   64101

Benhar Products Company, Inc.
5825 National Blvd.
Culver City, California   90230

Bernina Sewing Machine Company, Inc.
70 Orchard Drive
North Salt Lake, Utah   84054

L.L. Bean, Inc.
Freeport, Maine   04033

Bonny Products, Inc.
1175 West Broadway
P.O. Box 356
Hewlett, New York   11557

The Cheney Company
3015 South 163rd Street
New Berlin, Wisconsin   53151

Cleo Living Aids
3957 Mayfield Road
Cleveland, Ohio   44121

Cosco Home Products
2525 State Street
Columbus, Indiana   47201

Davol Inc.
Box D
Providence, Rhode Island   02901

Delta Faucet Company
931 East 86th Street
P.O. Box 40668
Indianapolis, Indiana   46240

Ekco Housewares Company
9234 West Belmont Avenue
Franklin Park, Illinois   60131

Everest and Jennings, Inc.
1803 Pontius Avenue
Los Angeles, California   90025

Farberware
1500 Bassett Avenue
Bronx, New York   10461

Fulton Corporation
Fulton, Illinois   61252

Graco Children's Products
Eleverson, Pennsylvania   19520

Geddis Inc.
Dunedin, Florida

General Electric Company
1285 Boston Avenue
Bridgeport, Connecticut   06602

Grayline Housewares
1616 Berkley Street
Elgin, Illinois   60120

Hamilton Beach Division
Scovill Manufacturing Company
Scovill Square
Waterbury, Connecticut   06720

Help Yourself Aids
Box 15
Brookfield, Illinois   60513

M. E. Heuck Company
P.O. Box 23036
Cincinnati, Ohio   45223

Hobart Corporation
Troy, Ohio   45374

Hutzler Manufacturing Company, Inc.
Route 7 And Grace Way
Canaan, Connecticut   06018

International Paper Company
P.O. Box 555
Shawnee Mission, Kansas   66201

Lady Seymour Housewares
Lear Siegler, Inc.
Ninth and Chestnut Streets
Seymour, Indiana 47274

Lustro-ware Division
Borden Chemical, Borden Inc.
1625 West Mound Street
Columbus, Ohio   43223

Manville Manufacturing Corporation
5722 Tujunga Avenue
North Hollywood, California   91601

Maytag Corporation
Newton, Iowa   50208

Miles Kimball Company
41 West Eighth Avenue
Oskosh, Wisconsin   54901

Nesco Products, Inc.
650 Conklin Road
Binghamton, New York   13903

New York University Medical Center
Institute of Rehabilitation Medicine
Occupational Therapy Service
400 East 34th Street
New York, New York   10016

Nu-Line Industries
214 Heasley Street
Suring, Wisconsin   54174

Oster Corporation
5055 North Lydell Avenue
Milwaukee, Wisconsin   53217

J. A. Preston Corporation
71 Fifth Avenue
New York, New York   10003

Project Threshold
Rancho Los Amigos Hospital
7601 East Imperial Highway
Downey, California   90242

Questor Juvenile Furniture Co.
Kantwet Division

1801 Commerce Drive
Piqua, Ohio   45356

Regal Ware, Inc.
1675 Reigle Drive
Kewaskum, Wisconsin   53040

Reliance Products Corporation
108 Mason Street
Woonsocket, Rhode Island   02895

Rubbermaid Incorporated
1147 Akron Road
Wooster, Ohio   44691

Sears Roebuck & Company
Los Angeles, California   90051

Stanley Vemco
5740 East Nevada
Detroit, Michigan   48234

Strolee of California
19067 South Reyes Avenue
Compton, California   90221

Surburbanite
2 Central Street
Saxonville, Massachusetts   01701

Sunbeam Corporation
5400 West Roosevelt Road
Chicago, Illinois   60650

Tappan Appliances
250 Wayne Street
Mansfield, Ohio   44901

Texas Feathers Incorporated
P. O. Box 1118
Brownwood, Texas   76801

Toastmaster
Mc-Graw Edison Company
1200 St. Charles Road
Elgin, Illinois

Unique Efficiency
732 Valley Road
Upper Montclair, New Jersey   07043

Waring Products Division
Dynamics Corporation of America
New Hartford, Connecticut   06057

White-Westinghouse
Appliance Company
930 Fort Duquesne Boulevard
P. O. Box 716
Pittsburg, Pennsylvania   15222

Zim Manufacturing Company
2850-56 West Fulton Street
Chicago, Illinois   60612

SUGGESTED READINGS

PHYSICAL DISABILITIES

Aitken, George T. (Ed.): *Selected Lower-Limb Anomalies: Surgical and Prosthetics Management.* Washington, D.C., National Academy of Sciences, 1971.

Bleck, Eugene E., and Nagel, Donald A.: *Physically Handicapped Children: A Medical Atlas for Teachers.* New York, Grune and Stratton, 1975.

Bardossi, Fulvio: *Multiple Sclerosis: Grounds for Hope.* 381 Park Ave. South, New York, Public Affairs Committee Inc., 1971.

Cobb, Aldrena Beatrix: *Medical and Psychological Aspects of Disability.* Springfield, Illinois, Thomas, 1973.

Downey, John A., and Dooling, Robert C.: *Physiological Basis of Rehabilitation Medicine.* Philadelphia, Saunders, 1971.

Hardy, Richard E., and Cull, John G.: *Severe Disabilities: Social and Rehabilitation Approaches.* Springfield, Illinois, Thomas, 1974.

Hirschberg, Gerald G., Lewis, Leon, and Vaughan, Patricia: *Rehabilitation: A Manual for the Disabled and Elderly,* 2nd ed. Philadelphia, Lippincott, 1976.

Ince, Laurence P.: *The Rehabilitation Medicine Services.* Springfield, Illinois, Thomas, 1974.

Jokl, Ernst: *The Clinical Physiology of Physical Fitness and Rehabilitation.* Springfield, Illinois, Thomas, 1958.

Kramer, Diane: *Kinematics for the Handicapped: A Professional Handbook.* New York, Exposition Press, 1973.

Krusen, Frank Hammond: *Handbook of Physical Medicine and Rehabilitation,* 2nd ed. Philadelphia, Saunders, 1971.

Love, Harold D., and Walthall, Joe E.: *A Handbook of Medical, Educational, and Psychological Information for Teachers of Physically Handicapped Children.* Springfield, Illinois, Thomas, 1977.

Nichols, Philip, and Russell, John: *Rehabilitation Medicine: The Management of Physical Disabilities.* London, Butterworths, 1976.

Rusk, Howard A.: *Rehabilitation Medicine,* 4th ed. St. Louis, Missouri, Mosby, 1977.

PERSONAL CARE

Eastern Paralyzed Veteran's Association: *Spinal Cord Injury Manual,* 432 Park Ave. South, New York, no date.

Kondrasuk, Rosemary; Fahland, Beverly; and Stryker, Ruth P.: *Self-Care for the Semiplegic,* Minneapolis, Minnesota, Sister Kenny Institute, 1977.

Krenzel, Judith R., and Rohrer, Lois M.: *Paraplegic and Quadriplegic Individuals (Handbook of Care for Nurses)*. 333 N. Michigan Ave., Chicago, Illinois, The National Paraplegia Foundation, 1966.

Lawton, E. B.: *Activities of Daily Living for Physical Rehabilitation*. New York, McGraw-Hill, 1963.

Roach, William L.: How to put on socks, trousers, and shoes with "hook sticks." *Accent On Living, 17:*54-55, Fall 1972.

Sister Kenny Institute: *Nursing Care of the Skin*, 1800 Chicago Ave., Minneapolis, Minnesota, 1975.

KITCHEN PLANNING

Burton, Alice M.: *Easy to use Mixing Center*. Lincoln, Nebraska, University of Nebraska College of Agriculture and Home Economics, no date.

———: *Easy to use Kitchens*. Lincoln, Nebraska, University of Nebraska College of Agriculture and Home Economics, no date.

———: *Easy to use Cooking and Serving Center*. Lincoln, Nebraska, University of Nebraska College of Agriculture and Home Economics, no date.

———: *Easy to use Sink Center*. Lincoln, Nebraska, University of Nebraska College of Agriculture and Home Economics, no date.

Chasin, Joseph, and Saltman, Jules: *The Wheelchair in the Kitchen*. 7315 Wisconsin Ave., Washington D.C., Paralyzed Veterans of America Inc., 1973.

Continuing Education in Home Economics, University of Alabama: Plan safe, convenient kitchen for disabled. *On Your Own. 1:*1, February 15, 1971.

Continuing Education in Home Economics, University of Alabama: Three Work Centers Needed in the Kitchen. *On Your Own. 1:*1-2. February 22, 1971.

McCullough, Helen E., and Farnham, Mary B.: *Kitchens for Women in Wheelchairs*. Urbana, Illinois, University of Illinois, 1961.

United States Department of Housing and Urban Development, *Designing Kitchens for Safety*. Washington D.C., United States Government Printing Office, June 1976.

Wheeler, Virginia Hart: *Designing Kitchens for the Handicapped Homemaker*. New York, The Institute of Physical Medicine and Rehabilitation, New York University Medical Center, no date.

COOKING

Baron, Henrietta: *Everybody Can Cook: Techniques for the Handicapped*. Seattle, Washington, Special Child Publications, 1977, vol. 1.

Continuing Education in Home Economics, University of Alabama: Cooking via microwaves: assistive to the handicapped. *On Your Own. 8:*1-2. June 1978.

Foott, Sydney (Ed.): *Kitchen Sense for Disabled or Elderly People*. London, William Heinemann Medical Books Ltd., 1976.

Kondrasuk, Rosemary, and Grendahl, Beth: *Homemaking Aids For The Disabled*. Minneapolis, Minnesota, Sister Kenny Institute, 1967.

Klinger, Judith Lannefeld: *Mealtime Manual for People With Disabilities and The Aging.* Box (MM) 56, Camden, New Jersey, Campbell Soup Company, 1978.

CLEANING

Burton, Alice M.: *Cleaning Supplies: Keep Them Handy,* Lincoln, Nebraska, University of Nebraska College of Agriculture and Home Economics, no date.

Disabled Living Foundation: *Cleaning Equipment: A Guide Towards Choosing Equipment For The Physically Handicapped.* 346 Kensington High St., London, W. 14, no date.

Grant, Russell W.: Principles of Rehabilitation, London, E. & S. Livingston Ltd., 1963. pp. 37-43.

LAUNDRY

Bevacqua, Katherine, M. Gerhold, Marilyn Q., and Ruth, Honey Ruef: *Sewing and Housecleaning Units for Cardiac Homemakers,* University Park, Pennsylvania, Pennsylvania State University, 1960.

Continuing Education in Home Economics, University of Alabama: Careful Arrangement Facilitates Laundry Tasks, *On Your Own,* 8:1-2, April, 1978.

Continuing Education in Home Economics, University of Alabama: Homemaker Can Do Family Laundry, *On Your Own, 1:2,* May 17, 1971.

Continuing Education in Home Economics, University of Alabama Simplify Home Laundry, *On Your Own, 2:1,* 1972.

Disabled Living Foundation: *Laundry Equipment: A Guide Towards Choosing Equipment For The Physically Handicapped.* 346 Kensington High St., London, W. 14, no date.

McCullough, Helen E.: *Laundry Areas: Space Requirements and Locations,* One East Saint Mary's Road, Champaign, Illinois, University of Illinois, 1957.

Woman's Day: Complete home laundry center and how to plan it. *Woman's Day Kitchen and Bath Guide, 1:65-80,* May 1978.

STORAGE

Agan, Tessie, and Luchsinger, Elaine: *The House: Principles/Resources/Dynamics,* rev. ed. Philadelphia, Pennsylvania, Lippincott, 1965.

Bradford, Barbara Taylor: *The Complete Encyclopedia of Homemaking Ideas.* New York, Meredith Press, 1968.

Burton, Alice M.: *No-Stoop, No-Stretch, Kitchen Storage,* Lincoln, Nebraska, University of Nebraska College of Agriculture and Home Economics, no date.

Continuing Education in Home Economics, University of Alabama: Proper Kitchen Storage Can Save You Time. *On Your Own. 3:1,* February 1973.

Laird. Jean E.: *Around The House Like Magic.* New York. Harper & Row. 1967.

United States Department of Health. Education. and Welfare. *Can Your Kitchen Pass The Food Storage Test?* Washington D. C.. United States Government Printing Office. 1977.

Rasbach. Roger: *The Provident Planner: A Blueprint for Homes. Communities and Lifestyles.* New York. Walker & Company. 1976.

Tasker. Grace E.: *More Space for Storage.* Ithaca. New York. New York State College. 1973.

STRUCTURAL MODIFICATION

Anio. E.. and Loversidge. R. D. Jr.: *Access For All: An Illustrated Handbook of Barrier Free Design For Ohio.* Columbus. Ohio. The Ohio Governor's Committee on Employment of the Handicapped and Schooley Cornelius Associates. Architects/Engineers/Planners. 1977.

American Society of Landscape Architects Foundation: *Barrier Free Site Design.* Washington D. C.. United States Government Printing Office. 1976.

Burton. Alice M.: *The Bathroom Made Safe and Usable.* Lincoln. Nebraska. University of Nebraska College of Agriculture and Home Economics. no date.

Cary. Jane Randolph: *How To Create Interiors For The Disabled.* New York. Pantheon. 1978.

Chasin. Joseph: *Home In A Wheelchair.* Paralyzed Veterans of America. 7315 Wisconsin Ave.. Washington D. C.. 1977.

Continuing Education in Home Economics. University of Alabama: Bathroom Storage: Adaptations For Persons Who Are Handicapped. *On Your Own.* 6:1-2. January 1976.

Foott. Sydney: *Handicapped At Home.* 28 Haymarket. London. Design Council. 1977.

Goldsmith. Selwyn: *Designing For The Disabled.* London. Riba Technical Information Service. 1963.

Gutman. Ernest. M.. and Gutman Carolyn. R.: *Wheelchair To Independence: Architectural Barriers Eliminated.* Springfield. Illinois. Thomas. 1968.

Mace. R. L.. and Laslett. B.: *An Illustrated Handbook of the Handicapped Section of the North Carolina Building Code.* Special Office for the Handicapped. Department of Insurance. Raleigh. North Carolina. 1977.

Mace. R. L.: *Accessibility Modifications.* Special Office for the Handicapped. Department of Insurance. Raleigh. North Carolina. 1976.

Montalvo. A. and Weitzman. M. R.: *Bathroom Facilities Accommodating the Physically Disabled and the Aged.* Ann Arbor. Michigan. University of Michigan. 1977.

Schweikert. Harry A.. Jr.: *Wheelchair Bathrooms.* Paralyzed Veterans of America. 7315 Wisconsin Ave.. Washington D. C.. no date.

United States Housing Assistance Administration: *Housing For The Physically Impaired: A Guide for Planning and Design.* Washington D. C.. United States Government Printing Office. 1968.

United States Department of the Army: *Design For The Physically Handicapped.* Washington D. C., Military Construction Civil Works, 1976.

CLOTHING

Hoffman, Adeline M.: *Clothing for the Handicapped, the Aged, and Other People with Special Needs.* Springfield, Illinois, Thomas, 1979.

Rusk, Howard A., and Taylor Eugene J.: *Functional Fashions for the Physically Handicapped.* Department of Physical Medicine and Rehabilitation, New York, New York University-Bellevue Medical Center, 1959.

Talon Consumer Education and Velcro Corporation: *Convenience Clothing and Closures.* 41 East 51 Street, New York, no date.

United States Agricultural Research Service. *Clothes for the Physically Handicapped Homemaker With Features Suitable for All Woman.* Washington D. C., United States Government Printing Office, 1974.

Yep, Jacquelyn: *To Fit Your Needs (for the physically limited).* Ames, Iowa, Iowa State University, 1974.

CHILD CARE

May, E. E.: A letter to mothers who are disabled. *On Your Own,* 1:1—2, March 22, 1971.

Waggoner, N. R., and Reedy, G. W.: *Child Care Equipment For Physically Handicapped Mothers.* Storrs, Connecticut, University of Connecticut, School of Home Economics, no date.

Wall, Jessie S.: *Play Experiences Handicapped Mothers May Share With Young Children.* Storrs, Connecticut, University of Connecticut, no date.

United States Department of Health, Education, and Welfare. *Young Children and Accidents in the Home.* Washington D. C., United States Government Printing Office, 1977.

MISCELLANEOUS

Braunel, Laura M., James, Carole A., Stovall, Janice D.: *M. S. Is a Family Affair.* 2023 W. Ogden Ave., Chicago, Illinois, The National Easter Seal Society For Crippled Children And Adults, 1972.

Bruck, Lilly: *Access: The Guide To A Better Life For Disabled Americans.* New York, Random House, 1978.

Dickman, Irving, R.: *Independent Living: New Goal for Disabled Persons.* 381 Park Ave., South, New York, Public Affairs Committee, 1975.

Gilbert, Arlene E.: *You Can Do It from a Wheelchair.* New Rochelle, New York, Arlington House, 1973.

Hodgeman, Karen and Warpeha, Eleanor: *Adaptations and Techniques for the Disabled Homemaker.* rev. ed. Minneapolis, Minnesota, Sister Kenny Institute, 1973.

Klinger, Judith Lannefeld: *Self-Help Manual For Arthritis Patients,* 475 Riverside Drive, New York, The Arthritis Foundation, 1974.

Lowman, Edward W., and Klinger, Judith Lannefeld: *Aids To Independent*

Living. New York. McGraw-Hill. 1969.

May, Elizabeth E., Waggoner, Neva R., Hotte, Eleanor B.: *Independent Living for the Handicapped and the Elderly.* Boston, Massachusetts, Houghton Mifflin Co., 1974.

Robinault, Isabel Pick, (Ed.): *Functional Aids for the Multiply Handicapped.* Hagertown, Maryland, Medical Department, Harper and Row, 1973.

Washam, Veronica: *The One-Hander's Book: A Basic Guide To Activities of Daily Living.* New York, John Day Co., 1973.

INDEX

A

Abilities, analysis of, 9-13
Accessibility checklist, 261-262
Acne, 49
Adjustable Helper shelf, 221
Ambulatory disabilities, 16
Analyze daily tasks, 90, 95
Antiperspirant, 49
Aphasia, 17, 29
Appropriate location for work, 91, 95
  accessible location, 91
  comfortable location, 91
  height factor, 91
  safety factor, 91
Armchairs, 246
Arthritis, 22-25, 30
  beds for persons suffering from, 244
  defined, 22
Artificial limbs, types of, 27
Assistance, call for, 91-92, 96
Ataxia, 24-25
Atherosclerosis, 17, 29-31
Athetosis, 24
Attendant, 19, 88
  firing, 86
  hiring, 85-86
  manner of payment, 84
  relationship with, 85
  rolling over in bed, 32-33
  services rendered by, 84-85
  sitting up in bed, 34-35
Automatic dryer, 194-195, 206
  accessible filter, 195
  advantages, 194-195, 206
  cooling cycle, 195
  electric, 195, 206
  front-loading, 193, 195
  gas, 195
  installation cost, 195
  large knobs, 195
  selecting right model, 195
Automatic washing machine (*See* Washing
  machine)

Awkward gait, 16

B

Babies (*See* Child care)
Baby-Tenda safety feeding table, 292
Back brush, 53-54
Back dryer, 54-55
Banking procedures, analysis of abilities
  for, 13
Bar stool, 109-110, 113
Basic figuring, analysis of abilities for, 13
Basinet for baby, 283, 308
Bathing aids, 49-54
Bathing hints, 49-54
Bathing of baby, 288-290, 308-309
  kitchen sink, 289
  small tubs, 288-289
  tubs, 289-290
Bathing of spinal cord injured persons, 21
Bathroom laundry, 181
Bathroom storage, 225, 228
  blotters in medicine cabinet, 225
  frequently used articles, 225
  hooks, 225
  peeling labels, 225
Bathrooms, 231-242, 263 (*See also specific
  topics*)
  accessories, 241-242, 263
  bathtubs, 238
  electric outlets, 242
  faucets, 240-241
  lavatory, 236-238, 263
  lighting, 242
    switches for, 242
  linen closet, 242
  medicine cabinets, 241
  overhead exhaust fan, 235
  questions to be answered in designing,
    231
  safety bars, 235
  size, 232, 263
  toilet, easy-to-use, 232-235, 263
  toilet paper holder, 241-242

towel racks, 241-242
wheel-in stall shower, 239-240
window, 240
Bathtub (*See* Tub)
Beating foods, 142-146, 165-166
Bedrooms, 242-245, 263
  beds, 243-244
  chairs, 245
  closets, 243
  design considerations, 242-243
  doorways, 251
  furniture, 243-245
  Gatch spring, 244
  hospital bed, 244
  lamps, 244
  linens, 245
  mattress pads, 244
  mattresses, 244 (*See also* Mattresses)
  mirrors, 244
  night tables, 244
  signal bell, 244
  windows, 243
Beds, 32-36, 243-244
  comfort, 87
  making up, 178
  mobility of spinal cord injured, 21
  moving forward and backward, 35-36
  rolling over, 32-34
  sitting up, 34-35
  wheelchair transfers in and out of, 36-38
Beds for babies, 283-284, 308
  adjustable springs, 284
  basinets, 283, 308
  casters, 283
  construction, 283
  cribs, 283, 308
  drop-down sides, 284
  height adjustments, 284
  latches, 284
  Port-a-crib, 284-285
  size, 283
Belts, 215
Better-Grip wooden reacher, 169
Biological clocks, 90
Blackboards and chalk for children, 300-301, 309
Bladder control, 19
Bladder infections, 46
Bladder stones, 46
Blankets, 217
Blenders, 131-132, 165

base height, 131
container, 131
controls, 131
Blouses
  hot weather, 275
  raglan sleeve, 275
  tailored, 275
Blue jeans, 271-272
Bonny Top-Off jar opener, 123, 125
Bony spurs, 23
Bottle and Can Dispenser, 222
Boutonniere, 23
Bowel care, 46-48, 87
  agents, 47-48
  chemicals, 47-48
  digital stimulation, 47
  enemas, 48
Bowel control, 19
Bowl holder, 119-120, 139, 165
Braces (*See* Leg braces and casts)
Bread holder, 121-122
Breadboard, 122
Breaking an egg, 146-147, 166
  dropping, 146-147
  fingertips, 146
  separation, 147
  upright position, 147
Broom holder, 226-228
Broomstick closet rod, 216-217
Buttoners, 68-69
Buttons, 269-270, 278
  devices for, 68-69

C

Can openers, 125-128, 165
  electric, 125-127
  manual, 127-128
Carafes, 141, 165
Card Dialer for telephone, 257, 264
Cardiac conditions, 16, 28-31 (*See also* Heart disease)
Care of body, 32-88, 321-322 (*See also* *specific topics*)
  attendant, hiring and firing of, 84-86, 88
  bed, 32-36, 87
  bowel care, 46-48, 87
  cosmetics, 62-64, 87
  dressing guidelines, 68-73, 87-88
  drinking aids, 80-83, 88
  eating with less effort, 73-80, 88

eyeglasses, 67-68, 87
hair grooming, 59-60, 87
manicuring nails, 56-59
shaving, 60-62, 87
skin, 48-56, 87
tooth decay prevention, 64-67, 87
urinary management, 42-46, 87
wheelchair transfers, 36-42, 87
Care of child (*See* Child care)
Care of clothing, 277-278
  general considerations, 277
  Velcro, 277
  zippers, 277-278
Carpeting (*See* Floor coverings)
Carports, 247, 263
Carriage for baby, 293-294
Carrying child, 293-295, 309
  carriage, 293-294
  Gerry Kiddie Pack, 294-295
Carrying items, 26-27
Carrying pans, 28
Carrying without spilling, 114-115, 163
Casts (*See* Leg braces and casts)
Catheters
  changes, 43
  Foley, 43
  indwelling, 43, 45-46
  retention type, 43
Catheter kit, 43
Catheterization, 19, 30
  equipment, 44
  females, 42-43
  males, 42-45
  menstrual flow, 49
  need for, 42
  procedure, 44-45
  twice daily irrigation, 45-46
Cerebral anoxia, 17
Cerebral hemorrhage, 17
Cerebral palsy, 3-4, 17
  definition, 24
  incoordination, 24
  types, 24
Cerebral thrombosis, 17
Cerebrovascular accidents, 17
Cervical region damage, 19
Chair lift, 258-261, 264
  porch lift, 261
  stairway chair lift, 258-259, 264
  wheelchair platform lift, 258, 260-261, 264

wheelchair stair lift, 258-260, 264
Chairs in bedroom, 245
Changing baby, 295-296
Changing work habits, 93-94, 96
  body position, 93
  end product, 94
  equipment, 93
  place of work, 93-94
  range of motion, 93
  raw materials, 94
Checking account procedures, analysis of
  abilities in, 13
Cheese cutter, 134-135
Cheney Wheelchair Lift II, 260
Child care, 279-310, 325 (*See also specific topics*)
  analysis of abilities, 13
  assessment sheet, 280-281
  bathing baby, 288-290, 308-309
  bed for baby, 283-284, 308
  carrying child, 293-295, 309
  deciding on a family, 279-281, 308
  diapering child, 295-296, 309
  discipline, 306-307, 310
  dressing child, 292-293, 309
  equipment selection, 282-295, 308
  explaining parent's disability, 304-305, 310
    language understood by child, 305
    medical aspects, 305
  feeding baby, 290-292, 309
  free time for, 281-282
  gates for safety, 286, 308
  general guidelines, 282-283
  major problem areas, 282
  play experiences, 297-304, 309
  playpen, 285-286, 308
  procedures, 282-295
  self-reliance, 307-308, 310
  toilet training, 287-288, 308
Children (*See* Child care)
Cholesterol level, 29
Choose good time for work, 95
Circuit breakers, 254
Clay for children, 302, 309
Clean-up Caddy, 226-227
Cleaning, 167-179, 323
  attitude about, 175, 179
  bed making, 178
  canes, 169, 179
  dust accumulation, avoidance of, 173,

179
  dusting, 172, 176, 179
  easier performance, 173-175
  equipment, selection of, 167-172
  flexibility in standards, 174
  floor care, 177-178
  improvement in methods, 174-175, 179
  kitchen, 175-176
  long-handled dustpans, 168-169, 179
  mop holder, 226-228
  mop pails, 170-172
  mops, 170-171, 179
  mop sticks, 169, 179
  new commercial products, 175
  organization of work, 173, 179
  picking up objects, 176
  pickup scissors, 169, 179
  plan order of work, 174
  polishing, 172, 179
  select proper tools, 174
  simplifying each chore, 175-178
  think about one chore at a time, 174
  vacuum cleaner, 167-168, 178
  wiping up spills, 177
Cleaning supplies, 226-229
  aids, 226-228
  broom and mop holder, 226-228
  Clean-up Caddy, 226-227
  disabilities to be considered, 226
  duplicate items, 226
  easy access, 226
  location, 226
Cleaning tasks, analysis of abilities for, 10-11
Cleaning up after meals, 162-165
  portable dishwasher, 163-164
  sponge-head dish mop, 163, 165
  suction bottle brush, 163, 165
Closet storage space (*See* Home storage areas)
Closets, 243
  doorways, 251
  linen, 242
Cloth diapers, 296
Clothes-folding clips, 184
Clothesline drying of clothes, 195-196, 206
Clothing, 265-278, 325
  accentuation of personal features, 267
  attractiveness, 266-267, 278
  bright colors, 266
  care, 277-278

comfort, 265
convenience, 266
crutches and, 267
disabilities and, 267-268, 278
easy-on and easy-off fastenings, 268-270
  (*See also* Easy-on and easy-off fastenings)
fabric patterns, 266
general considerations, 265-267, 278
leg braces or casts, 268, 278
limited hand, elbow and shoulder motion, 267-268
lines in garments, 266-267
men's fashions, 270-273 (*See also* Men's fashions)
mobility, 265, 278
safety, 266, 278
serviceability, 265, 278
storage (*See* Home storage areas)
taking off and putting on, 69-70
type of cloth, 265-266
wheelchairs, 268, 278
women's fashions, 273-278 (*See also* Women's fashions)
Clothing Research Design Foundation, 271
Clothing suppliers, 313-314
Coat hanger covers, 216
Coffee table, 246
Colace, 47
Comfortable clothing (*See* Clothing)
Comforters, 216-217
Commode chairs, 40-41
Communication handicap, 17
Confidence, 6-7
Congenital abnormalities, 18
Continental Grater 'n Bowl, 136-137
Cooking, 114-166, 322-323 (*See also* specific topics)
  analysis of abilities, 11-12
  basic activities, 114-147 (*See also* subtopics hereunder)
  blenders, 131-132, 165
  bowl holder, 119-120, 139, 165
  bread holder, 121-122
  breadboard, 122
  breaking an egg, 146-147, 166
  can openers, 125-128, 165
  carafes, 141, 165
  carrying without spilling, 114-115, 163
  cheese cutter, 134-135
  cleaning up after meal, 162-163

cookware with heat-resistant handles, 149, 166
cutting, 128-131, 165
cutting boards, 118
electric grinders, 136-138
electric knives, 128-130, 165
electric mixers, 142-144, 165
electric skillets, 154-156, 166
food processors, 131, 133
gas appliances, 148, 166
glass stabilizer, 119
graters, 135-137, 165
Grip 'n Mix bowls, 141, 165
beating, 142-146, 165-166
hints, 147-162 (*See also subtopics here-under*)
hot pots, 160-162, 166
juice pourer, 138-139, 165
kettle stand, 139, 165
lapboards, 115, 117
long-handled kitchen tools, 149-150, 166
loosening bottle tops, 123-125, 164-165
microwave ovens, 149, 151-153, 166
milk carton holders, 140, 165
mixing, 142-146, 165-166
one-handed food chopper, 134-135, 165
open handled knife, 133-134
opening containers, 123-128, 164-165
oven mitts, 149-150, 166
ovens, 148-149
package or box of food, anchoring of, 121
pan stabilizer, 119, 121
pan strainer, 142, 165
peeler, 133-134, 165
pitchers, 140, 165
portable broiler ovens, 156-160, 166
pouring liquids, 138-142, 165
Presto Whip, 145, 166
ranges, 148-149, 166
scissors, 133
serving carts, 115-116
slant-handled egg beater, 146, 166
slicers, 130-131, 165
stabilizing foods, dishes and pans, 115, 118-122, 164
stirring, 142-146, 165-166
suction stand or cup, 119-120
table on wheels, 115, 117
table range, 153-154, 166
unscrewing jars, 123-124

wire whisk, 145, 166
Cooking center in wheelchair kitchen, 104-105, 112
built-in cooking top, 104
burner switch knobs, 104
combined cooking tops and ovens, 104
electrical installation, 104
remote controls, 104
separate oven, 104-105
Cookware with heat-resistant handles, 149, 166
Cosmetics, 62-64, 87
aluminum tubing mount, 63-64
lipstick tubes, 63-64
mascara tubes, 64
powder puff holders, 63-64
Cotton Mitt-Mop, 170
Crayons for children, 301, 309
Creative art activities, 300-302, 309
blackboards and chalk, 300-301
clay, 302
crayons, 301
finger-painting, 301-302
free-hand cutting, 302
materials around house, 302-304
paste, 302
water colors, 301
Crib for baby, 283, 308
modification into playpen, 285-286
Crutches, 16, 26-27, 30
clothing and, 267
Cutting boards, 118
Cutting foods, 128-131, 165
Cutting with knife, 28

D

Death of parents, preparation for, 7
Deciding on a family, 279-281
consider limitations, 280-281, 308
genetics, 279-280, 308
timing, 280, 308
Decubitus ulcers, 19
prevention, 55-56
Definitions (*See specific terms*)
Deodorants, 49
Dermis, 48
Desk, 246
Diaper pail, 186-187, 205, 296, 309
Diaper rash, 296
Diapering child, 295-296, 309

changing baby, 295-296
cloth or disposable diapers, 296
diaper pails, 295
fastenings, 296
table on wheels, 295-296
Dining area, 246-247, 263
furniture, 246-247
height of table, 247, 263
location, 246
opening to kitchen, 246
Discipline of children, 306-307, 310
build child's respect, 306
sense of humor, 306-307
Dishmaster, 103
Dishwasher, 103-104, 112
portable, 163-164
Dislocations, 18
Disposable diapers, 296
Distributors, 315-320
Doors (*See* Doorways)
Doorways, 250-253, 263
accordion doors, 250-251
children and, 297
closing devices, 251-253
dimensions, 250
door fastenings, 251-253, 263
entry doors, 250-251
interior doors, 251
kickplate, 251
knobs, 251-253
level approach inside and outside, 251
rubber doorknob lever, 251-252
sash door closing, 252-253
screen doors, 251
side-hinged door, 250-252
sliding door, 250-251
tight spaces, 251
wheel-in stall showers, 240
Double Burner Table Range, 154
Drawer dividers, 224
Dresses
hot weather, 274-275
shirtwaist, 274
year-around, 274
Dressing
analysis of abilities, 10
spinal cord injured, 21
Dressing guidelines, 68-73, 87-88
buttons, 68-69
lower extremity garments, 70
shoes, 71-73

socks and stockings, 70-71
upper garments, 69-70
Dressing infant or toddler, 292-293, 309
Drinking aids, 80-83, 88
bilateral glass holder, 81
bulldog straw clip, 83
glassholder, 82
plastic-handled mug, 82
straws, 83
Wonder-Flo drinking cup, 81
Drying oneself, 54-55, 87
Dulcolax suppositories, 47
Dust mops, 170, 179
Dusting, 172, 176, 179

E

Easy-on and easy-off fastenings, 268-270, 278
buttons, 269-270
grippers, 269-270
hooks and eyes, 269-270
Velcro, 270-271
zippers, 268-270
Easy way to work, 92, 96
Eating
analysis of abilities, 9
spinal cord injured, 21
Eating with less effort, 73-80, 88
adjustable swivel utensils, 78
bent spoons, 76
built-up handle utensils, 74
extension forks, 76
food guards, 79
horizontal palm self-handle utensils, 75
level spoons, 77
limitations, 73-74
Little Octopus suction holders, 80
long-handled utensils, 78
rocker knife, 78
round scoop dish, 79
sandwich holder, 77
vertical palm self-handle utensils, 75
Efficiency in doing work, 89
Electric grinders, 136-138
Electric knives, 128-130, 165
controls, 129
handle design, 129
weight, 128-129
Electric mixers, 142-144, 165
portable, 143-144

standard counter models, 144
Electric skillets, 154-156, 166
    advantages, 154-155
    aluminum, 155
    easy-to-operate controls, 155
    heat-resistant handle, 155
    square lightweight, 155
    stainless steel, 155
    well-designed cover, 155-156
Electrical service, 253-254, 263
    cooking center installation, 104
    delayed action switches, 253
    meter panels, 254
    outlets, 242, 254
    switches, 253-254
    two-way switches, 253
Embolus, 17
End tables, 246
Enemas, 48
Energy level
    heart conditions, 29, 31
    wheelchair homemaker, 26
Epidermis, 48
Eyeglass care, 67-68, 87
Eyeglass holder, 67-68

F

Farberware Open Hearth Broiler, 160-161
Farberware Turbo Oven, 158-159
Fastenings (*See also* Easy-on and easy-off
    fastenings)
    diaper, 296
    door, 251-253, 263
    shoes, 72
Fatigue, avoidance of, 89-90
Faucets
    bathroom, 240-241
    kitchen sink, 101
    lever-handle, 240-241
    Scald-guard, 240-241
    single handle, 240-241
    water spout, 240
        goose neck, 240
        straight, 240
        swivel, 240
    wringing clothes with, 193-194
Feather duster, 172, 179
Fecal matter elimination, 19, 30
Feeding baby, 290-292, 309
    bottles, 290

feeding tables, 292, 309
    high chairs, 290-292, 309
    plastic infant seats, 290-291, 309
Feeding tables for babies, 292, 309
Financial management, analysis of abili-
    ties in, 13
Financial resources, 8-9
Fine motor skills, 30
    problems, 25
Finger painting for children, 301-302, 309
Fireside matches, 148
Fistulas, 46
Fleet enemas, 48
Flexible shower hose, 53-54
Floor care, 177-178
    mopping, 177-178
    polishing, 178
    sweeping, 177
Floor coverings, 255-256, 263-264
    ambulatory individuals, 255-256
    carpeting, 255
    chairbound persons, 255, 264
    indoor-outdoor carpeting, 255
    linoleum, 255
    nonskid materials, 255
    nylon rugs, 255
    wheel-in shower stall, 240
    wood, 255
Floor designs for kitchens, 97-98, 112
    corridor plan, 97-98
    L plan, 97-98
    U plan, 97-98
Foley catheter, 43
Food processors, 131, 133
Fractures, 18
Freedom, 3-5
Friedreich's ataxia, 25
Furniture
    bedroom, 243-245
    dining area, 246-247
    living room, 245-246

G

Garages, 247-248, 263
    door openers, 248
Gas appliances, 148, 166
Gatch spring, 244
Gates for child safety, 286, 308
General Electric slicing knife, 129
Genetics, 279-280, 308

Genitourinary complications, 46
    fistulas, 46
    infections, 46
    stones, 46
    urethral stricture, 46
Gerry Kiddie Pack, 294-295
Glass stabilizer, 119
Gloves, 215
Glycerine suppositories, 47
Grab-All extension arm, 224
Graters, 135-137, 165
Grip 'n Mix bowls, 141, 165
Grippers, 269-270, 278
Grocery shopping, 26
Gross motor skills, 30
    deficiencies, 25

H

Hair grooming, 59-60, 87
    adjustable mirrors, 59-60
    brushing, 59
    combing, 59
    extension comb, 60-61
    finger ring hairbrush, 60-61
Hamilton Beach blenders
    Fourteen Speed, 131-132
    Seven Speed, 131-132
Hamilton Beach Food Converter Set, 137-138
Hand laundry, 192-194, 206
    faucet used to wring clothes, 193-194
    not too much dirt in clothes, 193
    small amounts, 193
    soak clothes overnight, 192-193
    wrap garments in towel, 193
Hand sewing, 202
    needle threader, 202-203, 206
Heart disease, 16, 28-31
    beds for persons suffering from, 244
Heavy household tasks, analysis of abilities
    in performing, 12
Heberden's nodes, 23
Hemiplegia, 16-18, 21, 29-30
    urinary management, 42-46
High blood pressure, 29
High chairs, 290-292, 309
High thoracic lesion, 19
Holding objects, 28
Home adaptation, 230-264, 324-325 (See
    also specific topics)

accessibility checklist, 261-262
bathrooms, 231-242, 263
bedrooms, 242-245, 263
carports, 247, 263
chair lift, 258-261, 264
communications, 256-257, 264
cooling, 256
dining area, 246-247, 263
doorways, 250-253, 263
electrical service, 253-254, 263
exterior considerations, 230-231, 262-263
floor coverings, 255-256, 263-264
garages, 247-248, 263
heating, 256-264
home areas, 231-248, 263-264 (See also
    subtopics hereunder)
intercom, 256-257, 264
living rooms, 245-246, 263
mobility handicaps, 256
other structural modifications, 248-264
    (See also subtopics hereunder)
ramps, 231, 262-263
sidewalks, 230, 262
steps, 230-231, 262
telephone, 257, 264
windows, 248-250, 263
Home storage areas, 214-228
    bathroom, 225, 228
    belts, 215
    blankets, 217
    brighten dark closet, 215
    broomstick closet rod, 216-217
    cleaning supplies, 226-229
    closet areas, 214-217 (See also subtopics
        hereunder)
    coat hanger covers, 216
    comforters, 216-217
    corner storage, avoidance of, 214, 228
    dividers for closets, 216
    fasten garments securely, 214
    fresh smelling, 217
    gloves, 215
    guest closet kept dry, 216
    jewelry tangling avoided, 215
    kitchen, 218-224 (See also Kitchen stor-
        age)
    ladies' hat holder, 215
    laundry, 225-226, 229
    linens, 217
    mildew protection, 215
    purses, 215

seasonal garments put away, 215
separate clothes, 214
sheets kept organized, 216
shelves divided into sections, 216
shoe bag, 214, 216
shoes, 214
  plastic bags, 215
slacks, 215-216
smoothing pleats, 214
wax closet rods, 216
Hooks and eyes, 269-270, 278
Hospital bed, 35, 244
Hot pots, 160-162, 166
Hygiene for spinal cord injured, 21
Hypertension, 29-31

I

Incoordination, 24-25, 30
Independence as goal, vii
Independent living, 3-15
  death of parents, preparation for, 7
  definition, 5, 15
  financial resources, 8-9
  interpersonal relationships, 5-6
  living arrangements, 14
  physical disabilities and, 16-31
  program, 4
  readiness for, 7-15
  reasons for, 5-7
  self-reliance, 3-5, 15
  time factor, 14
Indoor play, 297-298, 309
Indwelling catheter, 42-43
Infections, 18
  bladder, 46
Initiative, 6-7
Insta-Clean can opener, 126
Intercom, 256-257, 264
Interpersonal relationships, 5-6
Invisible disabilities, 16
Iron, 198-199, 206
  base, 198
  cord, 199
  cord holder, 199, 206
  easy-to-use controls, 198
  grip, 198
  insulated handle, 198
  sole plate, 198-199, 206
  steam, 198
  weight, 198

Ironing, 196-199, 206
  avoiding stress, 196
  basic concepts, 196, 206
  board, 196-197
  correct accessories, 196
  holding iron, 196
  kitchen table, 197-198
  oven mitt, 196, 206
  pad, 197
  purchasing equipment, 198-199, 206 (*See also* Iron)
  reducing number of times garment is turned, 196
  sensation impairments, 196, 206

J

Jewelry, 215
Juice pourer, 138-139, 165
Jumbo-handled can opener, 127-128

K

Kettle stand, 139, 165
Kidney stones, 46
Kitchen cleaning, 175-176
Kitchen laundry, 181
Kitchen planning, 97-113, 322
  ambulatory homemaker, 108-112
  appliances, 111, 113
  bar stool, 109-110, 113
  bending and reaching ability, 99-100, 111
  consider disability, 98-100, 111
  continuous work surface, 109, 113
  floor designs, 97-98, 112 (*See also* Floor designs for kitchen)
  lighting, 111, 113
  mobility, consideration of, 98-99, 111
  opening to dining area, 246
  reduce walking, 108-109
  security strap, 99
  sit down to work, 109-110, 113
  ventilation, 111, 113
  wheelchair homemaker, 100-108, 112 (*See also* Wheelchair homemaker)
  work triangle, 108-109, 112
Kitchen storage, 218-224, 228
  Adjustable Helper shelf, 221
  aids and devices, 219-224
  aluminum foil, 219
  bottle rack and can dispenser, 222

cabinet door kept shut, 218
cabinets, best use of, 218-219
cardboard dividers, 219
drawer dividers, 224
Grab-All extension arm, 224
knives in wooden spools, 219
lighten shelves, 219
pantry for foods, 218
paper bags, 218
plate rack, 220
raised shelves, 218
shoe bag to hold items, 218
Sliding Pot 'n Pan Rack, 221
Spacemaker Drawers, 222
spice rack, 220
turntables, 223
vegetable storage bins, 223
Wrap and Bag Organizer, 219
Kitchen table ironing, 197-198

L

Ladies' hat holder, 215
Lamps, 244, 246 (*See also specific types*)
Lapboards, 115, 117
Large table lamps, 246
Latches for baby's bed, 284
  hand buttons, 284
  knob into slot locks, 284
  recessed safety locks, 284
  toe releases, 284
Latches on windows, 250
Laundry, 180-207, 323
  analysis of abilities, 12
  automatic dryer, 194-195, 206
  clothesline, 195-196, 206
  collecting and sorting, 185-188, 205
  designing area for, 180-185, 204-205 (*See also* Laundry area)
  diaper pail, 186-187, 205
  dirty clothes classification, 187-188
  dishpan, 185-186, 205
  drying clothes, 194-196, 206
  hand washed, 192-194, 206 (*See also* Hand laundry)
  ironing, 196-199, 206 (*See also* Ironing)
  laundry cart, 185-186, 205
  mending area, 199-202, 206 (*See also* Sewing area)
  pillowcases, 186, 205
  plastic bag in hamper, 186, 205

sewing area, 199-202, 206 (*See also* Sewing area)
sorting bins, 187-188, 205
storing clothes, 202-204, 206
washing dirty clothes, 188-194, 205 (*See also* Washing machine; Washing dirty clothes)
Laundry area, 180-185, 204-205
  bathroom, 181
  chutes, 185, 205
  countertops, 183-184, 205
  electricity, 182, 205
  installing washer and dryer, 181-182
  ironing equipment space requirement, 183, 205
  kitchen, 181
  laundry room near kitchen or bathroom, 181
  LP gas, 182, 205
  multipurpose room or hall, 181
  natural gas, 182, 205
  passageways, 183, 205
  planning location, 180-181
  plumbing, 181-182, 205
  sinks, 184-185, 205
  space requirement, 182-185, 205
  venting, 182, 205
  washing and drying equipment space requirement, 183, 205
Laundry cart, 185-186, 205
Laundry rack, 204
Laundry room near bathroom or kitchen, 181
Laundry storage, 225-226, 229
Lavatory, 236-238, 263
  countertop units, 236
  height, 236
  location, 236
  porcelain basin, 237
  steel basin, 237
  vitreous china basin, 237
  wall-hung units, 236
  wheelchair, 237-238
Laxatives, 47-48
Leg braces or casts
  clothing and, 268, 278
  men's fashions and, 270-273, 278
Linen closet, 242
Linens, 245
  fitted, 245
  muslin, 245

organization, 216
percale, 245
slide-out shelves, 217
slippery materials, 245
storage, 217
unfitted, 245
wrinkling, 245
Living arrangements, 14
Living rooms, 245-246, 263
  armchairs, 246
  bay window, 245
  coffee table, 246
  desk, 246
  end tables, 246
  furniture, 245-246
  large table lamps, 246
  size, 245
  sofa, 245
  standing lamps, 246
  wall lamps, 246
  writing lamps, 246
Living skills profile, 9-13
Long-handled dustpans, 168-169, 179
Long-handled kitchen tools, 149-150, 166
Loosening bottle tops, 123-125, 164-165
Loss of sensation, 17-18, 29

M

Make body work effectively, 94-96
  casters, 95
  gravity, 95
  momentum, 95
  other muscle groups, 94
  smooth and jerky movement, 94-95
Manicuring nails, 56-59
  assistive devices, 56-59
  bicycle nail clipper, 59
  cable nail clipper, 58-59
  fingernail cleaning, 56
  mounted clipper, 58
  professional manicure or pedicure, 59
  sandpaper files, 56-58
  toe nails, 56
Manufacturers, 315-320
Marketing abilities, analysis of, 13
Materials around house for playing, 302-304
Mattress pad, 244
Mattresses, 244
  foam rubber, 244

moving forward and backward on, 36
principles in selection, 244
rolling over in bed, 34
solid upholstered, 244
upholstered innerspring, 244
Maxi-Mite Baby carrier, 290-291
Maytag four-pronged knob on washing machine, 191-192
Mealtime Manual for People With Disabilities and the Elderly, 94
Medicine cabinet, 241
  blotters in, 225
Men's fashions, 270-273
  braces, 270-273, 278
  wheelchairs, 270, 273, 278
Mending area (*See* Sewing area)
Menstrual flow, 49
Meter panels, 254
Microwave oven, 149, 151-153, 166
Mildew protection, 215
Milk carton holders, 140, 165
Milk of magnesia, 47-48
Mirrors, 244
  adjustable, 59-60
Miscellaneous readings, 325-326
Mixing foods, 142-146, 165-166
Mop pails, 170-172
Mopping floors, 177-178
Mops, 170-171, 179
Moving forward and backward in bed, 35-36
  board and rope, 36
  mattress to shift weight, 36
Multiple sclerosis, 21, 25
  urinary management, 42-46
Multipurpose items, 210
Multipurpose room or hall for laundry, 181
Muscular dystrophy, 21
Musical experience with child, 299-300, 309
  instruments, 299-300
  listening, 300
  singing together, 300

N

Nails (*See* Manicuring nails)
National Electric Code, 253
Needle threader, 202-203, 206
Neurofibromatosis, 280
Night tables, 244
Nonambulatory disabilities, 16

Nu-Line Mesh Pressurge Gate, 286
Nursery chairs, 287-288

O

One-hand wringing method, 193-194
One-handed food chopper, 134-135, 165
Open handled knife, 133-134
Opening containers, 123-128, 164-165
Osteoarthritis, 22-23, 30
Osteogenesis imperfecta, 280
Outdoor play, 297, 309
Oven cleaning, 176
Oven mitts, 149-150, 166
  ironing with, 196, 206
Ovens, 148-149
Oversized easy-to-turn key can opener, 127

P

Packages or boxes of food, anchoring of,
  121
Pampers, 296
Pan stabilizer, 119, 121
Pan strainer, 142, 165
Parkinson's disease, 21, 25
Paraplegia, 18-19, 30
  defined, 18
Patient lift, 51
Peelers, 133-134, 165
Penal fistulas, 46
Penoscrotal fistulas, 46
Personal care (*See* Care of body)
Personal finances, analysis of abilities to
  handle, 13
Personal grooming, analysis of abilities
  in, 9-10
Pets, 299, 309
Physical disabilities, 321 (*See also specific
  types*)
  arthritis, 22-24, 30
  cardiac conditions, 16, 28-31
  crutches, 16, 26-27, 30
  hemiplegia, 16-18, 29-30
  incoordination, 24-25, 30
  independent living and, 16-31
  paraplegia, 18-19, 30
  problems encountered, 16-31
  quadriplegia, 18-19, 30
  spinal cord injury, 18-21, 30
  upper extremity amputees, 27-28, 30

  upper extremity weakness, 19-22, 30
  wheelchair homemaker, 16, 25-26, 30
Picking up objects, 176
Pickup scissors, 169, 179
Pitchers, 140, 165
Plastic infant bathing tub, 288-289
Plastic infant seats, 290-291, 309
Plastic pitchers, 140, 165
Plastic shoe bags, 215
Plate rack, 220
Play experiences and the disabled mother,
  297-304, 309 (*See also specific topics*)
  active indoor play, 297-298, 309
  creative art activities, 300-302, 309
  doors and your youngster, 297
  enjoying outdoors, 298-299, 309
  household pets, 299, 309
  monitoring children's play, 297, 309
  musical experiences, 299-300, 309
  selecting toys, 298
  stories, 302, 304, 309
  supervising outdoor play, 297, 309
  teach child to clean up, 298, 309
  visitor's house, animal or insect, 299, 309
Playpen for child, 285-286, 308
  modification of crib into, 285-286
Playtex Nurser Kit, 290
Pledge spray, 172
Polio, 21
Polishing
  floors, 178
  furniture, 172, 179
Poly Insta-Hot, 162
Porch Lift, 261
Portable broiler ovens, 156-160, 166
  countertop models, 157-160
    broiling pan, 157
    controls, 157-158
    door, 158
    element, 157
    insulation, 158
    interior, 157
    power output, 158-160
    rack and rack supports, 157
  open models, 160
    disassembling, 160
    rack design, 160
Portable urinals, 288
Port-a-crib, 284-285
Pouring liquids, 138-142, 165
Pressure sores, 19

Presto Whip, 145, 166
Prosthesis, 27, 30
Protect-o seat ring trainer, 287
Purses, 215

Q

Quadriplegia, 4-5, 18-19, 25, 30
  bowel care, 47-48
  defined, 18
  drinking aids, 80-83

R

Ramps, 231, 262-263
  handrails, 231
Ranges, 148-149, 166
Reading lamps, 244
Readiness for independent living, 7-15
Readings, 321-326
Refrigerator in wheelchair kitchen, 105-106, 112
  door swing, 105
  freezer compartment, 105
  frost free, 106
  ice cube maker, 105-106
  shelves, 105
Resources, 315-320
Retention type catheter, 43
Rheumatoid arthritis, 22, 30
Rigidity, 24
Rolling over in bed, 32-34
  attendant, 32-33
  headboard and mattress, 34
  pillows, 32-33
  rope, 34
  wheelchair, 33-34
Rope
  moving forward and backward in bed, 36
  rolling over in bed, 34
  sitting up in bed, 35
  wheelchair transfers in and out of bed, 36-37

S

Scissors
  cooking, 133
  pickup, 169, 179
Seasonal garments put away, 215
Section Eight Housing Program, 8-9

Security strap, 99
Self-reliance, 3-5, 15
  child, 307-308, 310
  confidence, 6-7
  initiative, 6-7
  reasons for, 15
Senekot, 47
Serving carts, 115-116
Serving meals, analysis of abilities in, 12
Sewing abilities, analysis of, 12
Sewing area, 199-202, 206
  equipment, 200
  hand sewing, 202
  sewing machine for handicapped, 201-202, 206 (*See also* Sewing machine for handicapped)
  solid surface, 200-201
Sewing machine for handicapped, 201-202, 206
  electronic sewing speed regulator, 202
  finger guard, 202
  inserting needle, 201-202
  operating knobs, 202
  presser-foot lifter, 202
  threading, 202
  winding bobbin, 201
Shaving, 60-62, 87
  battery powered shavers, 62
  electric razor, 62
  universal electric shaver holder, 62
Shoe bag, 214, 216, 218
  plastic, 215
Shoe storage, 214-215
Shoes, getting in and out of, 71-73
  elastic shoelaces, 72
  Kno-Bows, 72-73
  long-handled shoe horns, 72
  zipper fastening, 72
Short-handled mops, 179
Sidewalks, 230, 262
Sidewinder high chair, 291-292
Signal bell, 244
Simplifying housework, 89-113
  analyze daily tasks, 90, 95
  assistance, 91-92, 96
  changing work habits, 93-94, 96
  choose good time, 95
  easy way, 92, 96
  find appropriate place, 91, 95
  make body work effectively, 94-96
  simultaneous chores, 92-93, 96

Simultaneous performance of chores, 92-93, 96
Single-button telephone sets, 257, 264
Sink
  baby bathed in, 289
  laundry, 184-185, 205
Sink in wheelchair kitchen, 100-103, 112
  Dishmaster, 103
  faucets, 101
  modification, 106-107
  rear drains, 101
  shallow sink, 101
  side faucet sinks, 101-102
  spray hose, 102
  Triple Concept stainless steel sink, 102
Sitting up in bed, 34-35
  attendant, 34-35
  pushing with forearms in hospital bed, 35
  rope and wheelchair armrest, 35
Skin care, 48-56, 87
  anatomy, 48
  antiperspirants, 49
  bathing hints, 49-54
  cleanliness, considerations for, 48-49
  creams, 49
  decutibus ulcers, prevention of, 55-56
  deodorants, 49
  drying oneself, 54-55
  functions, 48
  gentleness, 48
  lotions, 49
  soap selection, 48-49
Skirts
  gored with side openings, 275-276
  open in center front, 275-276
  wraparound, 275-276
Slacks, 215-216 (*See also* Trousers)
Slant-handled egg beater, 146, 166
Slicers, 130-131, 165
Sliding Pot 'n Pan Rack, 221
Soap ball, 53
Soap selection, 48-49
Socks and stockings, 70-71
Sofa, 245
Soft-bristled brush on pole, 172, 179
Spacemaker Drawers, 222
Spasticity, 24-25
Speakerphone, 257, 264
Spice rack, 220
Spinal abscesses, 18

Spinal cord injury, 18-21, 30
  decubitus ulcers, prevention of, 55-56
  limitations, 21
  rolling over in bed, 32-33
  sitting up in bed, 34-35
  urinary management, 42-46
Sponge-head dish mop, 163, 165
Squeez-a-matic, 170-171
Stabilizing foods, dishes and pans, 115, 118-122, 164
Stair Glide Delux, 258-259
Stairway chair lift, 258-259, 264
Standing lamps, 246
Stay-Put Grater, 135-136
Steps, 230-231, 262
  handrails, 230, 262
  railings, 231
Stirring foods, 142-146, 165-166
Stocking aid, 71
Stockings, 70-71
Stool softeners, 47
Storage, 208-229, 323-324
  accessible space for frequently used items, 212-213
  analyze space for, 209-210, 228
  discarding unused items, 209, 228
  group things together, 211
  home areas, 214-228 (*See also* Home storage areas)
  list items, 211-212, 228
  multipurpose items, 210, 228
  near where items are used, 211, 228
  only what is needed, 208-209, 228
  organizational principles, 208-213 (*See also subtopics hereunder*)
  plan space wisely, 212, 228
  return things to proper places, 213
  take inventory, 209, 228
  three basic questions, 209-210, 228
Storage areas, 22 (*See also* Home storage areas)
Storing clothes, 202-204, 206
Strokes, 17
Strolee Travel Trio, 294
Structural modification (*See* Home adaptation)
Suction bottle brush, 163, 165
Suction stand or cup, 119-120
Sunbeam Mixmaster, 144
Sunbeam Today Iron, 199-200
Supplemental Security Income program

(SSI), 8
Swan's neck, 23
Sweeping, 177

T

Table on wheels, 115, 117
Table range, 153-154, 166
    controls, 154
    cooking element, 153
    double burner, 154
    height, 153
Tappan Tap 'n Touch, 152-153
Telephone, 257, 264
Time factor, 14
    importance of, 89
Toastmaster Push-Button Oven Broiler,
    158-160
Toilet training child, 287-288, 308
    nursery chairs, 287-288
    portable urinals, 288
    special seats, 287
Toileting
    analysis of abilities, 9-10
    spinal cord injured, 21
Toilets, 232-235, 263
    built-in ventilation systems, 232
    close-coupled, 232
    corner, 232, 234
    elongated bowls, 232
    five basic types, 232
    handrail mountings, 233-235
    height, 235
    one-piece, 232
    placement, 235
    raised bowl, 235-236
    reverse trap, 235
    siphon jet, 235
    trapeze, 235, 237
    two-piece, 232-233
    wall-hung, 232-234
    washdown, 235
    water action classification, 235
Toilets, getting on and off
    armrests, 40
    free-standing grabbars, 40
    raised seats, with or without, 38-39
    straight chair as bridge, 39-40
    wheelchair transfers, 38-40
Tooth decay prevention, 64-67, 87
    built-up handled toothbrush, 64-65

electric toothbrush, 64
suction denture brush, 66-67
toothbrush, type of, 64-66
tube squeezer, 66-67
Trapeze, 235, 237
Traumatic injuries, 18
Tremor, 24
Trevo Lifter, 52-53
Tri-Pan Fry Pan, 156
Triple Concept stainless steel sink, 102
Trousers (*See also* Slacks)
    men's fashions, 271-273
    women's fashions, 276-277
        pedal pushers, 276-277
        slacks, 276
Tub
    baby bathed in, 289-290
    grab bars, 238
    horizontal rails, 238
    installation, 238
    patient lift, 51
    safety rail, 49-50
    Trevo Lifter, 52-53
    wheelchair transfers, 40-41
Tumor, 17-18
Turntables, 223

U

Ulnar deviation, 24, 30
Unscrewing jars, 123, 164-165
    drawer, 123-124
    hot water, 123
    pliers, 123
    tap the cap, 123
    Zim jar opener, 123-124
Upper extremity amputees, 27-28, 30
    carrying pans, 28
    cutting, 28
    holding objects, 28
    washing dishes, 28
Upper extremity weakness, 19-22, 30
    cosmetics, application of, 62-64
    garments, putting on and taking off,
        69-70
    shaving, 60, 62
Urethral stricture, 46
Urinary management, 42-46, 87
    genitourinary complications, 46
    twice daily irrigation, 45-46
Urinary physiology, 42

Utility stick, 70

V

Vacuum cleaner, 167-168, 178-179
  attachment storage, 168
  attachments, 168
  bag release, 168
  bumpers, 168
  canister, 168, 179
  casters, 168
  cord, 168
  cord rewinder, 168
  dealer reliability, 167
  disposable dust bags, 168
  foot-operated switch, 168
  manufacturer reliability, 167
  soil container, 168
  upright, 168, 178
  use to be made, 167
  wheels, 168
Vacuum cleaning, 26
Vegetable storage bins, 223
Velcro fasteners, 270-271, 278
  care of, 277
Visible injuries, 16
Vocational Guidance and Rehabilitation
  Service, 271-273

W

Wall lamps, 246
Waring Delux 12 Speed Hand Mixer, 143-144
Waring Food Processor II, 131, 133
Waring Thin Slicer, 130
Washing dirty clothes, 188-194, 205 (*See also* Washing machine)
  automatic washing machine, 190-192, 205-206
  bleaching, 190, 205
  bluing, 190, 205
  detergent container, 189, 205
  detergent measurement, 189, 205
  hints for, 188-190, 205
  loading washing machine, 189, 205
  prepare garments for, 188, 205
  rinsing, 189-190, 205
  soaking time, 188, 205
  soft water, 189, 205
  sort clothes, 188, 205

  starching, 190, 205
  timing, 189, 205
  water temperature, 188-189, 205
Washing dishes, 28
Washing machine
  bleach dispensers, 191
  capacity, 190
  controls, 191-192
  delicate fabric cycle, 191
  easy-to-reach filter, 192
  economical operation, 190
  fabric softeners, 191
  front-loading, 192-193
  general guidelines in selection of, 190-191, 205-206
  loading, 189, 191, 205
  meter-filled, 191
  number of cycles, 190-191
  permanent press cycle, 191
  prewash and presoak cycles, 191
  special considerations, 191-192
  top-loading, 192
  tub, 191
  unloading, 191
  water safety lid, 191
  woolens cycle, 191
Water colors for children, 301, 309
Wet mops, 170, 179
Wheelchair, ability to push
  spinal cord injured persons, 21
Wheelchair homemaker, 16, 25-26, 30
  beds for, 243-244
  clothing and, 268
  crutches, use of, 27
  energy level, 26
  extended footrests, 25
  hair grooming, 59-60
  height considerations, 25
  men's fashions, 270, 273, 278
  ramp entrances, 26
  reduced leverage for opening doors, 25-26
  rolling over in bed, 33-34
  sitting up in bed, 35
  space limitations, 25
Wheelchair kitchen
  cooking center, 104-105, 112 (*See also* Cooking center in wheelchair kitchen)
  countertop depth, 100, 112
  countertop height, 100, 112
  countertop space, 100, 112

different work space, 106, 108
dishwasher, 103-104, 112
refrigerator, 105-106, 112 (*See also* Refrigerator in wheelchair kitchen)
remodeling not possible, 106-108, 112
sink, 100-103, 112 (*See also* Sink in wheelchair kitchen)
space for legs, 106
Wheelchair lavatory, 237-238
Wheelchair platform lift, 258, 260-261, 264
Wheelchair stair lift, 258-260, 264
Wheelchair transfers, 36-42, 87
bed, in and out of, 36-38
spinal cord injured, 21
toilet, getting on and off, 38-40
tub, 40-41
Wheel-in stall shower, 239-240
carpeting, 240
door, 240
hand-held shower head, 240
location, 239
seat, 240
sunken floor, 239-240
wall railing, 240
window, 240
Windows, 248-250, 263
awning, 249
bathroom, 240
bedroom, 243
casement, 249

cleaning, ease in, 250
double hung, 249-250
four basic designs, 249-250, 263
height, 248-249, 263
latches, 250
sliding, 249-250
Wiping up spills, 177
Wire whisk, 145, 166
Women's fashions, 273-278 (*See also specific topics*)
blouses, 275
collars, 273
cut of garment, 273
dresses, 274-275
fabrics, easy-to-care for, 274
necklines, 273
skirts, 275-276
sleeve lengths, 273
trouser garments, 276-277
Work areas, 22
Work triangle, 108-109, 112
Wrap and Bag Organizer, 219
Writing lamps, 246

Z

Zim jar opener, 123-124
Zippers, 72, 268-270, 278
care of, 277-278